1,000
WINE and BEERMAKING Hints and Recipes

BEN TURNER

PELHAM BOOKS
LONDON

THE WINEMAKER'S GRACE

For good food
for good wine
and for good friends
may we be truly thankful
Amen

First published in Great Britain by
Park Lane Press 1985

This edition published by
Pelham Books Ltd
44 Bedford Square
London WC1B 3DP
1986

Text copyright: © Ben Turner 1985

All rights reserved. No part of this publication may
be produced, stored in a retrieval system, or transmitted,
in any form or by any means, electronic, mechanical,
photocopying, recording or otherwise, without the prior
permission of the copyright holder.

British Library Cataloguing in Publication Data

Turner, B.C.A.
1000 wine and beer making hints and recipes.
1. Wine and wine making – Amateurs' manuals
2. Brewing – Amateurs' manuals
I. Title
641.8'72   TP548.2

ISBN 0 7207 1646 2

Drawings by the Hayward Art Group

Printed and bound in Great Britain by
Billing & Sons, Worcester.

Contents

Quantities in the recipes 5
Introduction 6
The Law 8
Hygiene 10

WINEMAKING **13**
The History of Wine 13
Styles of Wine 18
Equipment and Hygiene 21
Coping with Stains 31
Base Ingredients 35
Other Ingredients 47
The Importance of Yeast 57
Colour and Flavour
    Extraction 64
The Hydrometer 71
Acid Control 80
Making the Wine 85
Winemaking Problems:
    Causes and Cures 106
Wines from Kits 116
Traditional Country Wines 121
Modern Table Wines 138
Second-run Wines 155
Social Wines 157
Easy Wines from
    Juices, Jams and Canned
    Fruits 168
Sparkling Wines 183
Sherry-style Wines 193
Dessert Wines 204

Fortified Wines 218
Wines for the Diabetic 222
Grape Wines 226
Serving Wine 231
Keeping Records 238

BREWING BEER **242**
The History of Beer 242
Styles of Beer 245
Equipment and Hygiene 248
Ingredients 251
Principles of Brewing 256
Brewing Problems:
    Causes and Cures 261
Kit Beers 264
Malt Syrup Beers 271
Grain-mashed Beers 280
Fruit and Other Beers 292
Serving Beer 298

CIDERMAKING **300**
The History of Cider 300
Using a Kit 302
Equipment and Hygiene 304
Ingredients 306
Making the Cider 308
Cellarcraft 312
Cidermaking Problems:
    Causes and Cures 314
Serving Cider 316

MEAD 318
The History of Mead 318
Honey 320
Other Ingredients 322
Equipment 324
Making Mead 325
Serving Mead 336

LIQUEURS 337
Commercial or home-made? 337
Equipment and Hygiene 339
Ingredients 340
Methods and Recipes 343
Serving Liqueurs 350

VINEGARS 351
What is Vinegar? 351
Equipment and Hygiene 354
How to make Vinegar 356

SOCIETIES AND
SUPPLIERS 359
Clubs and Competitions 359
Sources of Supply 365

Glossary 367
Index 381

Quantities in the recipes

- These have been closely equated. With these recipes you can mix imperial and metric quantities in the same recipe if you wish.
- Each recipe is designed on the unit of six standard bottles of wine. You can increase this quantity as long as you also increase each ingredient, except yeast, *pro rata*. A sachet of dried yeast granules or a compressed yeast tablet, or a phial of liquid yeast, is enough to ferment from 1 to 6 gallons.
- Some containers of fruit juice or fruits may contain a little more or a little less than the amount in the recipe. These will make no difference to the finished wine. Use the entire contents and adjust the amount of water if you need to.
- The quantity of water given can only be approximate, depending on the amount of juice you extract from the fresh fruit, the size of the container of canned fruit or juice, the size of the fermentation vessel and so on. If you produce more must than your container will hold, ferment the surplus in a bottle and use it for topping up.
- All 5 ml spoonsful are level unless stated otherwise.

Comparative liquid measures

The only difference between British and American liquid measures is the number of fluid ounces in the pint. The British pint contains 20 fl oz, the American pint contains only 16 fl oz.

British	American	Metric
1 gallon	$1\frac{1}{5}$ gallon	4.5 litres
1 pint	$1\frac{1}{4}$ pints	560 ml
$\frac{1}{2}$ pint	$\frac{5}{8}$ pint	280 ml
$6\frac{2}{5}$ pints	**1 gallon**	3.6 litres
$\frac{4}{5}$ pint	**1 pint**	454 ml
$\frac{2}{5}$ pint	**1 cup ($\frac{1}{2}$ pint)**	227 ml
$8\frac{3}{4}$ pints	$11\frac{1}{4}$ pints	**5 litres**
$1\frac{3}{4}$ pints	2 pints $3\frac{1}{4}$ fl oz	**1 litre**
$17\frac{1}{2}$ fl oz	1 pint $1\frac{1}{2}$ fl oz	**500 ml**
$8\frac{3}{4}$ fl oz	1 cup $\frac{3}{4}$ fl oz	**250 ml**
1 tsp	1 tsp	**5 ml**

Introduction

WHY MAKE YOUR OWN?

There is almost no limit to the number of different alcoholic drinks you can make at home. What, however, are the advantages of doing so? The most significant is often the great saving in cost. But please don't go to the extreme and use poor-quality ingredients just because you can get them cheaply – the results may simply not be worth drinking. For many people making wine, beer and other drinks is also an enjoyable hobby that can be shared by all ages.

THE INGREDIENTS

A vast range of ingredients can be used, either alone or in combination. Almost every fruit can produce a wine of one kind or another, although a better wine can usually be made when several are used together. Vegetables, flowers, leaves, herbs, spices, grains and honey may all be added to the fruits to improve the body, bouquet and flavour. The choice is yours, although hints will be given on combinations worth developing.

DIFFERENT BEVERAGES
Mead
Made with different honeys, mead is a delightful drink which everyone should make at some time. Honey can be blended with any fruit, both juice and flower, spice or herb to vary the flavour. It can be made for drinking at table – both dry and sweet – and as a social or dessert beverage. Alternatively it can be sparkled or warmed and served as a mull.

Cider
Cider is becoming increasingly popular. It is made exclusively from the juice of apples but the flavour depends entirely on the variety used. Since there are some 2000 of these the range of flavours is therefore enormous. Cider too can be produced both dry and sweet as well as sparkling. It can also be warmed with spices and served as a fine mull at Hallowe'en or, indeed, at any time of the year.

Beer
The basic ingredients of malt and hops can be varied with many adjuncts in different combinations and quantities to produce different beers. These can vary in colour from the palest straw through every shade of gold, copper and brown to a domino black. They can be light in body and alcohol or as strong as wine. Some beers taste best when chilled, others when spiced and warmed.

Vinegar
Wine, mead, cider and beer are also the base ingredients for different vinegars. These can be further flavoured with fruits, herbs or spices.

The key to success
Of all the hints and tips in this book a handful seem to me to hold the key to success. They will be discussed in detail in the pages which follow but they are so important that they are worth repeating here.

Cleanliness: Equipment must *always* be cared for and sterilized before use and containers left covered at all times to avoid airborne infection from spoilage organisms. Care in hygiene will prevent most wine and beermaking problems.

The best-quality ingredients: A silk purse was never made from a sow's ear. It is false economy to use any ingredients less than the best.

The correct yeast: Always use a *pure* wine or beer yeast. Never use a beer yeast for wine and never leave out the yeast. A Champagne wine yeast may be used for certain lager beers and barley wines.

Sulphite (Campden tablets): Never use these in beermaking – on the other hand, always use them sensibly when making wines, meads and ciders.

FELLOWSHIP
Home winemaking and brewing is the most gregarious of hobbies. Having made drinks at home you will certainly want to share the results with others and discuss how you made them. Joining one of the many wine clubs will make you new friends who share your enthusiasm.

The Law

Throughout this book all references to wine and other drinks mean home-made products unless otherwise stated, although many of the recipes make drinks similar in style to and reminiscent of the commercial products. They must never, however, be passed off as the legitimate commercial product.

Wine labelling

European Economic Community legislation concerning wine is now being applied more strictly in the UK. Wine is officially defined as the product of the fermentation of the freshly pressed juice of the grape.

To comply with the law all labels stuck on to bottles of home-made wine should describe the contents as such, i.e. Home-Made Wine, Elderberry Wine or whatever. Names such as Red or White Table Wine, Champagne, Burgundy, Claret, Hock, Sherry, or Port can only be used on the labels of commercial products.

Selling: In the UK there has never been any legislation governing the making of wine at home for drinking by members of the household or their friends. There are regulations, however, should you wish to sell your wine.

Before making any attempt to sell your wine, registration must be made with the Customs and Excise Department to ensure that you pay the appropriate duty and possibly VAT as well. Registration must also be made with your local authority so that the environmental health officer can check that your premises are suitable.

Incidentally, the donation of a bottle or two of wine for a prize in a raffle or tombola is also construed as selling if money is paid for the tickets.

In Australia, New Zealand and South Africa at the time of writing there is no tax on wine and you may make wine at home from grapes or from other fruits or ingredients. You may also contribute bottles to charitable causes.

In the USA and Canada the law varies from one state to another. In the USA relics of Prohibition still remain and you have to get a licence even to make wine for your own consumption. It is normally granted only to the head of the household and for not more than 200

US gallons a year. In Canada each state has different laws, notably permissive in the predominantly French-speaking areas and prohibitive in the areas where alcohol can only be bought from a state liquor shop.

In Muslim states alcohol in any form is forbidden.

Beer, mead and cider

Brewing beer at home was controlled in the UK between 1880 and 1963 when it was necessary to register an intention to brew and to obtain a licence. Excise duty was also payable on the alcohol content of the brew which was calculated from the specific gravity of the wort before fermentation started. By the 1960s the problem of issuing licences and checking the gravity of a few gallons of beer had become an uneconomic nuisance. The law was repealed and there is now no control other than that for home-made wine, i.e. only if you attempt to sell your beer. The same applies to mead and cider.

Spirits

Liqueurs are made in the home with spirits upon which duty and VAT have been paid at the time of purchase. It is *forbidden* in almost every country in the world, however, to make spirits in the home, whether by distillation or by freezing.

Warning: All alcohols are poisonous, some much more so than others. Home-made spirits could easily contain too high a proportion of methyl alcohol and/or fusel oil. When imbibed in sufficient quantity – which could be less than half a bottle – these can cause blindness and even death.

   Please do not attempt to make spirits. The law quite rightly forbids the practice for your own protection.

Hygiene

There is no doubt that a failure in cleanliness is the cause of most of the off-smells and taints found in home-made wines and beers. Fortunately there is no need today, as in the past, to use brimstone with its choking sulphur fumes or to risk breaking glass jars and bottles by scalding them with boiling water. Instead, we have simple bactericides that effectively sterilize all our equipment.

STERILIZING EQUIPMENT
Wash it first
- Do buy new equipment when you are starting out and use it exclusively for your winemaking and brewing.
- Always wash all equipment thoroughly in hot water containing detergent before you use it to remove surface dirt. Then rinse off the detergent several times with cold water. This advice applies to all your equipment whatever it is made of, whether it be a wooden press, a glass jar, a polythene bin or a stainless steel container.
- If necessary, use a bottle brush to clean the shoulders of bottles and jars and to get into the corner where the upright joins the base.

Store it carefully
- After you have cleaned and dried your equipment, store it in a dry and airy place until you need it.
- Lightly plug bottles and jars with cotton wool or a tissue to keep out insects and spoilage organisms. Air will still flow in and out, thus preventing a stale atmosphere.
- You can cover large pieces of equipment, such as a press, with an old sheet. Smaller items can be kept in a drawer or cupboard.

Sterilizing with Chempro or bleach
Every piece of equipment should be sterilized before use. Chempro, a chlorine-based agent, is extremely effective but it must be rinsed off with plenty of cold water. A weak solution of household bleach can also be used.

Warning: Great care must be taken when using either Chempro or bleach; if the solution comes into contact with acid, toxic fumes can be released.

Sterilizing with sulphite

A somewhat safer, equally effective agent, and the one most widely used, is metabisulphite, whether associated with potassium or sodium. The sulphite works even better when mixed with an acid.

How to buy it and make it up: Sulphite can be bought as a white crystalline powder in 100 g ($3\frac{1}{2}$ oz) and larger packs. For most people the 100 g pack is adequate. It can be made up into a 10% solution by dissolving it in some cold water, say 250 ml (9 fl oz) or thereabouts – the precise figure is not important – and then making the total quantity up to 1 litre ($1\frac{3}{4}$ pints). Kept in a dark bottle in a cool place this solution will remain effective for several months. If you think that this quantity is more than you are likely to use, make up any quantity you wish in the same proportion. One 5 ml spoonful of this solution is the equivalent of 1 Campden tablet.

Sterilizing with sulphite: (1) Wash all equipment using a brush if necessary. (2) Make a sterilizing solution using sulphite and citric acid (do not inhale the sulphur dioxide which is produced). (3) Pour the solution into a jar and swirl it about. (4) Return it to the jug for use with all other pieces of equipment.

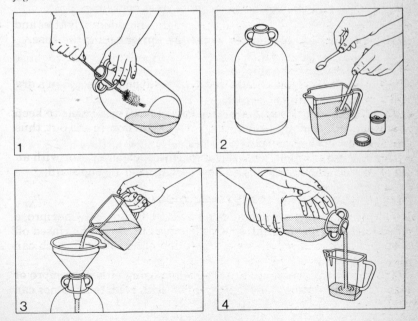

Sterilizing with Campden tablets

Campden tablets are a compressed form of sodium metabisulphite. Each tablet contains a precise quantity of sulphite that in solution releases just over 50 parts per million of the bactericide sulphur dioxide. *Take care to avoid inhaling the sulphur dioxide, especially if you suffer from a bronchial condition.* Four tablets crushed and dissolved in 500 ml (18 fl oz) of cold water, together with 5 ml (1 tsp) citric acid crystals make a strong solution that can be used to sterilize bottles, jars, corks, bins, straining bag, trial jar, funnel and so on during the course of a single session of, say, three hours.

- Pour the solution into a bottle, close it with your hand, shake it gently, wetting every inner surface many times, then empty the solution into another bottle or jar and repeat the process.
- Drain the bottle, jar or piece of equipment but do not rinse it in water or dry it with a cloth. The small trace of solution adhering to the surface is beneficial to the wine.
- Remember that because of the addition of citric acid the solution will not remain effective for longer than a single sterilizing session, and will not keep overnight or for several hours.

THE WINERY

Good hygiene should be maintained throughout the area where the wine is made and stored. In a commercial organization you would be required to cover your hair and wear protective clothing. Whilst this is not necessary at home, do take note of the principle and do all that you can to maintain good hygiene.

Do keep the floor clean and wash it regularly with a bactericide such as a weak solution of bleach.

Do clean up any spilt must or wine at once and wipe the surface over with a clean cloth that has been soaked in a sulphite solution.

Do wipe the outside of bins and jars with a cloth soaked in sulphite from time to time.

Do remember always to wash your hands, rinse them free of any perfume in the soap and dry them on a clean towel before you clean, crush, strain or press fruit.

WINEMAKING

The History of Wine

THE EARLIEST BEGINNINGS

Archaeological evidence suggests that wine has been made from fermented grape juice for some 8000 years. The vine, *Vitis vinifera*, grew wild in the area that used to be called Asia Minor and the inhabitants of the upper valleys of the Euphrates and Tigris no doubt learned that the juice from the berries was good to drink. All that was then needed was for some of the juice to be left in a gourd overnight for fermentation to begin.

Vine cultivation

By 4000 BC the vine was under primitive cultivation. The planting of vines and the making of wine from grape juice spread slowly through

> **British beverages**
> ● In Celtic Britain honey was diluted with water and fermented into mead. Variations were made by adding fruit juices, flowers and leaves for flavouring. Cider was also popular among the Celts.
> ● Although sugar was available as early as the fourteenth century, it was very expensive. Honey continued to be used for sweetening until the arrival of cheap sugar from the West Indies during the eighteenth century. It was then that country winemaking from fruits and other ingredients really started.
> ● Imported grape wine was fairly cheap but not always as good as Hereford cider; ale always has been the common drink.

Palestine to Egypt, thence to Thrace and Crete, and later to southern Greece and Italy. The vine reached Marseille in southern France in about 500 BC and Bordeaux in about 50 BC.

EARLY WINEMAKING METHODS

- The introduction of sugar in the eighteenth century spawned a wealth of recipes including the 'improvement' of imported grape wines with home-produced fruit wines. Many books of instruction appeared but few contained any technical knowledge.
- Boiling water was usually poured over the ingredients to extract the colour and nutritious elements. Although this killed the wild yeasts, after a few days spoilage moulds often infected the must. It was customary to leave crushed fruits and water in an open vessel until they became covered with a green mould!
- Muslin was spread over crocks of steeping fruit for protection and fermentation-on-the-pulp was seldom practised. Hessian or linen bags were used for pressing the pulp after it had been strained through a colander.

Sugar
Different kinds of sugar, called candy or preserving sugar, were used. They were not quite as pure as the sugars of today but substantial quantities were used – often as much as 1.8 kg (4 lb) to the gallon. This resulted in very sweet, low-alcohol wines that had to be well laced with brandy from France to prevent them from turning to vinegar.

Fermentation
Bread yeast was spread on a slice of toast and floated on the pressed juice until fermentation started. The must was then poured into a cask that was filled to the brim so that the fermentation could 'boil over' and take with it much of the unwanted debris containing pulp, dead yeast and so on. This was called the 'tumultuous ferment'. When it settled down a large pebble was sometimes placed over the bunghole to keep out insects, mice and other small animals during the secondary fermentation.

Cellarcraft
Racking was regarded for a long time as the great cure all, especially among commercial winemakers. Most housewives who made country

wines seem to have been aware of the need to use clean containers but a sulphur match was the only form of sterilization then available for home use.

The early winemakers
Most farmers' wives made wine, usually in quantities sufficient to fill a 9- or 18- gallon cask. Cottagers who made wine in smaller quantities used earthenware crocks and jars. Cups or basins were inverted over the jars to keep out flies, as there were no airlocks.

Rubber tubing was used to siphon the finished wine into bottles. These were usually closed with flanged stoppers, since the bottles were rarely laid on their sides and the wine was always drunk far too young.

Trial and error
Experimentation was as active then as it is today and all kinds of ingredients were used. It is from the results of some of these experiments that we know what not to use today.

Lead poisoning: This was fairly common because earthenware crocks and jars glazed with a lead slip were widely used. Fortunately most vessels are now glazed with a salt slip. Surprising as it may seem, lead-glazed vessels were in common use until about 1950.

THE NEW BEGINNING
In the early 1950s there was a dramatic change and many of the standard items used in winemaking today were introduced.
Polythene dustbins of varying sizes and colours became available. Their loose-fitting lids made muslin obsolete.
Glass demijohns appeared, often from laboratories which had bought the chemicals they originally contained.
The first airlocks were blown.
Hydrometers were offered for sale in chemists' shops.
Campden tablets had been used since the 1930s for preserving fruit; now a new use was found for them.
Wine yeasts were developed for making wines in a style similar to the various commercial wines.

A revolution in home winemaking had occurred and more and more people were starting on this new hobby.

Winemakers' clubs and competitions

In the late 1950s a monthly magazine for winemakers was started by C.J.J. Berry of Andover and the first clubs were also formed at this time. In 1959 the first wine competition was held, organized by Mr Berry in Andover. In 1961 the first nationally organized conference and competition was held in Harrow.

Winemaking today

Since 1959 our knowledge of winemaking has increased substantially. Much has been learned from the commercial winemakers who also benefited from a similar revolution in their own technology and equipment.

Do take the trouble to find out as much as you can because a wealth of knowledge, much of which you will hopefully find in the pages which follow, is available at every level.

THE BENEFITS OF WINE

In the ancient Egyptian and Greek civilizations, wine was reserved for the rich. As the therapeutic qualities of wild herbs and plants became known, the leaves, flowers or roots were either steeped in wine to extract their beneficial qualities, or their juices were mixed with wine to mask their bitter flavour. Wine was used not only as a medicine that relaxed tension, reduced inhibitions, aided digestion and generally toned up the system but also as a vehicle for taking other medicines.

HOW WINE WAS DRUNK

The Romans mostly drank their wine with water, usually in the proportion of nine measures of water to three of wine, which produced 560 ml (1 pint) of fluid containing some 3% alcohol. Men sometimes drank their wine and water half and half or, on occasions, three of water to nine of wine. Only the young rakes of the day drank their wine neat but then everyone drank a lot and drunkenness was rife. The intoxicating effects of wine had been discovered as early as Biblical times, as the story of Noah shows.

WINE AS MEDICINE

From the Middle Ages and up to the turn of the nineteenth century, countryfolk made wines from different ingredients as a specific for different ailments, notably elderberry wine for coughs and colds. Wine's intoxicating effects were also used to good effect in early operations to anaesthetize the patient. Both wine and vinegar were used to sterilize wounds.

In Elizabethan times

William Turner, physician to Queen Elizabeth I, wrote the first book on wine to be published in England in 1568. He described how red wine heated the blood and caused the development of stones in the kidney and bladder. He recommended German white wine instead, to cool the blood, prevent the formation of stones and flush the offending particles from the system. 'The stone' was then a prevalent and very painful ailment and the red wine of Bordeaux was widely imported and drunk in the taverns and inns in much larger amounts than the wines drunk today.

Today

In recent years research into the therapeutic qualities of wine has been extensive. In France Dr Maury has prescribed specific French wines for different ailments. In the USA scientists have discovered that wine dilates the blood vessels and is therefore beneficial to those suffering from heart trouble. They have also shown that people who drink about $\frac{1}{2}$ litre (17 fl oz) of wine a day live longer than others who either drink less or to excess.

The tonic effects of all wines have long been recognized and one can still buy a number of different wines that contain extra mineral salts and other medicinal additives from wine merchants. Doctors often recommend convalescents to take a glassful of such wine before their main meal each day.

Easy does it

All wine contains alcohol. Taken in moderation and in conjunction with the many acids, mineral salts, vitamins and trace elements in wine, alcohol is beneficial. In excess, however, alcohol is poisonous and continued excessive drinking damages both the liver and the brain and, in the most extreme cases, can cause death. Wine is good for you, so drink it regularly and enjoy it – but in moderation.

Styles of Wine

THE SIMPLEST CLASSIFICATIONS
Some people might say that the only definition that matters is whether a wine is sweet or dry. Palates are, however, becoming more sensitive and some further classification is necessary.
Colour: Wines can be red, white, rosé or tawny. Each colour has a range of distinctive variations that we can make at home.
Use: Wines can be suitable to drink before, during or after meals. Each purpose will cover wines from the total range of colours.

Of course, you can drink any kind of wine at any time and with any type of food, but if you want to get the best out of your wine you will know that particular wines are more suitable for particular occasions. So before making your next wine, think about the circumstances in which you will be drinking it.

APERITIFS
The charming French word *apéritif* is usually translated into English as the rather less mellifluous 'appetiser'. It is the generic classification for wines suitable for drinking in relatively small quantities before lunch or dinner to cleanse the mouth and to stimulate the appetite.

Sweet wines
These tend to dull the appetite because they contain so much sugar in addition to the alcohol. They are best left until later in the meal.

Medium-sweet to dry wines
- These are preferable to sweet wines. Since the purpose of an aperitif is partly to cleanse the mouth, the wine should contain enough acid for it to taste fresh and clean.
- A slight herby bitterness, usually associated with vermouth, is often appreciated, especially as it stimulates the gastric juices.
- The 'nutty' flavour of an oxidized wine is also popular. This is best exemplified by the dry and medium sherries so widely served as aperitifs.

Dry wines
On a very warm day a glass of cold, dry, white wine can be very stimulating, especially if it is drunk out of doors. Such a wine needs not only freshness and youthfulness from sufficient acid but also a fruit flavour that is slight rather than dominant but nevertheless noticeable. Commercially the wines from Alsace made from Riesling or Traminer grapes are very suitable.

Sparkling wines
For special occasions nothing is better than a glass of sparkling wine. The bubbles cleanse the mouth, stimulate the appetite and raise the spirit into anticipation of the meal to follow.

TABLE WINES
This generic term covers a multitude of wines suitable for drinking with all kinds of foods. Wine and food should enhance one another and accompany each other naturally. Neither should be so strongly flavoured as to dominate the other. The acid, tannin and texture of the wine should be appropriate to the food. The alcohol content should not be so high as to cause inebriation after two or three glasses. The wine should taste clean and be pleasantly flavoured with no bitter aftertaste.

White wines
These traditionally accompany white food such as fish, pork and poultry. They should be pale to medium straw in colour, dry to medium sweet and not too full bodied. The acid content should be low to medium: 4.5–6 parts per thousand, and the alcohol from 10 to 12% by volume. Sweeter, golden, stronger and full-bodied white wines should be saved for the dessert course.

Rosé wines
- So popular at parties and picnics, these should be a pretty pink in colour with no hint of orange, nor yet of too much red.
- The texture should be medium to light, the acidity fresh and clean, the flavour subtle and pleasant, the alcohol low to medium (10–11.5%). There should be just sufficient sweetness to be noticeable, enough to prevent the wine being called dry but not enough to be even medium-sweet.

Red wines
- These traditionally accompany red meats, game and cheese. They should be dry without any noticeable sweetness. The colour should be a deep red without blue tints, which indicate extreme youthfulness and therefore immaturity, and without brown tints which indicate oxidation. Very slight hints of brown at the rim suggest advanced age and are acceptable if the wine is otherwise sound.
- The wine should contain enough acid and tannin to balance the texture of the meat which will of course vary. A rump steak, jugged hare or a thick lamb chop will need a wine with more acid, tannin and alcohol than, say, a thinly carved rib of beef, veal cutlets, or a shoulder of lamb. Acidity can vary from 5 to 7 parts per thousand and alcohol from 11 to 13% by volume with the lower figure suitable for the lighter meats and the higher figure for the heavier ones. All the wines should taste smooth and the good fruity flavour should be mellow.

Dessert wines
- These wines are not actually meant to accompany the dessert course of a meal but are drunk at the end of the meal. They may be a rich red in the style of port wine, a full tawny in the style of Madeira, or deep golden in the style of muscat.
- Dessert wines should all be fairly strong – 16–20% alcohol – with a relatively low acidity of from 4.5 to 6 parts per thousand. They should be full bodied and with a sweetness that is neither marked nor cloying – that job is left to liqueurs. The dessert wine should round off the meal satisfyingly. It should possess character, a quality immediately recognizable in the right wine but almost impossible to describe.

Social wines
- Wine does not have to be drunk only at mealtimes. It serves for many other social occasions too. Social wines may be red or white, light enough to be drunk without food or with just a cheesy biscuit or potato crisp.
- They may also be stronger in flavour and alcohol – up to 14% – and can often be exemplified by wines made from a single base ingredient such as elderberry or parsnip, that becomes the talking point of the conversation. Many people prefer these wines to be at least off-dry and even medium-sweet.

Equipment and Hygiene

BASIC EQUIPMENT

To the beginner winemaking equipment may conjure up visions of enormous vats, jars, bottles, pipes, a press and similar extensive paraphernalia. Happily these are not required. People new to making wine at home need only acquire a few small items to get started. Other equipment can be obtained as their interest and experience increase.

The beginner's kit

At most Home-Brew centres, you can purchase a winemakers' beginner's kit. The precise contents will vary from one manufacturer to another but are likely to be something like this:

- a 4.5-litre (1 gallon) glass demijohn.
- a bored bung to fit into the neck of the demijohn and an airlock to fit into the bored bung.
- a plastic funnel and a length of plastic tubing, possibly with a small tap attached.
- half a dozen bottles and corks and some decorative labels on which to write the name and year of the wine.
- a sachet of yeast.
- a sachet of Campden tablets.
- a container of concentrated grape juice.

Only water and, usually, a small quantity of sugar are needed in addition to get you started. Within a few minutes your first gallon of wine can be under way. There is available a great range of concentrates to make red and white grape wines, including sherry- and vermouth-style wines, as well as some for country fruit wines such as apple, blackberry and elderberry.

22 · WINEMAKING

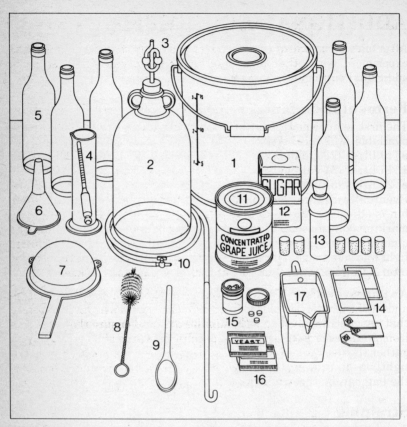

All the basic winemaking equipment you will need: **(1)** plastic bin for pulp fermentation; **(2)** fermentation jar (demijohn); **(3)** airlock in a bored bung; **(4)** hydrometer and trial jar; **(5)** wine bottles; **(6)** plastic funnel; **(7)** nylon sieve; **(8)** bottle and jar brush; **(9)** wooden spoon; **(10)** J tube siphon; **(11)** concentrated grape juice; **(12)** sugar; **(13)** corking tool and corks; **(14)** labels for bottles and jars; **(15)** Campden tablets; **(16)** sachets of yeast; **(17)** plastic jug.

EQUIPMENT AND HYGIENE · 23

ADDITIONAL EQUIPMENT

After making up one or two wine kits it is likely that you will want to experiment with other ingredients. For these you will need some additional equipment.

Fermentation bin

The first requirement is for at least one fermentation bin. These are available in several sizes:
- 10 litres ($2\frac{1}{4}$ gallons)
- 15 litres ($3\frac{1}{3}$ gallons)
- 25 litres ($5\frac{1}{2}$ gallons)

Eventually all three may be useful but for most purposes the 15-litre bin is adequate. Buy one with a fitting lid and graduated quantity markings on the side. This scale is most helpful for controlling the quantity of water required. A carrying handle is provided. The bin is light and safe to use. It can be easily sterilized and cleaned and dried after use. Small items may be stored in it when not in use.

An improvised bin: If you need an extra bin in an emergency a large and strong plastic bag placed in a cardboard carton will do. Make sure that you sterilize the bag with sulphite first and ensure that it is free from pinholes or weak seams. Be careful not to overfill the bag. Then gather the neck together and fasten it with a rubber band but not so tightly as to prevent the fermentation gas from escaping. After use, the bag can be thrown away.

Straining

A **nylon straining bag** will be needed for most items. The bags are available in two sizes – small and large – and in two meshes – coarse and fine. One large, fine-mesh bag covers most needs, but a back-up is always an asset. A **nylon sieve** is also useful.

Stirring and cleaning

A **long-handled plastic spoon** is necessary for stirring and a **long-handled brush** for cleaning bottles and jars. Different-sized **funnels** may be helpful too.

Hydrometer

Perhaps your most important acquisition at this stage is a hydrometer and trial jar for testing the specific gravity of the must or wine. You can buy a plastic one with a flat chart or a glass one with the chart in a tube.

Plastic or glass? There is not much to choose between the two. The plastic hydrometer is virtually unbreakable but the graduation is not quite so fine as that of the glass one which can be broken if it is handled carelessly. There is a more sophisticated glass hydrometer fitted into a tube which has a nozzle at one end and a rubber bulb at the other. The bulb is squeezed to expel the air and the nozzle dipped into a sulphite solution. The pressure on the bulb is released and the tube fills with the sterilizing solution. After one minute the bulb is squeezed to expel the sulphite solution and the same process is repeated with the must or wine to be tested. The hydrometer floats in the usual way and a reading is taken, then the sample is returned to its container. This type is more expensive but quicker, simpler and safer to use.

Thermometer

A long thermometer with a range from 0 to 100°C (32 to 212°F) is often required to find out the temperature of a must or wine before it is checked with a hydrometer and also before a yeast starter is added. Keep the thermometer in a protective plastic case when not in use.

More jars and airlocks

- More fermentation and storage jars will be required. The brown jars are best for storage. Glazed earthenware jars are especially useful for storing wines that need long maturation. They are so thick that they insulate the wine from sudden changes in temperature. Cork or rubber bungs may be used with them.
- Additional bored bungs and airlocks will also be required if you wish to ferment several musts at the same time. There are a number of different shapes and sizes of airlocks available in both glass and plastic to suit all needs.

Warming devices

- If wine is to be made in an unheated room in winter, or in one where there is a substantial difference between daytime and night-time temperatures, it may be necessary to use a **heating pad** on which to stand the fermenting jar.
- Sometimes these can create rather too much warmth, so check the temperature of the must after it has been on such a pad for, say, 8 to 10

EQUIPMENT AND HYGIENE · 25

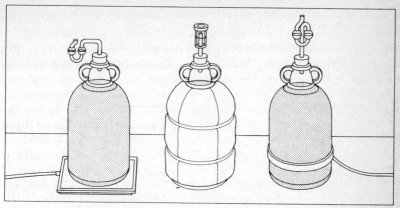

Various warming devices (*from left to right*): electric thermal pad, thermal demijohn cover and electric thermal belt.

hours. If the temperature is above 21°C (70°F) place two thin pieces of wood across the pad and stand the jar on these. This will then allow the air to circulate, reduces the temperature slightly and produces better wine.
* An alternative to a thermal pad is a **thermal belt** that fits around the jar. The same precautions need to be taken.
* An **immersion heater** lowered into the must and then coupled to a **thermostat** can also be used. But, again, keep an eye on the temperature. The thermostat is not very finely gauged and may cause 5°C (10°F) fluctuations of temperature in the must.
* Once fermentation has started, some heat is generated by the activity of the enzymes. A simple teacosy-like **padded cover** with a tiny outlet for the airlock is likely to be just as effective and much cheaper than an electrical gadget. A little care will be needed to keep the cover clean and free from spills of fruit juice or wine.

Jar labels
There are now some very good plastic write-on, rub-off labels that can be fitted on to the neck handles of fermentation and storage jars. Accurate labelling is important. When you make several wines at a time it is very easy to become confused as to which wine is which.

Bottles
Wine bottles can of course be bought but it is often possible to obtain them free from licensed restaurants. Soak off the labels and wash the bottles before sterilizing them. As far as possible store wines in dark brown or green bottles to keep out the light.

Corks and corkers
Cylindrical corks are essential for storing bottles of wine on their sides. When softened they can easily be inserted into the bottles with the aid of a corking tool. This consists of a wooden cylinder with a hole in its side in which to place the cork and a piston that pushes the cork into the bottle. There are several differently designed tools including a bench model with a single-pull lever.

Wine labels and capsules
A splendid selection of attractive **labels** and **neck collars** can be bought as well as coloured foil or plastic **capsules** to fit over the mouth of the bottle and cork to provide a professional finish.

Storage
A **bottle rack** becomes necessary if you make wine regularly or in any quantity but a **bottle carton** placed on its side will do for one dozen bottles.

Siphons
The plastic tube provided with the beginner's kit is a basic siphon but improvements can be made by attaching to one end a glass or plastic **J tube**. This causes the clear wine to be sucked *down* into the tube instead of *up* from the bottom of the jar with the risk of disturbing the sediment.
• Another version has a blocked end and several holes pierced into the tube about 12 mm ($\frac{1}{2}$ in) from the end. This causes the wine to flow in from the side, again with less disturbance of the sediment and it can also be used in a bottle that contains a heavy sediment. The outlet end of the siphon can be controlled with a small tap or a piece of rubber tubing that can be more easily squeezed than the plastic.
• A more sophisticated version with larger tubing incorporates a pump in the middle of the tube. It is particularly useful in siphoning from larger containers.

EQUIPMENT AND HYGIENE · 27

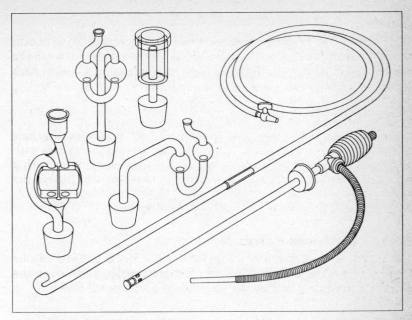

Assorted airlocks and siphons.

Filter kits
Winemakers who exhibit their wines often use a filter to ensure that their wines are crystal clear. There are several on the market, some using a mixture of powders, others papers or pad. A **stand** that fits over a **receiving jar** is often very useful for this. The wine can be passed through the filter more quickly with the aid of a **pressure pump** or by a **vacuum pump** attached to a cold-water tap.

Records
Detailed records should be kept of each wine made and for this you can use printed cards stored in a ring binder.

IMPORTANT STOCK ITEMS
Metabisulphite: A stock of this, both in powder and tablet form, is essential for sterilizing equipment and ingredients.

28 · WINEMAKING

Chempro: Some Chempro should be kept for removing stubborn stains and for sterilizing jars and certain other non-plastic pieces of equipment.

Pectic enzyme: Bought under a trade name such as Pectozyme or Pectinol, this reduces the pectin in fruit musts. The white powder has a longer shelf life than the brown liquid.

Diammonium phosphate and/or ammonium sulphate crystals: These will be required as nutrient for the yeasts. Proprietary brands of mixed nutrients, including names such as Tronozymol, are also available. Vitamin B_1, sold as 3 mg Benerva tablets, is another valuable nutrient.

Tannin: Brown grape tannin powder will enhance the character of many red wines. The liquid tannin seems to be less effective.

Acids: A small stock of citric, malic and tartaric acids should always be available to the serious winemaker to supplement the acids in the musts. **Acid-testing paper** that assesses the degree of acidity, or an **acid-testing kit** that measures the quantity of acid in a must, is also necessary.

Fining agents: These help a wine to clear and are widely used. Apart from proprietary brands of fining gels, the most popular agents are bentonite and isinglass. Keep a little in stock for the stubborn wine that is slow to clear.

Flavourings: Unfortunately a few wines may fail to please. There may be nothing wrong with the wine, just a lack of appealing bouquet and flavour. A range of flavourings is available to help you. They include essences for port-, sherry- and vermouth-style wines, as well as flavourings for apricot, cherry, orange, peach and mead, and the list is increasing steadily.

SPECIALIZED ITEMS
Casks
Shavings of oak wood and oak sticks are now available to impart an oaky flavour to red wines made in 4.5-litre (1 gallon) quantities. Small oak casks are occasionally used. The smallest that is safe to use has a capacity of 25 litres ($5\frac{1}{2}$ gallons). Make sure that it has been specially prepared for wine and has never held vinegar or beer. Unfortunately casks are quite expensive.

Crushers and presses
- For large quantities of fruit, especially grapes, gooseberries and apples, a fruit crusher is an asset. Its stainless steel blades quickly pulp the fruit ready for pressing.
- Another version consists of a stainless steel blade attached to a shaft that fits into an electric drill. The drill must be a powerful one, however, or the pressure from the hard fruit will stop the electric motor.
- There is a range of different-sized presses available including a small one that can be used for many fruits.

Juice extractors
- Juice extractors are becoming increasingly popular. Attachments can often be fitted to existing kitchen equipment such as food processors, blenders or mixers.
- Heat can be used on a double-saucepan principle in the Saftborn juice extractor, although some people feel that a stewed taste is imparted to the wine.

Mincers and shredders
Stainless steel mincers or fine shredders are also useful.

Handy gadgets
Many gadgets can be made by the home handyman to meet a particular need. For example, some dowel rods stuck into a plank of wood makes a splendid **rack** on which to drain bottles.
- A **torch bulb** soldered to a length of wire connected to a small battery is also helpful when examining the inside of a glazed earthenware storage jar for cleanliness.

Bag-in-the-box
- One of the most interesting developments of recent years has been the bag-in-the-box. This is a double-skinned, sealed, plastic bag inside a cardboard box. The outer skin is sometimes surfaced with a thin coating of foil and the inner coating is impervious to vapours. Ordinary polythene bags are unsuitable since, although they are airtight, they are not vapour proof and over a period of time there could be a loss of aroma, bouquet and sulphur – all required in the wine and not out of it!

● Welded to the bag is a rubber tap that can be removed while the bag is being filled with wine. The tap is then replaced and the wine is ready for serving, either by the glass or the carafe. By using the bag-in-the-box you not only save all the business of bottling but also consume only as much wine as you want in the confident knowledge that the rest will not spoil.

HYGIENE
Sterilizing ingredients
● Fruit should always be washed in a weak solution of sulphite to inhibit the growth of the micro-organisms that have settled on the surface.
● 5 ml (1 tsp) of the 10% solution or 1 crushed Campden tablet in up to 4.5 litres (1 gallon) of cold water is adequate for good-quality fruit. Twice as much should be used for bruised, damaged or slightly over-ripe fruit.
● The need for a clean must continues after the fruit has been washed and crushed. Add 5 ml (1 tsp) of the 10% solution or 1 crushed Campden tablet to each 4.5 litres (1 gallon) of must with the pectic enzyme. This protects the must from infection during the 24 hours allowed for the pectic enzyme to reduce the pectin and also prevents oxidation of the crushed fruit.

Keep everything covered
Whole fruit may need only a cloth over it. Store in a cool place.
Crushed fruit should be put straight into a fermentation bin with sulphite and covered with a close-fitting lid.
Pressed fruit should be disposed of promptly and not left about to attract fruit flies. Swarms of these tiny insects seem to appear from nowhere whenever fruit is being crushed, must is being stirred or strained, or indeed at any moment of the day or night when must or wine is receiving attention. These flies often carry bacteria on their feet, particularly acetobacter, which turn a weak wine into vinegar.
Musts and **wines** should be kept effectively covered at all times to keep out flies and insects. A thick cloth or sheet of plastic secured with an elastic band is best for this. Anything more lightweight will be ineffective.

Coping with Stains

When winemaking it is very easy to stain yourself, your clothes, floors, walls and other things unless you are very careful. Here are some hints on how to avoid doing so and on how to get rid of any accidental stains.

PROTECT YOURSELF

- Take especial care when picking, cleaning and crushing the following fruits and vegetables: beetroot, blackberries, black cherries, blackcurrants, black plums, damsons and, of course, elderberries; also when straining, pressing and racking musts and wines made from them.
- It is sensible to wear an apron to protect your clothes and thin rubber gloves to protect your hands. Otherwise the dark fruit and acid colouring gets beneath and around fingernails as well as into patches of rough skin.
- Prevention is better than cure here because these stains are very difficult to remove and you may sometimes have to wait for them to wear off. Very dark dyes also stain porous material such as wood and wool and even some plastic surfaces.

PROTECT YOUR HOME

- It is best to make your wine and beer in an outhouse converted for the purpose. Many home winemakers now have their own small winery. The fruit can then be prepared and the wine made in hygienic conditions and splashes and spills will not wreak havoc with the decor.
- Alternatively use a utility room, the kitchen or bathroom where water is readily to hand to wash down mishaps.

Mind the floor – and the walls!

Spread newspaper on the floor to absorb the juice from any crushed fruit that got away. This is important when stripping elderberries from their stalks and when straining and pressing fruit pulp.

- Other areas to watch: Beads of juice sometimes squirt out of the side of a straining bag, whether in a press or held in your hand. Even if you are careful you can occasionally make 'a right mess' on the floor – and on the walls. Straining bags can also sometimes burst under too much pressure.

Filling bins
- Never fill polythene bins with carrying handles to the brim, even if they have a fitting lid. When the bin is picked up its shape is slightly distorted and must or wine can easily be spilled.

Siphoning
- It is never easy to stop the flow of wine completely and at precisely the right moment when racking and bottling. All too often a bottle is over filled or the siphon is not sealed sufficiently when moved from one jar or bottle to another and wine is spilled.
- To prevent staining, stand the sterilized empty jars or bottles in the sink and the container of wine on an upturned bin on the draining board. This will provide the necessary height to effect an adequate flow of wine. If this is not possible, stand the empty jars or bottles on old newspapers that will absorb any spilled wine.

Serving wine with care
- A little extra care taken when serving wine can save a great deal of effort later in trying to get rid of stains. When pouring wine from a carafe or decanter at the table do watch out for drops that dribble down the outside of the vessel on to the tablecloth. Why not use an attractive ceramic tile, perhaps with a wine motif, as a decanter coaster? You can even have a kitchen paper towel handy to absorb that dribble before it starts sliding downwards.
- Always stand glasses on coasters. It is amazing how often filled glasses leave dark rings on the surface on which they have been standing.

PROTECTING EQUIPMENT
- After a period of regular use, notably in hard-water areas, a hazy discoloration appears on much winemaking equipment. Chempro SDP and domestic bleach are effective at removing this, particularly from glass jars, bottles, carafes and decanters.

- Make up the solution according to the instructions supplied, fill the container and leave it for 24 hours or so.
- A good rub with a jar or bottle brush also helps, but sand, gravel or similar substances are not recommended since they tend to roughen the surface and make further staining more likely.

Enamel saucepans
- Enamel saucepans sometimes stain, especially when heating black and dark red fruits.
- Leave the pan full with a weak solution of Chempro or bleach overnight and the stain will probably disappear.

First aid when things go wrong
If juice or wine is spilt on tablecloths, serviettes, clothes or the carpet, this is what to do:
1 Absorb it as much as possible by sprinkling salt onto the juice or wine. Paper serviettes, paper handkerchiefs or kitchen towels are alternative blotters. Use a plucking action which will help to confine the area rather than spread it.
2 Dilute the stain with cold water, soda water, or even a little white wine. Pluck at the stain again with absorbent material.
3 Wash articles that can be as soon as possible. Take items which must be drycleaned to the cleaner without delay. Point out the stain and describe its nature to the assistant.
4 Stains from white fruit juices and white wines are less serious but should still be treated in the same way. Prompt treatment is essential because old stains which have dried into a fabric are much more difficult to remove.

Further treatment
- Stains from **white** juices and wines are often less noticeable than red ones and after prompt first aid, washing or drycleaning, there is a good chance that they will be entirely removed.
- The **reds** are much harder to remove completely. Depending on the material and position of the stain it may be worth dabbing it later with a weak solution of Chempro SDP or domestic bleach. This works particularly well on stone floor tiles, lino, wood block and similar materials.

- When you empty out the bleaching solution, rinse the jar, bottle or saucepan frequently with clean cold water to remove all traces of the chlorine.

Polythene bins/funnels
- Don't use Chempro or bleach to clean these. Polythene surfaces are less smooth than glass and there is a slight risk that the chlorine will taint the polythene and anything that subsequently comes into contact with it.

Nylon straining bags
- These discolour quite quickly, but do not soak them in a bleach solution. Although the bleach is very effective it tends to damage or weaken the fibres and after a short while the bag will begin to come apart at the seams.
- Simply wash the bag clean in plenty of cold water and dry it in the air before putting it away. As long as it is carefully sterilized in a sulphite solution immediately before use it will be quite safe and the discoloration will have no harmful effect on either the must or the wine.

Base Ingredients

You can make wine from a very wide range and combination of ingredients. Palates differ as to the most suitable ones and these also vary with the style of wine. During the past 40 years I have made wine from a great number of ingredients and have had very few complete failures. I do suggest that at first, however, you use only the popular ingredients. When you feel sufficiently experienced you can begin to experiment. This chapter will give you many hints on what to choose and what to combine.

FRUITS

The outstanding merit of fruit, whether fresh, frozen, canned, dried, jammed or as juice, is that it not only makes good wine as a single ingredient but also blends well with other ingredients to make even better wine.

Fresh fruits

All fresh, edible fruits can be made into wine, including the many tropical fruits now widely available. Choose ripe culinary varieties for preference and select the best quality for the best results.

Fruits grown in the garden: These are ideal as you can harvest them at the most suitable point of ripeness. They can then be washed and crushed whilst they are still absolutely fresh.

Pick your own fruit farms: Their fruit will also be very fresh. Take plenty of containers with you so that you can bring the fruit home in shallow layers without being damaged. Organize your trip so that you can get home in time to wash and crush the fruit the same day whilst it is still really fresh.

A trip to the country: Here you can gather blackberries, elderberries, rosehips or sloes from the hedgerows and the same recommendations apply. Try to avoid collecting the fruit from places close to busy roads as they will be covered by a haze similar to that which dulls the brilliant surface of a car. And when you are picking do have a thought for next year and be very careful not to damage the bush.

The greengrocer: If you have to rely on the greengrocer for fresh fruit be choosy, avoid stale produce and decline damaged offerings.

36 · WINEMAKING

A selection of fresh fruits and vegetables which can be used in winemaking.

The only over-ripe fruit worth buying is the banana, at its best for winemaking when the yellow skin is heavily speckled with brown spots. The fruit is then usually perfectly sound, albeit a little soft underneath the skin. All other fruit should be sound, ripe, freshly delivered and look good.

The market: Sometimes a sealed box of fruit fresh from the market is less expensive to buy than loose fruit. These boxes often contain enough fruit to make from 13 to 18 litres (3 or 4 gallons) of wine and can be an excellent purchase.

Fruits from the freezer

Although wine can be made all year round, August and September in the northern hemisphere and February and March in the southern hemisphere are the busy months when most fruit is just ready for harvesting. Unfortunately it isn't always possible to make the wine just when the fruit is at its peak of perfection. Sometimes all your containers are in use or you do not have the time. Happily, the fruit need not be wasted because frozen fruit is excellent for winemaking. The freezing process causes the water in the juice to expand and burst the surrounding cell wall and, as a result, better juice extraction is obtained. Indeed, some winemakers deliberately freeze some hard fruits such as gooseberries to soften them when thawed. In addition varieties of fruit which do not ripen at the same time can be used in combination from the freezer.

Home-frozen fruit: This should be used in the following way:
- Before putting fresh fruit into a home freezer, stalk, wash and stone if necessary. Then pack it into small polythene boxes or bags. The small sizes both freeze and thaw more quickly and reduce the possibility of oxidation.
- When you take the fruit out of the freezer, you should empty it into a bin containing the water, sulphite and pectic enzyme required for making the wine. The sulphite also prevents oxidation and the fruit will remain as fresh as when it was packed.
- Freeze the fruit in the way in which it is to go into the must. If possible, it should be crushed as it will take up less space and unwanted air will be excluded.
- It is very difficult to clean and prepare fruit for winemaking after it has been frozen straight from the tree. It is almost impossible to clean elderberries properly and the small cap stems make the wine taste too bitter if left on. By the time stone fruit has thawed enough for the stone to be removed the flesh of the fruit has become brown and oxidized. Plums are notorious in this respect.

Commercially frozen fruit: Bought from a supermarket, this may also be used for winemaking. Get everything ready at home so that when you return with the frozen fruit it can be used immediately. Sometimes you can buy frozen fruit, such as morello cherries, which are not otherwise available in their fresh state.

Before putting fresh fruit into the freezer, stalk, wash and stone it if necessary and then pack it into small polythene boxes or bags.

Bottled and canned fruits

These make excellent, light table wines although none are really suitable for the heavy dessert wines. They may be used alone or in combination. For some reason wine made from canned fruits matures more quickly than wine made from fresh fruits and this is a very real advantage for those who need to make a fast-maturing wine.

- Use at least three 440 g (15½ oz) cans per 4.5 litres (1 gallon) of wine and ideally 250 g (9 oz) concentrated grape juice or a bottle of pure grape juice.
- If you want to make larger quantities of wine, catering packs from a cash-and-carry wholesaler are ideal.
- Read the small print on the can label and only buy fruit that contains nothing but a light sugar syrup or even fruit in its own juices.
- Avoid cans that contain preservatives, colourings or sweetening agents other than sugar. These agents are unfermentable and cause the wine to remain sweet.

Dried fruit

There are many dried fruits available to the home winemaker apart from raisins and sultanas and most can be obtained from specialist home-brew centres. The drying process concentrates the sugar and flavour of the fruit but some acid is lost.

Dried fruits, canned or bottled fruits, and cartoned juices all make good, pleasant-tasting wines.

Dried fruits to choose

Prunes make a splendid sherry-style wine or you can add a few to a must from which a red dessert wine is to be made. The prunes impart body as well as enriching the flavour.

Figs make good wines, especially in combination with rosehips and parsnips. A few mixed into plenty of raisins make a fine Madeira-style wine.

Dates have a high sugar content and enhance any tawny-style wine. They blend particularly well with high-acid fruits such as lemons and rhubarb.

Dried apricots and **peaches** make delightful wines in their own right but a few can also enhance most other wines.

Raisins and **sultanas** also make good wines on their own as well as improving all other wines. Approximately two-thirds of their weight is fermentable sugar, so allow for this when adding them to a must. Before use they should be washed clean of the mineral oil with which they have been sprayed which prevents them from lumping together and keeps them looking good.

Elderberries can pick up an infection when being dried, so wash them in a sulphite solution first. This also helps to clean them from dust and cap stems.

Bilberries, although very expensive, make a fabulous addition to red wine musts. As few as $100\,g$ ($3\frac{1}{2}\,oz$) per gallon make a tremendous improvement to the colour and flavour of red wines. Rinse them in plenty of cold water containing a little sulphite first.

Muscatels are also expensive but they do impart a wonderful aroma to a wine. Mix them with sultanas to make a sweet and fragrant wine to accompany the dessert.

Dried fruits to avoid

Dried apples and **pears** are hardly worth using. The flavour is too slight and you would need to add a prohibitive amount.

Dried orange peel is not recommended because it imparts a bitterness to wine that most people find unacceptable.

Fruit, jams and jellies

All fruit jams and jellies can be used to make wine. Bramble or redcurrant jelly mixed with concentrated grape juice is particularly good, so too is strawberry jam.

- Use at least three jars to the gallon and add a double dose of pectolytic enzyme to break down the pectin.
- Make sure that no preservatives, colouring or added pectin have been used in the making of the jam or jelly. Home-made jam that has gone a little sugary is fine.
- Fine-cut marmalades make attractive aperitifs but coarse cuts contain too much bitter pith.
- Gelatine flavoured with fruit essence is, of course, not suitable for making into wine.

Fruit juices

Supermarket shelves always contain a good stock of cartoned, canned or bottled fruit juices. The most popular are apple, orange, grapefruit and pineapple. Sometimes a mixture of several fruit juices is also on sale. All of them make good, light table wines.
- Use 2 litres ($3\frac{1}{2}$ pints) to the gallon and include some concentrated or fresh grape juice.
- Make sure that the fruit juice is unsweetened and that it does not contain preservative.
- Always add a pectolytic enzyme to the must.
- Occasionally you can buy other fruit juices, especially concentrated orange juice and blackcurrant juice. Less common are apricot, passion fruit, redcurrant and strawberry juice. These are often concentrated syrups so make sure that sugar, and not saccharin or sorbitol, has been used in the preparation of the 'nectar', the term often used to market this type of juice.

FLOWERS AND LEAVES

Flowers

Fresh flower petals and leaves have long been used to flavour alcoholic drinks. Before country wines were made, flowers and leaves were added to meads. Violet and strawberry leaves were popular.
- Remember that flowers and leaves can only impart flavouring to a wine; the rest of the usual constituents must still be added.
- As they contain no acid, sugar or body these must come from some other source. Traditionally, sultanas are and still can be used but concentrated grape juice is easier to handle.
- Remember also that the leaves, stem and calyx all impart a bitter taste to the wine and have to be excluded. In effect only the flower petals are used.

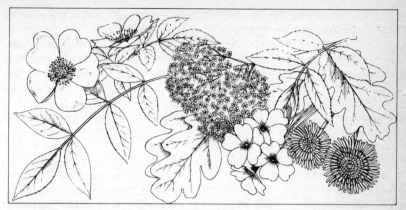

Fresh flower petals and certain leaves are excellent for flavouring both wine and mead.

Dried flowers

When fresh flowers are not available you can use a small packet of dried flowers instead: 50–60 g (approx 2 oz) is enough for 1 gallon. Often a wider range of dried flowers can be bought than can be obtained fresh.
- Again, use these in even smaller quantities than fresh ones to enhance the aroma and flavour of what might otherwise be a rather dull wine.

Poisonous plants

Some flowers are poisonous so please take *great care when you pick wildflowers*. A list of plants, vegetables and fruits known to be dangerous is given on page 46.
- Please use only the well-known flowers, such as the rose, elderflower, dandelion and primrose.

Leaves

The young leaves and tendrils of the vine and bramble are sometimes used to make a wine called a 'folly', derived from *feuille*, the French word for leaf.

- They can be chopped up and boiled to make a wine or frozen, then thawed, crumbled and added to a must to improve another wine.
- Blackcurrant, oak and walnut leaves may also be used as they contain a great deal of flavour. Add these in small quantities, say one handful per gallon, to red wine musts; the oak and blackcurrant leaves impart tannin as well as flavour.
- Wash young leaves that are just fully grown. They should be green and fresh and, of course, free from insecticide spray.
- Tea-leaves can be used to make wine and cold strong tea is sometimes used instead of grape tannin.

HERBS

The therapeutic qualities of herbs have long been appreciated and infusions of herbs in wine were once commonplace. Many herbs, however, have a bitter flavour that is only acceptable in a wine if you believe that it is going to improve your health.
- Please remember that these are only herb-flavoured wines: *they are not herbal medicines and should not be taken for any ailment without first consulting a doctor*. Nevertheless, like other wines, taken regularly and in moderation they cannot do you any harm.
- Use only the flowers, leaves or roots of the herbs as specified in the recipes.
- If you cannot obtain fresh herbs you may safely use a small packet, 50–60 g (approx 2 oz), of dried herbs to 1 gallon.

GRAINS

Although the Japanese have for centuries produced an internationally recognized wine from rice grains (*sake*), cereals are not a very popular ingredient for making wine in the home.

Rice: Use brown rice rather than the polished white variety. Crush or liquidize it, using a coffee grinder or liquidizer. Rice is often combined with raisins.

Wheat: This should be crushed and is often combined with raisins.

Oats: These are best left for horses, although oatmeal is sometimes added to black worts to make stout.

Rye: This is best left for breadmaking.

Maize: This is sometimes used to make beer but is not very suitable for wine.

BASE INGREDIENTS · 43

- Use fungal amylase instead of a pectic enzyme with grains since this will convert some of the starch in the grain to a fermentable sugar.
- Also remember to use the 'cereal' yeast, *Saccharomyces diastaticus*. This yeast, available from most home-brew centres, is able to ferment a little starch as well as sugar.
- Grains contain no acid, so this must be added, but they do have plenty of nitrogen.

SPICES

Spices simply add flavour to a wine.
Ginger: This is the best known spice in winemaking; it enhances marrow, melon and similar bland wines.
Mixed spices and herbs: These can be bought in sachets to infuse in a must to make a vermouth-style wine. Other spices or herbs can be used to flavour mulls of wine, mead, cider and beer.

VEGETABLES

Many vegetables are suitable for winemaking. They contain no acid but some flavour, colour, body and a trace of sugar. These ingredients are extracted by boiling the vegetable until it is soft and tender but not mushy.

Root vegetables

- Take great care to ensure that these are thoroughly scrubbed clean from every trace of soil, for this would impart an earthy flavour to the wine.
- Cut away discoloured or damaged parts before cutting the vegetables into thin rings and boiling them.

Surface vegetables

Surface vegetables, such as pea pods, should be absolutely fresh and green, fleshy and juicy.

A general tip
There is little point in experimenting with ingredients that have proved unsuitable. It is far better to make original combinations from proven, successful ingredients, especially fruits.

THE MAIN CONTENTS OF POPULAR FRUITS

The table on page 45 indicates the contents of the popular fruits that are most used by winemakers. The figures are, of course approximate, for they vary slightly with the degree of ripeness, variety and the season.

The riper the fruit the more sugar and the less acid is contained in each kilogram of fruit. The quantity of juice expressed depends on how well the fruit is crushed and pressed as well as on its ripeness.

When formulating your own recipes, bear in mind the figures in the tables. They give you by deduction a fairly good idea of:
- how much extra water is required to make the total of soluble contents up to 1 gallon.
- how much extra sugar is required to produce the degree of alcohol strength appropriate for the type of wine being made.
- how much extra acid to add to the must.
- whether a pectic enzyme is needed.
- whether yeast nutrient is needed.

> ### A quick tip
> Many winemakers add a little enzyme and nutrient to every must as a matter of habit. It pays to be on the safe side.

> ### Key to table on facing page
> 3.5 g citric acid
> 3.4 g tartaric acid } = 1 level 5 ml spoonful
> 3.0 g malic acid
>
> 5 g acid = 1 part per thousand in 5 litres
> Average needs of must = 4–6 parts per thousand
>
> Water content: *without stone **without skin
>
> VH = very high   H = high   A = average   L = low   VL = very low
>
> For VH, H and A, add pectolytic enzyme.
> For A, L and VL, add nutrient.

FRUIT	SUGAR g per kg	SUGAR oz per 2 lb	ACID g per kg	PECTIN	NITRO-GEN	WATER % of weight
Apple						
Cooking	80–100	2¾–3½	9–14	H	VL	75
Eating	100–130	3½–4½	4–9	H	VL	
Crab	120–140	4¼–4¾	7–12	H	VL	
Apricot						
Fresh	60–70	2–2½	11–13	L	A	75 *
Dried	400–440	13½–14½	9–11	L	A	–
Banana	180	6	3–4	A	VH	60 **
Bilberry	50–70	1¾–2½	9–10	H	A	75
Blackberry	50–60	1¾–2	9–13	H	VH	75
Blackcurrant	70–80	2½–2¾	30–40	VH	H	66
Cherry						
Eating	100–130	3½–4½	4–5	L	A	75 *
Morello	90–110	3¼–4½	5–6	L	A	
Damson	80–100	2¾–3½	20–24	VH	A	75 *
Date (dried)	640	21½	2.5	L	A	–
Elderberry	100–130	3½–4½	8–13	L	VH	66
Fig (dried)	480–550	16–18½	7	L	H	–
Gooseberry						
Cooking	40–60	1½–2	14–20	H	H	80
Eating	80–90	2¾–3¼	14–20	H	H	
Grape	150–200	5–7½	4–13	VL	A	70
Greengage	100–120	3½–4¼	10–14	VL	A	75 *
Lemon	10–20	⅓–⅔	40–45	A	H	75 **
Logenberry	40–60	1½–2	15–25	A	VH	75
Mulberry	80	2¾	4–5	A	VH	75
Orange	90–100	3¼–3½	8–11	A	A	75 **
Peach	80–90	2¾–3¼	5–8	L	A	80 *
Pear	90–110	3¼–4	2–4	H	VL	75
Pineapple	120	4¼	8–13	VL	A	66
Plum						
Cooking	60–80	2–2¾	14–17	H	A	75 *
Eating	90–110	3¼–4	14–17	H	A	
Prune	440–485	15–16¼	15	H	A	–
Quince	70–90	2½–3¼	7–12	VH	H	75
Raisin	640–680	22–23½	6	VL	A	–
Raspberry	60–70	2–2½	15	A	VH	75
Redcurrant	50	1¾	20–25	A	VH	75
Rhubarb	10	½	10–20	A	A	85
Strawberry	50–60	1¾–2	6–15	A	A	80
Sultana	640–680	22–23½	6	VL	A	–

Poisonous ingredients

The following list, by no means exhaustive, is of plants, vegetables and fruits which contain some harmful substance. Not all of them will actually cause death but they will, at the very least, make you feel unwell. For this reason they are best avoided.

A acacia, aconite, alder, anemone, aquilegia, azalea
B baneberry, bay leaves, beech nuts, belladonna, berberis, bindweed, bitter almond, black nightshade, bluebell, box tree leaves, broom seeds, bryony, buckthorn, buddleia, buttercup
C campion, celandine, charlock, chrysanthemum, cineraria, clematis, clover, columbine, cotoneaster, cowbane, crocus, crowfoot, cuckoo-pint, cyclamen
D daffodil, dahlia, deadly nightshade, delphinium, dwarf elder
F figwort, fool's parsley, foxglove, fungi of all kinds
G geranium, gladioli, goosefoot, green potatoes
H all members of the helebore family, hemlock, henbane, holly, honeysuckle (both flowers and berries), horse chestnut flowers and conkers, hyacinth, hydrangea
I iris, ivy
J jasmine, jonquil
L laburnum, laurel, lilac, lilies of all kinds, lily-of-the-valley, lobelia, lucerne, lupins
M marsh marigolds, meadow rue, mezereon, mistletoe, monkshood
N narcissus
O orchids
P peony, pheasant's eye, poppy, privet
R ragwort, rhododendron, rhubarb leaves
S snowdrop, spearwort, spindleberries, spurge, sweet pea
T thorn apple, tobacco plant, tomato stems and leaves, traveller's joy, tulip
W wood anemone, woody nightshade
Y yew

Other Ingredients

WATER

Hard or soft? We do not yet know whether hard or soft water makes the best wine. We do, however, know that some types of water are better for winemaking than others.
Distilled water is unsuitable for winemaking.
Heavily chlorinated water should be boiled first to expel the chlorine.
Spring water is thought to be ideal.
Well water is safe, provided there is no possibility of contamination from seepage into the well of poisonous agricultural sprays.
Rainwater should be filtered and then boiled before use to remove dust, pollen, micro-organisms, sulphur molecules etc.
Tap water, if suitable for drinking, is usually suitable.

SUGAR

There is never enough sugar in most base ingredients to make even a light table wine, since only grapes in a really good year contain a sufficient amount. Sugar must always, therefore, be added.

Sucrose

Ordinary household granulated sugar (sucrose) is best. It is pure, dissolves easily, is relatively inexpensive and is universally available.

White sugars

Glucose and fructose may be bought separately and added to a must but they are much more expensive than sucrose. Caster sugar, icing sugar and cube sugar are also more expensive and have no advantage over granulated sugar. Nor does cane sugar have any advantage over beet sugar – chemically they are exactly the same and of equal purity.

Brown sugars

Whether light, dark, Barbados or Demerara, all brown sugars are chemically similar as far as fermentation is concerned but they are

> ## How sucrose becomes fermentable
> - Chemically, sucrose is a disaccharide. Its formula is $C_{12}H_{22}O_{11}$. It consists of two mono-saccharides in combination, **glucose** and **fructose**, each of whose formula is the same, $C_6H_{12}O_6$, although the atoms are attached to each other in slightly different patterns.
> - In its disaccharide form sucrose is not fermentable and it must first be split into its two components by the enzyme **sucrase**, more commonly known as **invertase**, which also involves one molecule of water (H_2O) in the process. This enzyme is secreted by wine yeast and is the first in action; hence the need to pitch an active colony of good yeast to get fermentation started without delay.
> - This process can be bypassed, however, by boiling the sugar in water containing a little acid for about 20 minutes. The usual ratio is 1 kg sugar and 5 ml citric acid to 620 ml of water to make 1.25 litres of syrup. (2 lb sugar and 1 level 5 ml teaspoonful of citric acid to 1 pint of water to make 2 pints of syrup with a specific gravity of 1.300.) When cool and diluted this syrup is immediately fermentable by the other enzymes in the yeast.

less refined. As a result they impart a slight caramel- or toffee-like flavour to a wine. This is desirable only in a Madeira-style wine.

Golden syrup
This may be used if necessary. It consists of sucrose and invert syrup but imparts a distinctive flavour. It is suitable for Madeira-style wines and, in small quantities, for elderberry dessert wines which have a pronounced fruit flavour.

Black treacle and molasses
These should not be used under any circumstances. The flavour they impart is most unpalatable.

Honey
Honey may be used because 75% of its weight consists of fermentable sugar, but an over-riding honey flavour is also imparted to the wine. A small quantity of, say, not more than 225 g (8 oz) per gallon could be used in strong dessert wines to make the bouquet and flavour more complex. But to many people the honey flavour would be noticeable and not necessarily enjoyable.

ACIDS

Without sufficient acid in a must yeast will not ferment well and the resultant wine will have no bouquet, the flavour will be bland and insipid and it could be prone to infection.

When formulating your own recipes bear in mind the quantity and type of acid in your base ingredient.

The quantity: This varies marginally with the season but more noticeably with the degree of ripeness of fruit as some acid is converted to sugar in the ripening process. In addition some fruits contain a much larger quantity of acid than others. Blackcurrants and lemons are both highly acidic, for example, while dates and bananas have very little. Other ingredients such as vegetables, flowers and grains contain virtually no acid.

The type: Ripe grapes contain a preponderance of tartaric acid, together with some malic acid and a little citric acid. In all other fruits either citric or malic acid is predominant and tartaric acid is not present.

How to use

- When acid has to be added to a must – and this is almost always necessary – you can safely use citric, malic or tartaric acid crystals.

Citric acid is the cheapest and stimulates a good fermentation.

Malic acid enhances the fruity bouquet and flavour of a wine; any excess may be converted to lactic acid by bacteria.

Tartaric acid is thought by some to produce a better wine flavour.

Some winemakers use a blend of all three and in specialist home-brew shops you can sometimes buy packets of an acid blend, a mixture of citric, malic and tartaric in the proportion of 1:2:2.

- If you always add some grape to your must you will automatically be adding some tartaric acid. From the table on page 45 you can see whether the fruit you are using contains citric or malic acid, and it is a simple matter to add the missing one. For the vast majority of wines, however, it is quite sufficient to add citric acid as a matter of course.

> **A general tip**
> Acid is the cornerstone of bouquet and flavour and keeps a wine in good condition. A little too much is better than not quite enough. Omit acid at your peril.

TANNIN

This is the somewhat bitter substance found in the skins, seeds and stems of certain fruits – notably the grape – and also in tea-leaves. It contributes to the character of red wines in particular, but also to some dry white wines in the Chablis and white Burgundy style. It also assists in the preservation of wine during maturation.

How to use

- Tannin is best added to a wine in the form of a reddish-brown powder produced from grape skins. A liquid tannin is available but it seems to be less effective than the powder.
- A strong infusion of Indian tea may be used but it is very difficult to know how much tannin is in the infusion and this method is not recommended.
- Home-made red wines often seem short of tannin compared with commercial red wines. It is advisable to add to each gallon of red must 5 ml (1 tsp) of grape tannin powder.
- If the wine is subsequently fined and/or filtered, a further half dose should be added. The problem with fining or filtering is that more is removed from the wine than the suspended solids – notably tannin – so this must be replaced.

OAK

The benefits of maturing red wine in oak casks have long been known. At one time larger oak casks were widely used for country wines but they seem to have disappeared and are now exceedingly expensive. Furthermore most people nowadays make quite small quantities of wine for which the larger oak casks are not suitable.

How to use

- The oaky flavour in wine, best exemplified by a good Rioja, is nowadays better appreciated, hence the desire to add an oaky flavour to home-made wines. But how much should you add, to what wines and when? The answers are as varied as the wines themselves.
- You can buy oak chips or rods suitable for insertion into a demijohn of wine. Oak essence is available and also oak leaves.
- Conduct your experiments when the wines have fallen bright and have had their second racking.

- Experiment first with small quantities of finished wine, perhaps as little as one bottleful. Palates vary enormously and the oakiness enjoyed by one person could be disliked by another. For example, try two or three new oak chips per bottle of clear, finished wine for 1 week. If that makes insufficient difference try more chips for a longer period.
- Don't overdo the oakiness – the result should be subtle rather than pronounced. Chips which have been used before could be added to those dry white wines where an even more subtle flavour is required.

Oak in commercial winemaking
Commercially new, small 225-litre (50-gallon) oak casks, from which the extract is removed more easily, are used each year for the new vintage of high-quality red wines. The wine is left in these for up to 18 months before bottling. Older and larger casks are used for those white wines needing oak since the oak extraction from these casks is significantly less than from the new casks.

PECTOLYTIC ENZYMES

All fruits and some vegetables contain pectin, the setting substance in jam. Some fruits contain much more pectin than others. Some have a pectin-reducing enzyme in their skin.

How to use
- To obtain the utmost extraction of juice and to prevent pectin from causing a haze in the finished wine always include 5 ml (1 tsp) of a pectolytic enzyme or of Rohament P in each fruit must.
- Those fruits that are particularly successful for jam-making and which are also used in jellies should have a double dose, particularly apricots.
- Fruit juices, frozen fruits, canned fruits and dried fruits also need treatment with pectic enzymes.
- Pectolytic enzyme works best in a warm temperature, 24–27°C (75–80°F). Allow 24 hours for this activity before making any other additions to the must, apart from a little sulphite and acid to protect it from infection in the meantime. The acid and sulphite will be destroying or inhibiting unwanted micro-organisms, while the enzyme reduces the pectin and extracts the juice.

- Do not add bentonite or other finings, tannin, nutrient salts or yeast with or before the pectolytic enzyme.
- Ensure that the pan is closely covered to keep out further infection from the air.

NUTRIENTS
How to use
- As soon as the pectolytic process is finished you can add the activated yeast, but first mix in some yeast nutrient. **Diammonium phosphate** crystals are most commonly used but **ammonium sulphate** or a mixture of both may also be used. 5 ml (1 tsp) per gallon is ample, as many ingredients naturally contain some nitrogenous material.
- One 3 mg **Benerva tablet** containing vitamin B_1 also helps to vitalize the yeast, especially in flower and vegetable wines.
- Grapes contain vitamin B_1, as well as other trace elements and minerals beneficial to the yeast. If you add enough sultanas or grape juice concentrate, you need not bother with artificial nutrients.
- High-alcohol wines need extra stimulus. Use **Tronozymol**, a proprietary brand of a multiple-ingredient yeast nutrient.

SULPHITE

Sulphite is the popular name for **potassium** and **sodium metabisulphite**, whether loose as a white crystalline powder or compressed as a Campden tablet. When dissolved in a liquid it releases sulphur dioxide (SO_2). Sulphur has been used to sterilize, make wholesome and 'sweeten' casks for centuries. Compressed and made into a candle or match, it was ignited and placed inside the cask and the fumes killed off the bacteria, moulds and fungi.

How to use
- Nowadays we sterilize equipment and ingredients with a sulphite solution. Add a small quantity, 50 parts per million, to all musts to protect and purify them while the pectic enzyme is working.
- A similar dose should be added to the new wine after the first racking, when fermentation is finished. This protects it from oxidation and infection. It is especially important for low-alcohol wines.
- Sulphite temporarily bleaches some red wines and prevents any malo-lactic fermentation.

SWEETENING

Dry wines tend to mature more effectively than sweet wines. It is therefore better to sweeten dry wines just before serving them. You can mature sweet wines if you wish, provided they are very strong and are fully fermented to the limit of the alcohol tolerance of the yeast; or if they have been treated with potassium sorbate and sulphite to kill the yeast.

Using non-fermentable sweeteners

- It is safest to sweeten a dry wine with a non-fermentable agent such as **sorbitol** or **saccharin**. Neither imparts any flavour.
- Liquid saccharin may be purchased and added according to the dosage recommended on the bottle.
- Saccharin pellets may be crushed, dissolved in a little wine and mixed in just before serving.
- The sweetening may be added to the bottle or decanter. One pellet per bottle smooths away any hard dryness, two pellets impart a recognizable sweetness, and three a positively sweet taste. It is best to add them singly, tasting the wine in between, until you have attained the degree of sweetness you require.
- Sugar granules may be added just before serving but it is harder to mix them in. It also results in wine which is considerably disturbed, with consequent loss of ethers.

Using natural sweeteners

- There is definitely something to be said for excluding as many artificial chemicals as possible from your wine. A pure and natural product is always preferable and you may like to sweeten your wines with either unfermented or concentrated grape juice.
- The actual quantities needed depend on the degree of sweetness required. One bottle of natural grape juice should be enough to sweeten three bottles of dry wine. Remember that concentrated grape juice is approximately four times sweeter than natural grape juice. One 250 g (9 oz) can should be enough to sweeten 1 gallon (6 bottles) of a dry wine.
- As in so many other instances it is best to experiment with a small quantity of wine first and to increase the proportion of sweetening to the bulk of the wine when you are satisfied with the result.

GLYCERINE

Some winemakers like to add glycerine to their sweet table wines and dessert wines as it imparts a smoothness and richness that can enhance the wine considerably.

How to use
- How much to add is again a matter of personal taste and the individual wine. Two, or at the most 3 tablespoonsful per gallon added after the wine has fallen bright should be sufficient.
- Be careful to use only British Pharmacopoeia (BP) quality bought from a chemist. Industrial glycerine should not be used.

FLAVOURINGS

The flavour of a finished wine is sometimes not as strong as you might wish. A number of fruit flavourings can now be bought from some specialist home-brew shops.

How to use
- Do be careful how you use them. Some have a rather artificial taste and can spoil a wine so add them very sparingly, using only half the recommended quantity to begin with.
- Leave the wine for a week or two, taste it, then add more flavouring if required. It is much easier to add a little more than to reduce an excess of flavour.
- Sherry flavouring is particularly difficult to get right and a quarter of the recommended quantity would be a safe starting point.

ESTERS

Esters are the subtle and complex flavourings that make good wines so enjoyable. A small phial of a colourless liquid containing many esters can be bought and added to delicately-flavoured white wines. There is no point in adding them to highly-flavoured wines such as elderflower, rose petal or gooseberry.

How to use
- If you wish to experiment, add a few drops of the liquid to sound and clean white wines which only lack flavour. This could include apple

or pear wines, and perhaps peach and wines made from canned fruits or fruit juices.
- The precise quantity to add will depend on your taste and the wine itself and may be a little more than that recommended. In the UK look for the Gervin label.

COLOURING

Some black/red fruits, notably plums, do not always produce as good a colour as is desirable. Colour can also vary with the variety, the season, the degree of ripeness and the method of colour extraction used. Boiling extracts the most colour but it can also impart a stewed flavour to the wine. Hot water poured on to the crushed fruit, followed by fermentation-on-the-pulp, is the next most effective method. The longer the pulp fermentation lasts, the greater the colour extraction in general. But by then unwanted bitterness may also be extracted. Getting the right degree of colour with the right extract of other ingredients is not always easy. This is when red colouring matter may be used to advantage.

How to use

- The quantity to use depends on the wine itself and your judgment of a good colour. Again, add only a little at first and gradually increase the amount until you are satisfied with the result.
- Colouring is best added when the wine has fallen bright and been racked a second time.
- Some wines, notably beetroot and blackberry, have a tendency to fade and are therefore suitable subjects for experiment. Store them in brown jars and bottles in a dark place to minimize fading.

STABILIZERS

When fermentation is finished and the wine is racked for the first time it is important to stabilize it and to prevent infection and oxidation.

How to use

- To stabilize wine add sulphite at a rate of 50 parts per million (1 Campden tablet per gallon). If the wine is not quite dry, i.e. if its specific gravity is 1.000 or above, double the quantity of sulphite should be added to prevent further fermentation of the residual sugar. Also remember to store the wine in a cool place.

- There is always a slight risk that a few yeast cells will survive and, with the intake of oxygen during racking, will reproduce and form a colony that will begin to ferment some of the remaining sugar. A blown cork or, at worst, a burst jar or bottle may result, especially if the surrounding atmospheric temperature increases.
- The safest way to avoid this is to add 1 ml ($\frac{1}{4}$ tsp) potassium sorbate per gallon to the wine with the sulphite. Sometimes the two are combined into a tablet and sold as stabilizing tablets.
- Whilst these can be added to any wine at any time there is no need to add them to a really dry wine nor to a very strong wine. They should, of course, never be added to a wine that is subsequently intended for sparkling.

The Importance of Yeast

THE MYSTERY OF FERMENTATION
Leaven and ale yeast have long been known to man – our first records come from the Ancient Egyptians and leaven is mentioned in the Bible. What actually caused dough to rise and wort to ferment, however, remained a mystery for centuries. Scientists held diverging opinions. The chemists among them thought that fermentation was caused by oxygen.

The microscope
- The development of the microscope enabled scientists to identify and isolate the cells that caused fermentation.
- In 1835 Cagniard de la Tour in France and Schwann in Germany discovered independently that beer and wine yeasts were living, spherical organisms able to reproduce themselves. Schwann called the cells *Zuckerpiltz* – German for sugar fungi; Van Meyer, another scientist, used the Greek term 'saccharomyces'.
- This was only the first step but it was realized that such cells were always present in a fermenting must or wort and that they multiplied in it.

Yeast as a catalyst
Jans Berzelius, an early nineteenth-century Swedish chemist, had discovered that some substances, simply by their presence, caused others to split or change without being changed themselves. He called these substances 'catalysts' from the Greek 'katalysis' – dissolution. In 1839 he suggested that yeast was such a catalyst since in a sugar solution it caused a reduction of the large sugar molecules into ethyl alcohol and carbon dioxide in almost equal proportions without being changed itself.

Pasteur
In 1857 Louis Pasteur proved conclusively that if yeast cells cultured in an otherwise sterile medium (i.e. one in which no cells of any other kind were present) were introduced into a beer wort that had been

sterilized by heating it, then fermentation quickly started and yeast cells multiplied. There could be no doubt that it was the yeast cells alone that caused the fermentation of sugar into alcohol and carbon dioxide.

HOW YEAST WORKS
Enzymes
It was subsequently discovered that yeast cells secreted a number of enzymes and that these were the actual catalysts which caused fermentation. Some dozen enzymes are now known to be involved in the fermentation of sugar, although originally only one, zymase, was recognized. This collection of enzymes is called the **apo-zymase complex**. Each enzyme has a co-enzyme, the latter to stimulate the change and the former to receive the moving atom and pass it on to the appropriate molecule.

The shape and size of yeast cells
Wine yeast cells are quite invisible to the naked eye. They measure about $\frac{1}{1000}$ mm across and, seen under a microscope, are elliptical in shape. Other yeasts, equally small, are of mixed shapes that frequently vary with their age. Wild yeast, *Saccharomyces apiculatis*, is lemon-shaped. Some spoilage yeasts are hat-shaped, and others are long and narrow like sausages.

The mechanism of yeast cells
● Wine yeast is encased in a cell wall so fine that small molecules and enzymes can diffuse through it. Some enzymes, like invertase, diffuse out to convert the large sugar molecule, sucrose, into glucose and fructose. Other molecules diffuse in and are converted through a complicated chain of separate changes, each caused by a different enzyme, until alcohol and carbon dioxide are produced.
● These are not the only products of fermentation. Glycerine is produced and other higher alcohols – such as amyl, butyl and methyl – as well as acids – notably succinic, proprionic and valerianic.

What the cell needs to survive
The cell needs nitrogen as well as some vitamin B_1. It also needs oxygen so that it can reproduce itself. It obtains energy from the sugar which accounts for the small loss of sugar during fermentation and the emission of calories of heat.

Reproduction by budding
- When a viable cell is about 3 hours old and if it is in an aqueous solution containing oxygen, acid, nitrogen, vitamins and sugar, a tiny bud appears on the surface of the cell.
- This bud grows steadily over a period of about 3 hours. Then the nucleus in the mother cell splits and one half passes into the daughter cell.
- As soon as the daughter cell is mature that too starts to bud, as does the mother cell again.
- A cell can reproduce itself some twenty-five to thirty times before it dies, depending on the temperature and the quantity of oxygen, nutrient and sugar available. In the space of 24 hours one cell can become 256!
- A small sachet of dried yeast granules, sufficient to ferment from 4.5 to 22.5 litres (1 to 5 gallons) of must, could easily contain a staggering 100 million viable cells.

Reproduction by sporulation
- The yeast cell can live both **aerobically** (in the presence of air) and **anaerobically** (without air). In the presence of air the yeast reproduces itself readily. Without air the enzymes in the yeast cell continue to function but reproduction stops.
- In the absence of food and warmth, notably in winter, most yeast cells produce a tiny spore or seed which can remain viable for long periods until it comes into contact with moisture, food and warmth. The spore then grows into a cell and the life cycle starts again.

Death from sugar
In the past some winemakers added a large quantity of sugar to a must all at once at the outset. This often caused the death of the yeast cells.
Osmosis: Two-thirds of the cell consists of a watery liquid and, if the cell is surrounded by a very much heavier solution, the liquid in the cell diffuses out through the cell wall in an endeavour to thin the external solution and create an equilibrium. This process of osmosis applies to all compatible liquids. As a result the cell wall collapses on to the nucleus and the cell dies.
How to avoid this: Knowing this, we now make high-alcohol wines by dividing the total quantity of sugar into small portions and adding it to the must at intervals of several days until the alcohol tolerance of the yeast is finally reached.

WINE YEASTS

There are around 650 different enzymes and 1000 different yeasts but only a few will convert a sugary solution to alcohol.

Varieties

The best known of these is *Saccharomyces cerevisiae*, variety *elipsoideus*, or wine yeast. This yeast is elliptical in shape, hence its name, and has a number of strains that vary slightly in their enzyme systems and in their tolerance to alcohol. We tend to know them best by the name of the area or wine to which they are indigenous. The different yeast strains have different attributes and should be used to make wines similar in style to their name.

Bordeaux: This is widely used for very dry red table fruit wines.

Burgundy: This strain may be used either for dry red table wines or dry white table wines of the Chablis style.

Champagne: This has a remarkably high tolerance to carbon dioxide compared to other yeasts and remains active even at high gas concentrations. It ferments well under pressure and so is always used in the making of sparkling wines. It also conveys a pleasant taste to light white wines, particularly those made from apples and pears.

Hock: This is the name of the most widely used German yeast. It imparts a flowery bouquet to light white wines that are not quite dry or that are even medium dry/sweet.

Port: This is slightly less alcohol-tolerant than sherry yeast but contributes its flavour to a suitable red must.

Sauternes: This is used for sweet white wines since it ferments glucose rather slowly and reluctantly but readily converts fructose to alcohol. As a result extra glycerine is produced and some glucose remains unfermented, giving a richer and sweeter taste to the wine.

Sherry: This is often a combination of at least two strains and produces rather more acetaldehyde than usual. This contributes to the characteristic sherry flavour. It has a high alcohol tolerance and will produce 16 to 17% alcohol, given ideal conditions.

Tokay and Madeira: These yeasts are the most highly alcohol-tolerant of all the strains and are used to produce high alcohol dessert wines, both red and white.

General purpose wine yeast: This is used for those wines where the flavour of the ingredient is preferred, notably in simple country wines.

THE IMPORTANCE OF YEAST · 61

Yeast in its various forms (*from left to right*): dried yeast granules in a drum and in sachets; an activated yeast which is ready for use and yeast as seen under a microscope, the cells magnified 500 times.

Buying yeast

Dried wine yeast granules are now widely available sealed in foil sachets to keep them fresh. Some manufacturers market dried granules mixed with a little nutrient and sugar and describe it as 'compound'. Wine yeasts can also be bought as compressed tablets sealed in foil, others are available in tiny phials of distilled water and occasionally you can buy a yeast culture on an agar slant in a sealed test tube.

A general tip
Do not store yeasts for long periods and keep those that you have in a cool place.

ACTIVATING YEAST

All yeasts should be reactivated before being added to a must. The addition of a properly activated colony of yeast cells ensures a rapid start to the fermentation of the sugar. Yeast regenerates most quickly in tepid water.

The right temperature: It has now been proved that the best temperature for activating wine yeast is between 40 and 45°C (104 and 113°F) because the dried cell wall of the yeast more readily accepts the moisture and restores life to the cell within minutes. At lower temperatures some of the mitochondria and glycogens may be washed out of some of the cells before the cell wall is restored and a weaker colony results.

Never sprinkle a sachet of dried yeast granules on to the surface of a cool must. You will risk the loss of millions of viable cells and will delay the start of fermentation, leaving the must at the risk of infection in the meantime.

THE NEEDS OF ACTIVE YEAST
Warmth
Yeast is fairly heat tolerant and will ferment in the range of 10–30°C (50–86°F). Below or above these temperatures fermentation becomes sluggish and will eventually stop, although usually only until a more equable temperature is restored.

Nitrogen
Yeast needs nitrogen to survive. Grapes have plenty and some other fruits have sufficient for the fermentation of table wines, especially if a large quantity of the fruit is used. But too much of a particular fruit may cause too strong a flavour in the wine. It is important, therefore, especially when making dry wines, to include some grape or at least a small quantity of an ammonium salt such as diammonium phosphate from which nitrogen can be readily obtained.

Mineral salts, vitamins and trace elements
Grapes also contain a wide range of mineral salts, vitamins and trace elements that are beneficial to yeast growth and viability. If you add a small quantity of concentrated grape juice, sultanas or raisins, fresh grapes or grape juice to a must, you will stimulate fermentation and obtain a higher alcohol production.

A CLEAN MUST
In commercial winemaking
Commercially white grape juice is sometimes chilled, centrifuged or filtered, or all three, prior to the addition of a pure yeast culture. The

must is then spotlessly clean for the wine yeast to ferment the fruit sugars without hindrance. The result is a very clean-tasting wine in which the flavour of the grape is significant.

At home
We cannot do this at home but we do recognize the need to kill off weak micro-organisms and to inhibit others with sulphite before fermentation. Wine yeast has been developed to be more resistant to sulphur dioxide. Even so it is best not to add the active yeast until the sulphite has cleaned up the must and the sulphur dioxide has partially dispersed.

LOOKING TO THE FUTURE
New yeast strains
In various wine research institutes around the world zymologists are continuing their experiments into different aspects of the yeast cell. New strains are being developed and when proved to be superior to existing strains, are produced commercially.

Genetic experimentation
At least one zymologist is trying to vary the genetics of a wine yeast cell so that it can carry out a malo-lactic fermentation at the same time as the sugar fermentation. Another is studying the environment of yeast so that we can have a better knowledge of what constitues an ideal must.

Learning from the experts
- Every commercial winemaker is aware of the importance of the yeast cell. Only the best strain for the wine required is used. The culture must be pure and free from dead or mutating cells and especially from other micro-organisms. The must into which the culture is pitched is purified and hygiene is paramount at all times.
- As these experienced winemakers so wisely say: 'Look after your yeast and the wine will make itself.'

Colour and Flavour Extraction

There are a number of ways in which colour and flavour can be extracted from the base ingredients from which wine is made. These methods differ according to the ingredient and the quantity but first of all, you must prepare the ingredient.

CRUSHING

Before you can begin to extract colour and flavour you must first crush, chop or open up the ingredient in some way.

Grains
- Soak grains in water for an hour first to soften them; they can then be crushed by rolling them against a very hard surface with a heavy rolling pin.
- Alternatively a short spin in a liquidizer is effective. Be careful not to grind them into a flour!

Fruit
- To crush large quantities of fruit you should use a purpose-made crusher consisting of stainless steel teeth, bedded into rollers separated by a narrow gap, that are geared to rotate inwardly when the handle is turned. The crusher rests on a container into which the fruit pulp falls.
- You can also use a stainless steel blade fastened to the end of a shaft that fits into an electric drill. When the drill is switched on the blade spins round at high speed and will shred fruit placed in a suitable bin.
- Alternatively, place the fruit in a strong polythene bag and pound it with a mallet or steak hammer.
- Most electric food processors can have a shredder attachment fitted. These are very effective with suitable ingredients. As much as 50 kg (112 lb) of apples can be thinly sliced in as little as 15 minutes. This attachment is equally useful for certain vegetables.

COLOUR AND FLAVOUR EXTRACTION · 65

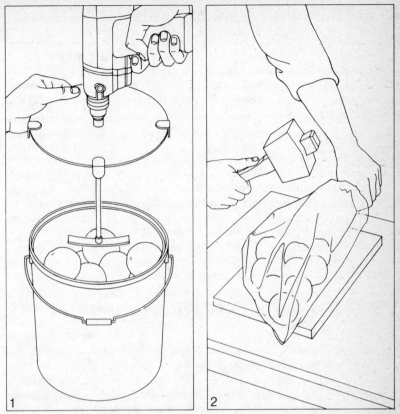

(1) This apple crusher consists of a stainless steel blade attached to a shaft passed through a lid and fitted to a powerful electric drill. Ensure that the apples are mellow and soft or cut up into quarters. (2) Mellow and soft apples can also be crushed with a mallet, but put them in a strong plastic bag to prevent splashing.

- A liquidizing attachment is also available and this is excellent for crushing soft and dried fruits.
- Some ingredients can be crushed in a stainless steel mincer.

FERMENTATION-ON-THE-PULP

After crushing, the juice can either be squeezed out of some fruits, as in the making of white wine from grapes, or fermented-on-the-pulp, as in the making of red wine from black grapes and other black fruits. This method is not reserved entirely for black fruits, as after crushing all fruits are best fermented-on-the-pulp for a few days to extract their flavour, sugar, acid and so on.

How it works
- The activity of the bubbling carbon dioxide moves the particles of pulp about in the liquid. The acids and developing alcohol also help to leach out the required ingredients.
- A significant difference is made by the addition of pectolytic enzymes to the crushed fruit. These dissolve the pectin surrounding the molecules of juice and thereby release them.
- Generally speaking, three or four days are long enough for pulp fermentation. Otherwise unwanted substances may be extracted that would make the wine taste coarse and harsh.

METHODS USING HEAT
Boiling
Colour and flavour can be extracted by boiling the ingredients (notably vegetables) in water.
- **Do** ensure that vegetables are boiled only until they are tender. If they become too soft and mushy, the minute solid particles in the liquid can be difficult to clear. Elderberries were traditionally boiled until they 'dimpled' and some winemakers still boil dried fruits. This is no longer regarded as wise, however, since a stewed flavour may be imparted to the wine.

The hot-water method
- Pouring boiling water on black and dried fruits is very effective and less likely to result in a poor flavour. Australian researchers have shown that if crushed black grapes are heated to 80°C (176°F), held there for 15 minutes and then cooled as quickly as possible, more colour, acid and sugar and less tannin are extracted than with pulp fermentation. The wine is smoother and matures more quickly.
- When the must is cool it can be pressed and the juice only used for wine, or it can be fermented-on-the-pulp before pressing.

COLOUR AND FLAVOUR EXTRACTION · 67

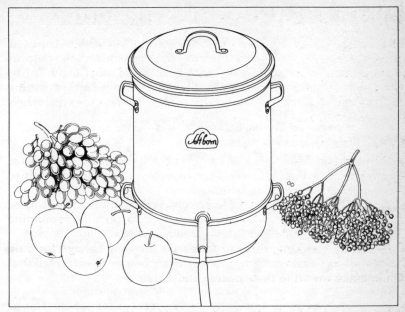

The Saftborn juice extractor. The fruit is heated by the steam rising from the boiling water in the pan beneath.

The double saucepan
An alternative method using heat is to use a double saucepan. The crushed fruit is placed in the pan above and heated by steam rising from the boiling water in the pan beneath. The Saftborn is specially designed for this and is available from specialist home-brew shops. There is an outlet for the juice beneath a wire mesh on which the fruit rests. The pan holds between 1.8 and 3.6 kg (4 and 8 lb) of crushed fruit and is very efficient.

JUICE EXTRACTORS
Electrically operated juice extractors are widely available and very efficient for small quantities of fruit or vegetables. The centrifuge leaves the pulp fairly dry and the juice can be used immediately. Unfortunately juice extractors are unsuitable for large quantities of fruit since they soon become clogged with residual pulp.

MACERATION

The flavour from flowers is best extracted by maceration.

Method

1 Pour hot water over the petals and rub these with the back of a plastic or wooden spoon against the hard surface of the vessel in which they are contained.
2 Rub the petals, a few at a time, with a firm circular motion to squeeze out the fragrant essences.
3 Repeat the process several times, keeping the container well covered in the meantime.

CARBONIC MACERATION

This is another method of extracting colour and flavour from black fruit.

Method

1 Crush a few fruits and, if necessary, add a little sugar.
2 Mix in pectic enzyme and an activated yeast. Then lay the rest of the uncrushed fruit on top.
3 Cover the bin with an airtight lid fitted with an airlock containing glycerine rather than water. Being heavier than water in the airlock, glycerine restricts the exit of the gas and marginally increases the pressure within the container.
4 As fermentation proceeds the carbon dioxide penetrates the skins of the fruits, releasing colour. Yeast cells carried up by the gas settle on the fruit and ferment the sugar, thus creating alcohol to leach out yet more colour.
5 After seven or eight days strain the juice away from the pulp. Press the pulp dry.
6 Ferment the resultant must with additional sugar etc. in the normal way.

The advantages

Carbonic maceration saves crushing, with its attendant risk of breaking pips and small stones. It is a particularly useful method for black grapes, black cherries and sloes, but bilberries, blackberries, blackcurrants, damsons, elderberries and black plums can also be used.

CITRUS FRUITS

There are always some exceptions to every method. Citrus fruits, in which the fruit pulp is surrounded by a highly pectinous and bitter-tasting pith, must be treated differently.

Method

1 Shave off the very thin coloured skin with a potato peeler or sharp knife, taking care not to remove any white pith.
2 As this skin contains most of the colour and much of the flavour, chop it up finely and add it to the subsequently expressed and strained juice.
3 To express the juice, cut the fruit in half across the centre and firmly rotate each half on a fluted lemon squeezer.
4 Strain the juice through a nylon sieve to exclude pips and particles of pulp.

(1) When preparing citrus fruits, first thinly pare the coloured skin with a potato peeler or sharp knife. (2) Then halve the fruit, squeeze out the juice and strain out the pips and pieces of segment skin.

FRUIT WHICH REQUIRES PEELING

Apples: The skins contain a little tannin and some winemakers recommend that they be peeled, but I find this unnecessary.
Bananas and **lychees:** Obviously these should be peeled and the skins discarded.

Peaches: These should be peeled and stoned. The fruit immediately around the stone is sometimes tainted and should be scraped lightly with a spoon.
Melons and marrow: These need not be peeled. They can be used whole, skin, flesh and pips.
Rhubarb: This needs only to be topped and tailed, then minced, shredded, liquidized or juiced.

PRESSING

Strain first: After crushing and extracting the colour and flavour, the base ingredient must be strained to separate the unwanted pulp from the juice. A nylon sieve or straining bag is best for this.
Firm pulp should be pressed to extract the entrained juice.
Soft, mushy pulp should be left to drain. Alternatively, it may be gently rolled about in the bag or sieve to release the trapped juice. Avoid squeezing or pressing.
Using the discarded pulp: Some pulps, such as sultanas, raisins, dried apricots etc. can be used to make chutney. Others, such as apple, elderberry, bilberry, blackberry and damson can be mixed together with more water to make a second-run rosé. Pulp from other musts need not be wasted entirely since it makes a useful addition to the compost heap and may be utilized to enrich the soil from which it came.

The Hydrometer

ITS DEVELOPMENT

● Winemaking at home is fundamentally a craft hobby but this single, simple-to-use scientific instrument can dramatically improve the quality of your wine.
● As far back as the sixteenth century an egg was floated in must by skilled winemakers to obtain some idea of the sugar content. Early attempts were also made to produce an instrument for the purpose.
● In its present form the hydrometer, or saccharometer as it is sometimes called, has been used to make wine since the beginning of the nineteenth century. In *The British Wine-Maker*, published in 1835, W. H. Roberts complained that many country winemakers made their wines far too sweet and he advocated the use of the saccharometer to control the sugar content. Alas his advice was, and is still, often neglected.
● The instrument we use today is an inexpensive, graduated float that measures the specific gravity of a liquid accurately.

THE ADVANTAGES

Producing dry wines: By using the hydrometer correctly you can control the alcohol and sugar content of your wine to make dry table wines of around 12% alcohol. Most people prefer to accompany the main course of a meal with a dry wine of modest strength rather than an excessively strong and sweet wine.
Preventing burst bottles: Bottles and jars that burst in the night with disastrous consequences need never occur if you use a hydrometer. By checking the specific gravity of a wine when fermentation appears to be finished you can find out whether any sugar remains that subsequent yeast activity could convert into still more alcohol and carbon dioxide. A stuck fermentation (see page 106) can be quickly diagnosed and dealt with.

SPECIFIC GRAVITY

Specific gravity is the absolute weight of different bodies of the same bulk. A cubic foot has been taken as the standard bulk of substances whose specific gravity must be ascertained. As a cubic foot of pure water at a temperature of 15°C (59°F) weighs nearly 1000 oz, it is considered to be sufficient for all practical purposes to call it so.

The base comparator

- When a hydrometer is floated in water at 15°C (59°F) the surface of the water crosses the chart at the 1.000 mark. By comparing the specific gravity, i.e. the density of weight of any must or wine to be tested with water, we can find its sugar content simply by looking at the table on page 75.
- The temperature of the liquid to be tested must be the same as that of the water at which the hydrometer chart was graduated. If this is not possible then you can allow for the variation.
- For convenience the comparative weights in the hydrometer tables are given both against the weight of 1 gallon and 1 litre of water.

HOW MUCH SUGAR DO YOU NEED?

- Most fruit musts contain the dissolved sugars that make the fruit taste sweet. But the precise quantities vary (see page 45). The table indicates the average sugar content of certain fruits, but this is only a general guide because of the variables of ripeness, variety and season.
- You should check the specific gravity of each must before adding any additional sugar. The recipes indicate the approximate quantity of sugar for the style of wine, but you may need a little more or even a little less. It is well worth checking to get the quantity as right as possible.

HOW TO USE A HYDROMETER

In liquid musts: The hydrometer should be used first just before mixing in the yeast. In all-liquid musts this is easy.
- Pour some of the must or wine into a sterilized trial jar containing the hydrometer. As soon as it floats freely and has stopped bobbing and twisting, read off the specific gravity figure on the hydrometer level with the surface of the must or wine.
- Remember that the surface of the liquid tends to climb up both the side of the trial jar and the hydrometer; looked at from eye level it resembles the shape of a saucer. Take the reading from the base of the 'saucer' rather than from the rim. This is known as the meniscus.

THE HYDROMETER

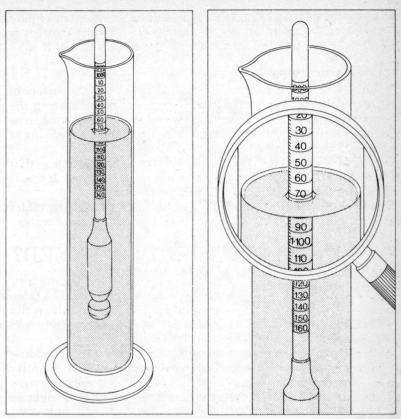

A hydrometer and trial jar used to test the must for its sugar content before adding the yeast and at the end of fermentation (*left*). The specific gravity reading should be taken from the bottom of the meniscus (*right*).

In musts containing pulp: Take a sample, squeeze it dry and then strain the must through very fine nylon to remove as much pulp as possible. Then test the liquid as described above.

Allowing for other substances: In addition to the sugar the must may contain a small quantity of pulp as well as some acids, tannins and soluble mineral salts. Allow perhaps 4 units for these and other substances to ensure an accurate calculation of the sugar content.

HOW MUCH ALCOHOL?

- Having ascertained the natural sugar content of a must it is easy to calculate how much extra sugar you need to produce the quantity of alcohol required. Approximately half the sugar is converted into alcohol and half into carbon dioxide.
- Theoretically 51.1% of the sugar could be converted into alcohol and 48.9% into carbon dioxide but this is biologically impossible to obtain since the yeast uses some sugar to provide itself with energy. In addition some acids and glycerine are produced. Some alcohol is also lost by evaporation, especially if the fermenting must is stirred or if the temperature of the must is high.
- In practice only 90–95% of the theoretical quantity of alcohol is produced, even by skilled winemakers. For those new to winemaking about 5% alcohol from 454 g (1 lb) sugar is usual.

ADDING THE SUGAR

To calculate how much sugar to add to a must, first decide how much alcohol you want to produce. Let us say, for example, that you want to produce a dry red table wine containing 12% alcohol by volume.

1 Check the specific gravity of the must prior to the addition of the yeast, nutrient and, if possible, acid and tannin. Other ingredients such as sultanas or concentrated grape juice should already be in the must since these contain sugar. Assume that the reading is 1.024.
2 Deduct 4 points for solids other than sugar and look down the specific gravity column of the hydrometer tables on the facing page until you find the figure 1.020. Looking to the right on that line you will see that this reading indicates that 1 litre of the must contains 51.9 g sugar (1 gallon contains $8\frac{1}{2}$ oz sugar).
3 Next look down the extreme right-hand column (probable % alcohol) until you find the figure 12%. Now look to the left and you will see that this is obtained from 235 g sugar in 1 litre of must ($37\frac{3}{5}$ oz sugar in 1 gallon of must).
4 Deduct the first quantity of sugar from the second to find the quantity that should be added to the must to produce 12% alcohol. Thus 52 g from 235 g leaves 183 g per litre ($8\frac{1}{3}$ oz from $37\frac{3}{5}$ oz leaves approximately 29 oz per gallon).
5 Multiply these figures by whatever quantity of wine you are making. For 9 litres of wine you would need $183 \times 9 = 1647$ g (for 2 gallons $29 \times 2 = 58$ oz = 3 lb 10 oz).

These calculations are not guaranteed to produce precisely 12% alcohol but the figure will be very close indeed. The difference would certainly be undetectable to the palate.

HYDROMETER – SUGAR/ALCOHOL TABLES

Specific Gravity	Sugar in 1 litre	Sugar in 1 gallon	Probable % alcohol potential
1.005	12.9 g	$2\frac{1}{10}$ oz	
1.010	26.0	$4\frac{1}{5}$	0.4%
1.015	38.8	$6\frac{1}{5}$	1.2
1.020	51.9	$8\frac{1}{3}$	2.0
1.025	64.8	$10\frac{2}{5}$	2.8
1.030	77.9	$12\frac{1}{2}$	3.6
1.035	91.2	$14\frac{3}{5}$	4.3
1.040	103.8	$16\frac{3}{5}$	5.1
1.045	117.0	$18\frac{2}{3}$	5.8
1.050	130.0	$20\frac{4}{5}$	6.5
1.055	143.1	$22\frac{9}{10}$	7.2
1.060	156.3	25	7.9
1.065	169.3	$27\frac{1}{10}$	8.6
1.070	182.3	$29\frac{1}{5}$	9.3
1.075	195.3	$31\frac{1}{3}$	10.0
1.080	208.5	$33\frac{2}{5}$	10.6
1.085	221.8	$35\frac{1}{2}$	11.3
1.090	235.0	$37\frac{3}{5}$	12.0
1.095	248.2	$39\frac{7}{10}$	12.7
1.100	261.4	$41\frac{4}{5}$	13.4
1.105	274.6	$43\frac{9}{10}$	14.2
1.110	287.7	46	14.9
1.115	301.0	$48\frac{1}{5}$	15.6
1.120	314.2	$50\frac{1}{3}$	16.3
1.125	327.3	$52\frac{2}{5}$	17.1

5 ml (1 tsp) of granulated sugar weighs approximately 5 g or $\frac{1}{6}$ oz.

TEMPERATURE VARIATIONS

- Hydrometer tables can be distorted by the temperature of the must when the reading is taken. Heat decreases the density of a liquid. So for any increase in the temperature of a must above that at which the hydrometer was calibrated you will need to make a small addition to the specific gravity reading.
- A comparable reduction must be made for temperatures below the calibrated figure. But this is a rare occurence and is usually disregarded.
- The table below shows the necessary subtractions or additions.

Temperature of liquid		Correction to specific gravity
°C	°F	
10	50	subtract 0.0006
15	59	no correction necessary
20	68	add 0.0009
25	77	add 0.002
30	86	add 0.0034
35	95	add 0.005
40	104	add 0.0068
45	113	add 0.0088
50	122	add 0.011

WHEN TO USE A HYDROMETER

It is important that hydrometer readings are taken and recorded at the following times:

1 Before the yeast is added.
2 After the pulp has been strained out and before the sugar is added.
3 After the sugar has been stirred in and completely dissolved.
4 When fermentation finishes.

All these figures help to provide information about the sugar and alcohol content of the finished wine. By adding together the total number of units fermented and by reference to the hydrometer tables a fairly accurate alcohol content can be ascertained.

STUCK FERMENT
- If the quantity of alcohol produced is less than that intended and the final specific gravity is higher than expected, then it is probable that something has caused the fermentation to stick. The reason for this and the remedy are dealt with on page 106.
- Without a hydrometer reading a stuck wine would probably be racked, sealed and stored. Eventually the yeast could become active again and start fermenting the sugar. The carbon dioxide would build up until the pressure was so great that the cork would be blown out or the glass container burst.

WHEN TO SEAL CONTAINERS
It is not generally safe to seal containers or bottles unless:
1 The specific gravity of the wine is down to 0.998 or below.
2 The wine has been fermented to a maximum alcohol content – 16% or above.
3 Fermentation has been artificially stopped with sulphite and potassium sorbate.

FACTORS AFFECTING THE HYDROMETER READING
- The tables on page 75 are for sugar alone in water. As mentioned on page 73, soluble acids, pulp and other substances would give a slightly higher first reading. To obtain a more accurate figure for the sugar alone remember to allow some 4 or 5 units for the other items. For example, a must specific gravity of 1.085 would be fairly close to a sugar specific gravity of 1.080.
- Towards the end of fermentation, when most of the alcohol has been formed and the wine is beginning to clear, the reading could also be distorted. Alcohol is thinner than water and therefore dilutes it. The difference is quite small but could be equal to the precipitated pulp. Furthermore, some of the sugar will have been converted into acids and glycerine that remain in solution.
- At the lower end of the scale it is difficult for the home winemaker to be absolutely precise; nevertheless the figures given are accurate enough for home use.

USING SPECIFIC GRAVITY

- There is no need to weigh the sugar accurately; after some practice it is quite possible to work in specific gravity alone.
- It is not always easy to measure accurately to the last gram the precise quantity of sugar you are adding to a liquid.
- Keep a record of the readings before and after the addition of sugar and count up the number of units fermented. The quantity of sugar used and the alcohol produced from it is not critical to a precise amount. The difference has to be fairly substantial to be detectable.

The volume of sugar: Remember that when sugar is added to a must it occupies some space and increases the volume. In fact, the addition of 1 kg sugar to a must increases the volume by 620 ml (2 lb increases the volume by 1 pint). By working exclusively in specific gravity you need not worry about the volume of wine produced. Ferment any small excess in a bottle alongside the main jar and use it for topping up after racking.

OTHER HYDROMETER SCALES

In the UK the hydrometer in use by winemakers records the specific gravity of the must or wine. In other countries hydrometers are used to record other aspects of the must.

The Brix hydrometer: This is used in the USA to indicate the percentage sugar content of a must. A reading of 18 on the Brix scale indicates that the must contains 18% sugar – equivalent to a specific gravity of 1.075.

The Baumé scale: This is used in France, Australia and many other countries to indicate the quantity of alcohol that would be formed if all the sugar were converted to alcohol. A grape juice may have a Baumé of 11.5, indicating that after total fermentation 11.5% alcohol will have been formed.

The Oechsle scale: This is used in Germany and it corresponds with our specific gravity without the preceding 1.0. Thus an Oechsle of 70° indicates that the must has a specific gravity of 1.070.

HYDROMETER COMPARISON TABLES

Specific Gravity	Degrees Brix	Degrees Baumé	Degrees Oechsle
1.000	0.0	0.0	0
1.005	1.2	0.7	5
1.010	2.5	1.4	10
1.015	3.7	2.1	15
1.020	5.0	2.8	20
1.025	6.3	3.6	25
1.030	7.6	4.3	30
1.035	9.0	5.0	35
1.040	10.0	5.6	40
1.045	11.2	6.3	45
1.050	12.5	7.0	50
1.055	13.8	7.6	55
1.060	15.0	8.3	60
1.065	16.0	8.9	65
1.070	17.1	9.5	70
1.075	18.2	10.1	75
1.080	19.3	10.8	80
1.085	20.4	11.4	85
1.090	21.6	12.0	90
1.095	22.8	12.6	95
1.100	24.0	13.2	100
1.105	25.0	13.8	105
1.110	26.0	14.4	110
1.115	27.0	15.0	115
1.120	28.0	15.6	120
1.125	29.0	16.1	125

A gentle reminder

Always check the specific gravity of a must before adding more sugar and add only sufficient for the approximate amount of alcohol you need.

Always check the specific gravity when fermentation has stopped and never seal bottles if any fermentable sugar remains in them.

Acid Control

THE IMPORTANCE OF ACID

Many factors are important in making a good wine, not the least being the balance between the acid, the alcohol, sugar, tannin and texture.
- Acid imparts freshness to the smell and taste of wine. Its absence impairs the bouquet and flavour, causing a certain flatness and lack of vitality.
- Added in excess, the wine will taste sharp and may combine with the tannin to cause astringency – a prickly feeling around the gums and cheeks.
- Without sufficient acid a wine will not keep; with too much, maturation takes longer.

FRUIT ACIDS

Types: There are three main acids present in fruit musts. Tartaric is found only in grapes, and malic and citric acids are predominant in other fruits.

Quantity: The chart on page 45 gives an indication of the average quantity of acid found in particular fruits, but this can vary with the variety and with the ripeness. Over-ripe fruits contain less acid than under-ripe ones, dessert varieties contain less acid than culinary varieties. Flowers, leaves, herbs, grains and vegetables contain virtually no acid.

THE RIGHT BALANCE

- Clearly adding the right quantity of acid is a critical factor. But a perfect balance is often difficult to achieve because other acids are formed during fermentation and the finished wine is usually more acidic than the original must.
- The quantity formed during fermentation is variable. From a must lowish in acid, say one containing 4 parts per thousand, an additional 2 parts per thousand may be formed. From a must high in acid, say 6 parts per thousand, 1 additional part may be formed. No definite figures can be given but some sort of control is essential.
- It is generally reckoned that a must should contain between 4 and 5

parts of acid per thousand parts of must, or put another way, the pH (the degree of acidity of the must), should be between 3 and 3.4.
● We can measure both the **quantity** of acid present and the **degree** of the acidity. Some acids taste sharper than others and professional winemakers often use pH rather than part per thousand because this reflects the taste of their wine more accurately. After a malo-lactic fermentation, for example, when some of the malic acid – very sharp – is converted to lactic acid – almost bland – the wine tastes softer and milder, although there is little change in the total quantity of acid present.

MEASURING THE QUANTITY OF ACID PRESENT

The quantity of acid present in the must is measured by a method called **titration**.

Acid-testing or titration kit

Inexpensive acid-testing kits with full instructions may be bought from specialist home-brew shops. The kit contains:
● a conical flask.
● a small bottle of phenolphthalein solution.
● a little pointed glass tube attached to a rubber bulb (used to add single drops of the solution at a time).
● a small bottle of a deci-normal solution of sodium hydroxide.
● a graduated glass tube with a pointed end and a tap.

How the test works

The hydroxide is an alkaline solution that neutralizes the acid in the must. The phenolphthalein solution changes colour between blue for acid and pink for alkali. The purpose of the test is to find out how much hydroxide must be added to a sample containing acid to neutralize it and from this we can calculate the quantity of acid in the sample. The critical moment is the cross-over point when the phenolphthalein changes from blue to pink.

Method

1 To test white must pour 10 ml (2 tsp) into the flask and add 2 drops of phenolphthalein.
2 Fill the glass tube (burette) to the graduated mark with the hydroxide and then slowly run it into the flask.

82 · WINEMAKING

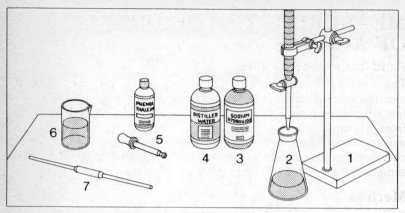

Ideal titration equipment: (1) burette and stand; (2) conical flask; (3) sodium hydroxide; (4) distilled water for diluting the colour of red wines; (5) phenol-thalein solution and dropper; (6) beaker; (7) pipette.

3 Agitate the flask gently until the instant the colour changes and remains stable.
4 Note the quantity of hydroxide used and repeat the process with a second sample of the same must. If there is any difference between the two results, then take the mean between them.
5 The resulting figure refers to sulphuric acid. To calculate the quantity of fruit acids present the result must first be halved and then multiplied by:

1.43 if the main acid present is citric
1.37 if the main acid present is malic
1.53 if the main acid present is tartaric

For example, if the first result of the titration was 6 ml and the second 8 ml, the mean would be 7. Half 7 is 3.5. Multiply this by 1.43 and the answer is 5. The sample of must containing predominantly citric acid contains 5 parts per thousand. If the predominant acid was malic the result would be 4.8 parts per thousand. If the predominant acid was tartaric the result would be 5.4 parts per thousand (3.5×1.53).

● **To test red must**, first dilute the colour with distilled water; use about 2 measures of water to 1 of must. This doesn't reduce the quantity of acid present but it does make it easier to ascertain the cross-over point. Continue as for white must from point No. 1.

MEASURING THE DEGREE OF ACIDITY

Acid-indicator papers

The degree of acidity is most accurately ascertained with an electronic pH meter, but this instrument is very expensive and very few winemakers have one. A fair guide can be obtained, however, from pH comparator papers. Those supplied in narrow ranges are the most suitable. They are strips of absorbent paper impregnated with a chemical that changes colour according to the degree of acidity in the sample tested. A colour chart is supplied.

Method

1 Dip a strip into the sample and leave it for a few moments to dry.
2 Compare its colour with the chart. The figures on the scale where the colours match is the pH of the sample.
3 Unfortunately, pH is affected by a number of mineral salts. It is best therefore to test the degree of acidity of a must before the addition of any sulphite, pectic enzyme and yeast nutrient.

An even more simple acid-indicator paper is available from chemists. Use it in the same way as a pH paper and compare it with the colour chart provided, to get an indication of whether the acidity is low, normal or high.

To check the degree of acidity in a must, dip a pH comparator paper into the sample (*left*). Leave it for a minute to dry and then compare its colour with the chart (*right*).

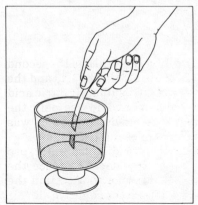
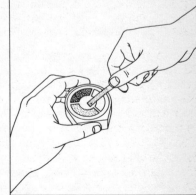

CORRECTION OF OVER-ACIDITY

● The quantity of acid present in an over-acid must can be reduced with a white powder called **potassium carbonate**. 5 ml (1 tsp) is sufficient to reduce the acid in 1 gallon of must by 1 part per thousand. The mixing in of the powder causes frothing, so leave plenty of headroom.

● If you use ripe fruit in the recommended quantities you should not need to add potassium carbonate. You may need it, however, when making wine from home-grown, outdoor grapes in a poor season. Without sufficient warmth in the ripening period there will be too much acid in the grapes and not enough sugar. The excess acid can be removed and sugar added.

CORRECTION FOR UNDER-ACIDITY

● It is more probable that you will need to add acid to ingredients that contain none, or to musts that contain insufficient. 15 ml (3 tsp) of citric, malic or tartaric acid is the approximate equivalent of 2 parts per thousand in 1 gallon of must; 250 g (9 oz) concentrated grape juice or sultanas in 1 gallon of must also contribute approximately 1 part per thousand of tartaric acid.

● When in doubt it is better to add just a little too much acid. The wine may take longer to mature but it will be the better for it.

Making the Wine

FERMENTING-ON-THE-PULP
In the making of commercial red wine, black grapes are crushed and the juice is fermented with the skins and pips until the winemaker judges that the colour is deep enough. The same principle has been adopted in the making of many country wines. After being cleaned and crushed the fruit is fermented for several days. This extracts the soluble constituents from all fruits as well as the colour from black fruits.

Adding pectic enzyme and sulphite
- All fruits, including grapes, contain pectin to a greater or lesser extent. Allow 24 hours for a pectic enzyme to break down the pectin before fermentation begins.
- To protect the must during this period, add sulphite at the rate of 50 parts per million (1 Campden tablet per gallon) with the enzyme.
- Cover the container and leave it in a warm place to stimulate the activities of the enzyme: 27°C (81°F) or thereabouts is the most suitable temperature.
- Treat white and golden fruits in the same way as red and black fruits, since otherwise the juice is difficult to extract. Steeping them in water first softens them and makes pressing out the juice easier and more effective.

Hot water or cold?
There are mixed views on this. Hot water about 80°C (176°F) is undoubtedly more successful than cold in extracting the colour from black fruits. It also kills off most, if not all, of the micro-organisms. Hot water may, however, dissipate some of the aroma constituents from the more lightly-flavoured fruits.
A sensible compromise: Use hot water on those fruits where the extraction of colour is important and cold water on the rest.
If using cold water: Do remember to wash the fruit in a sulphite solution before crushing and to include sulphite during the steeping. Sulphite inhibits yeast as well as spoilage organisms though, so *never add yeast to a must until at least 24 hours after adding the sulphite.* Even then it is advisable to give the must a good stir before mixing in

> ## The benefits of pulp fermentation
> Fermentation-on-the-pulp helps to extract colour, acid, sugar, tannin, mineral salts, vitamins, trace elements and so on.
> The creation of alcohol and carbon dioxide has two advantages:
> 1 Alcohol is a more efficient solvent of some constituents than water.
> 2 When the carbon dioxide bubbles rise towards the surface of the must they cause a constant agitation that stimulates the release of the elements required.

the activated yeast. This not only dissipates the free sulphite but also admits some air that will encourage the growth of the yeast colony.

Pressing down the fruit cap

- The rising bubbles also lift up the pulp. If it is not pressed down into the must it dries out and forms an ideal home for moulds, fungi and bacteria.
- Ideally the fruit should be kept in the must all the time and this can often be achieved by floating a china plate of a suitable size on the must. If need be, it can be weighed down with a flat bottle filled with water.
- Traditionally the fruit is pressed down with the back of a wooden spoon. Do not be too enthusiastic or you will dissipate some alcohol and esters and release them into the atmosphere.
- In between the few moments of pressing down the fruit cap, ensure that the container is well covered to keep out spoilage organisms, but not so tightly that the carbon dioxide cannot escape.

The correct temperature

- As far as possible the must should be fermented-on-the-pulp in an atmospheric temperature that is steady and around 20°C (68°F).
- In very cold weather in an unheated room, an immersion heater can be very useful in maintaining a steady temperature and a continuous fermentation. It is more efficient if coupled to a thermostat set at 20°C (68°F). But this is a last resort because the fruit closest to the heater gets too hot and becomes stewed unless it is stirred occasionally.
- Once fermentation has started it will generate some heat of its own. You can conserve this by insulating the container with newspapers or cloths.

The length of fermentation

Usually only a few days of pulp fermentation are necessary but count these from when fermentation begins and not from the moment the activated yeast is added.
White and golden fruits: Three days are probably enough.
Red and black fruits: These need four or five days to extract sufficient colour.
Apples: These often need six or seven days, but this is the maximum.

PRESSING

- After a short period of pulp fermentation the solid matter has to be strained out. If left in for too long it would disintegrate, impart unwanted bitterness or other taints to the must, and be extremely difficult to remove.
- It is helpful to have a second container available for this or at least a very wide-mouthed funnel and a demijohn. If you wish, the straining can be done twice: first through a coarse-meshed nylon bag and then through a fine-meshed one to remove as much of the pulp as possible.

Four hands or two?

Two pairs of hand are best, one pair to hold open the straining bag, the other to pour the must and pulp into it. An excellent stand is also available: the lower end fits over a demijohn, the upper end holds the funnel. A coarse sieve, colander or wide-mouthed nylon bag can be laid in the funnel and perhaps secured with a clothes peg.

Use a jug to help you

Rather than trying to pour direct from the bin, use a small jug or cup to transfer as much of the liquid must as possible. This can be done neatly and without mess. Then remove the solid particles in cupfuls rather than all at once. Otherwise the strainer may slip with calamitous consequences. It takes a minute or two longer to transfer the pulp in small quantities, liquid first and solids afterwards, but it is much less trouble in the end.

Method

1 You can press the pulp first with the back of a wooden spoon or a saucer to extract the more readily available juice. It can then be emptied into a straining bag quite easily.

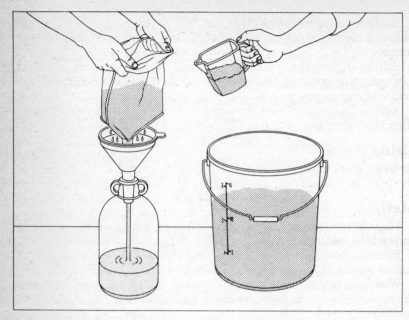

Two pairs of hands are easier than one when straining pulp.

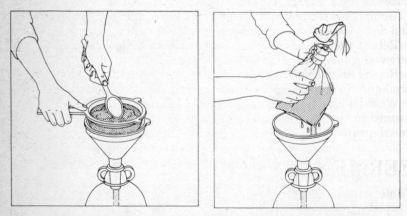

To extract the more readily available juice, first press a small quantity of pulp in a sieve with the back of a wooden spoon (*left*). For a larger quantity, put the pulp into a straining bag and squeeze it hard (*right*).

2 Gather the neck of the partially filled bag in one hand close to the pulp and twist the bag a few times. The juice will flow readily into the funnel.
3 Still holding the bag with one hand, squeeze the pulp with the other and watch the juice run. After a minute shake up the bag, take a lower grip and repeat the process.
4 Very soon the pulp will become quite dry and firm to handle; it can then be discarded.

Using a press
By using a small press you can extract three-quarters of the weight of the fruit in the form of juice.

Method
1 Place the straining bag in the press and arrange for the outlet to empty into another bin or into a funnel fitted into a jar.
2 Pour the loose juice through first and then the rest of the pulp, a cup or jugful at a time.
3 When all the pulp is in the bag, lift it up a little in the press and twist the neck of the bag to concentrate the pulp. Some hand pressing will easily remove much of the juice.
4 Fit the pressure plate and screw and turn this until close contact is made with the pulp. Turn the screw slowly but firmly until the flood of juice becomes a trickle.
5 Undo the screw, remove the pressure plate, lift out the bag of pulp and mix up the pulp in the bag.
6 Return the bag to the press, fit the pressure plate, twist down the screw and the juice will run freely again.
7 Repeat the process two or three times more until the pulp is dry and firm, and then discard it.
8 Wash and dry the press before putting it away. A small press can be washed in the kitchen sink; a larger one can be stood outside and hosed down.

FERMENTING THE JUICE

Table wines: The rest of the sugar should now be stirred in and completely dissolved.
Dessert wines and aperitifs: No more than half the sugar should be added. Pour all of the sweetened must back into the fermentation jar. The rest of the sugar is added later.

Surplus must: If the quantity of must is slightly in excess of the capacity of the jar, or likely to be so when any more sugar or syrup is added, pour the surplus into a suitably sized bottle and ferment this alongside the jar. Plug the neck of the bottle with cotton wool and fit an airlock to the jar.

Check the temperature
Continue the fermentation in an atmospheric temperature appropriate to the wine. For red table wines this is around 20°C (68°F), and for all others between 14 and 17°C (57 and 63°F).

Adding more sugar
To add dry sugar to high-alcohol wines:
1 Remove the airlock, pour or siphon some must into a bowl or jug containing the appropriate amount of sugar, and stir gently until all the sugar is dissolved.
2 Return the must through a funnel to the jar. Replace the airlock and resume the fermentation.
3 When mixing in a sugar syrup it is only necessary to remove the airlock and its bung and to pour in the syrup slowly.

Mind the frothing
Adding sugar to a must in any form causes an agitation, sometimes with high foaming. By pouring back a portion of sweetened must or of sugar syrup slowly, the must as a whole accommodates the sugar with no more than a substantial hissing.

An even temperature
Maintain as even a temperature as you can by using, for example, a padded demijohn cover (like a large teacosy) or by some other means. Remember that the fermentation itself creates some warmth. The ratio of surface to volume of must in a gallon glass jar is such that this warmth is dissipated as quickly as it is created. Lagging the jar will retain much of the warmth and at least protect the must from the substantial drop in atmospheric temperature usually experienced during the night.

Summer ferments
● A cool fermentation temperature is very important in the production of well-flavoured wines. It really is worth looking about your home for the best possible place to ferment your wines, whether you

make them from a kit of concentrated grape juice or from other ingredients.
- In summertime when the atmosphere temperature in the kitchen, utility room or garage is likely to exceed 21°C (70°F), it may be better not to start a white wine. You may be able to cool the must by standing the jar in a bowl, bucket or bin of cold water that you can change from time to time, as necessary.
- A cool fermentation takes longer than a hot one, perhaps as long as ten weeks or six at the least. Even so, the final result is well worth waiting for. Occasionally, fermentation stops prematurely. Should this happen, consult the next chapter.

RACKING

The next stage in winemaking is the removal of the finished wine from the dross of the fermentation process.

Cooling the wine

1 When you think fermentation is complete, i.e. when no movement can be seen in the wine, check its specific gravity with a hydrometer. A dry or a table wine should be 0.998 or lower. A high-alcohol sweet wine might be somewhere in the region of 1.020, give or take 4 or 5 units.
2 Gently stir the wine to release any entrained carbon dioxide molecules, then replace the airlock and stand the demijohn in as cool a place as you can find. Except in freezing conditions the jar can be left outside in a shady place for a couple of days to encourage the sediment to settle.
3 If you wish you can add wine finings during the stirring to ensure a clear and clean wine as quickly as possible.

Setting up the siphon

1 As soon as a deposit appears and the wine begins to clear, stand the jar on a convenient work surface and immediately beneath it put an empty and freshly sterilized jar of the same size.
2 Insert one end of a siphon into the jar of wine. It helps if the siphon has a J tube attached to the end or if the end is blocked and there are several holes in the wall of the tube. It also helps if a bored bung containing an air vent has been threaded on to the siphon.
3 The bung should be pushed into the neck of the jar and the siphon tube pushed gently down until the mouth of the J tube or the holes are

92 · WINEMAKING

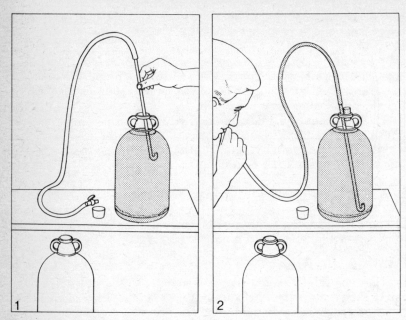

Racking: (1) Remove the bung from the full demijohn and put the inlet end of the siphon into it. (2) The siphon inlet should rest above the sediment. Wedge the tube to prevent movement. Suck the wine into the tube.

just above the sediment. Do this very carefully so as not to disturb the sediment.

4 If you do not have a vented and bored bung, the two halves of a bored bung cut down through the centre of the bore can be used to hold the tube still and so prevent disturbance of the sediment.

Suck it and see!

1 With the inlet end under firm control, pick up the outlet end. If it is finished with a little tap turn the handle to the open position, place the nozzle in your mouth, suck firmly and slowly and when the wine reaches the tap, turn the handle to the closed position.

2 Take the tap from your mouth, place the nozzle in the empty jar, turn the handle to open and the clear wine will flow slowly and steadily until the wine in the top jar falls below the inlet to the siphon.

MAKING THE WINE · 93

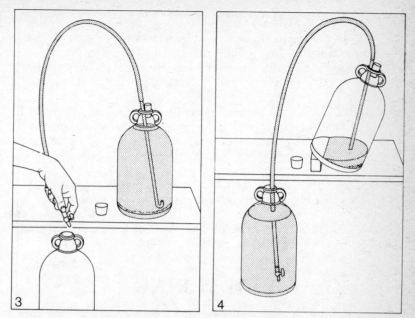

(3) Place the tap end into an empty, sterilized jar beneath the full jar above. (4) When the jar is nearly empty, tilt it carefully to remove as much clear liquid as possible.

3 If there is a considerable amount of clear wine left above the sediment, the jar can be tilted and the inlet moved in such a manner as to continue the flow. With experience and a firm sediment it is possible to remove all the clear wine.

Topping up
- There will still be some space in the receiving jar. Fill this with the wine fermented in the bottle beside the main supply.
- If you do not have any of this, use a similar wine, perhaps of another year or even from a different ingredient as long as it is sound, of the same colour and has a similar specific gravity.
- Never add a sweet wine to a dry wine, in case it causes further fermentation. In the absence of a suitable wine use cold boiled water or even sterilized glass marbles. The important thing is to fill the jar completely and exclude air.

Adding more sulphite
White wines: For all these wines 1 crushed or soluble Campden tablet, or the equivalent sulphite solution to produce 50 parts per million of sulphur dioxide, should be added without fail. This protects the wine from oxidation and infection during the period of maturation.
Red wines: These may be treated similarly unless you hope that a subsequent malo-lactic fermentation will occur to reduce some of the acidity. An airlock or safety bung should be used in this case.

Sealing
Bung the jar tight with a softened bung while a piece of plastic-coated wire or something similar is suspended in the neck of the jar. Withdraw the wire when the bung is in place. This prevents the loosening of the bung by expansion of the wine due to an increase in atmospheric temperature during maturation.

FINING AND FILTERING
I have found that if properly made, wines clear naturally. If the wine is a little veiled after the first racking, the suspended particles settle down during the following months and leave the wine crystal clear, although a thin deposit will be left on the bottom of the jar. A further racking easily removes this.

Fine first
Occasionally, however, you may come across a wine that is slow to clear or you may have one that you want to clear quickly. There are a number of proprietary brands of clearing agents available that are simple and quite effective to use, provided you follow the instructions on the pack. Chitosan will quickly clear most wines.

Filter second
Filtering is also possible and effective with the better filters. Indeed some winemakers prefer filtering to fining.
The advantages: Fining agents often combine with other substances – notably tannin – to form particles large enough to sink to the bottom of the jar. Wines that have been fined, especially red wines, therefore need the addition of a measure of tannin after fining. Wines that are filtered, however, lose only the micro-particles that cause the haze.

MAKING THE WINE · 95

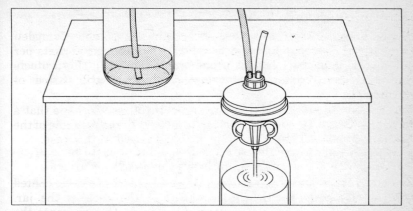

Filtering in progress to clear the wine of any suspended particles remaining after racking.

Filtering also removes the vast majority of the yeast colony and makes a secondary fermentation that much less likely.

Don't leave it too long: Unless filtering is effected fairly quickly, however, there is a strong possibility of infection and oxidation. It is important, therefore, to use a good filter system, preferably one aided by pressure.

BULK STORAGE

After clearing the wine it should be put away for a period of bulk storage, unless it is a fast-maturing one such as a fruit juice wine that is ready for bottling as soon as it is clear. Bulk storage is particularly important for red wines.

Containers to use

During storage chemical changes take place slowly between the different acids and alcohols and these seem to be more effective in larger containers – 1 gallon and upwards – rather than in bottles. This is also true of high-alcohol aperitif and dessert wines where a minimum period of two years' bulk storage is desirable before bottling.

Cool and dark

The optimum storage conditions are as follows:
1 Ideally the storage temperature should be around an even 10°C (50°F). The chemical changes are slower than they might be at a higher temperature but the wine develops finer rather than coarser flavours.
2 Keep the jars in a dark place or cover them to prevent the wine fading. Red wines tend to become tawny and white wines golden with hints of brown in both.
3 Store the jars where they are free from vibrations. In some urban areas close to main roads and railways this is not always easy.

Don't forget the labels!
All jars should of course be labelled with details about the wine. The labels should be of a type that is easy to read and does not come off easily and get lost.

BLENDING
Why blend?
Every time you start to make a new batch of wine you will be using all your experience and knowledge. Often this results in a splendid wine with which you are well pleased. Sadly, on some occasions it may not come up to your expectations. It is likely to be clean and sound but lacking in 'appeal'. Throughout the centuries winemakers have been coping with this problem. All kinds of additives have been tried from pinecones to honey but with limited success. Most have now been abandoned. The remedy that has proved most successful is blending. If winemaking is at least part science, then blending is all art.

Commercial blending
Commercial winebrokers are masters of the art of blending. They buy up small parcels of wine from different growers and then blend them with great skill into very attractive wines for everyday drinking.

Selecting your wines
When you find that you have a wine that you don't enjoy as it is, then look through your stocks for others. Set yourself a high standard and don't be afraid of admitting your shortcomings, at least to yourself.

Taste your wines critically and try to identify the cause of their lack of charm.

- Is the wine too dry or too sweet, too sharp or too bitter?
- Does it lack flavour or is the flavour too pronounced?
- Is it too thin or has it developed a faintly sherry-like taste?

Balancing the blend

A rule of thumb is to mix opposites together, but first consider how great the deficiency is. Should the blend be 50–50, 30–70 or some other proportion? At this stage you can make little more than an informed guess. Some winemakers mix the wines together in a glass first and taste the result, varying the mix until they produce one which they like.

- Keep an accurate record of each mix. After a few glasses you may not be able to remember very well and become muddled – if not fuddled!

Further changes

You must also remember that when two wines are blended together chemical changes will occur in the blend, even between the same sort of wine from different years. The wines won't remain just a mixture but will homogenize into a new and different wine. Sometimes a further fermentation will occur, either of the sugar or the malic acid. Sometimes a further deposit will be thrown showing tangible evidence of the changes that have been taking place.

... make it worthwhile

After making your blend, whether by mixing the wines in a glass or by intuition, fit an airlock to the jars and leave them in a cool place for about a month. A further taste will quickly reveal the level of your success. Blending is a remarkable equation. In my experience, having blended wines every year since 1952, the equation is not $1+1=2$, but $1+1=3$. The resulting blend has always been better than the wines that went into it.

Clever tricks

More than two wines can be blended; indeed, there is no limit to the number of wines that can be put into a blend if you can balance their reactions in your head. For example, during the season from August to December, you might have to make five or six different batches of apple wine, to meet both the use of the varieties of apples ripening at different times and the limitations of your equipment. By April of the following year all these different batches can be blended together to form one homogeneous wine based on many different varieties of apples. The result of such an operation has never failed to please me. I have frequently produced between 135 and 180 litres (30 and 40 gallons) of apple wine in this way.

Blending combinations

Sweet and dry wines: These may be blended to reduce the sweetness, but a further fermentation is likely to occur unless you prevent it by including some potassium sorbate and sulphite. Further fermentation will increase the alcoholic strength of the blend, so consider the present strength and the purpose of the wine. Otherwise the blend may become unbalanced.

White and red wines: These may be mixed forming lighter red wines or rosés as you wish.

Essential blending: Some wines, of course, have to be blended, notably sherry- and Madeira-style wines. The blends here are not only of similar-style wines but also of different years.

Naming the blend

- After blending and producing an enjoyable wine, give it a new name. Anagrams from the main ingredients may not be easy to invent! Commercial winemakers sometimes use bin numbers or just dream up fancy names.
- Do keep a note of the wines you blended and the result. The information will be of use at some other time.

The golden rules
- There are few rules to follow and of these the most important is commonsense: *never blend a bad or infected wine with a sound one.*
- A wine that is vinegarish, or one that has a smell or taste of rotting cabbage or of animals, such as mice, will *always* spoil any other wine with which it is mixed.
- Happily, these bad wines are few and far between and are usually caused by a lack of attention to cleanliness.

BOTTLING

- It must be clear from the outset that the word bottle in this context refers exclusively to a wine bottle, i.e. a bottle that has previously held commercially produced wine or that has been made especially for wine. Vinegar, beer, cider, mineral water and sauce bottles all have their own specific uses but that does not include wine.
- Wine is best preserved in brown- or green-coloured glass bottles. Other types of containers, including cans, cartons and plastics are being tested but these are for everyday wines and immediate drinking. They are not for storage while the wine continues to mature.

Bottle sizes

- Before selecting, sterilizing and filling the bottles, do think carefully about the kind of wine you are bottling and your drinking habits. It is often better to bottle some wines in half-size rather than standard bottles. It is a pity to open a standard bottle and to have to leave half the wine for another day. This applies especially to dessert wines where 'another day' may be a week or two away, by which time the wine is likely to have deteriorated. It is often better to use an assortment of sizes so that you have the right quantity available for your needs.
- Half bottles are especially useful for winemakers with small stocks. The temptation to open a bottle of a new wine that you believe to be good is often overwhelming. Soon the whole gallon is gone and the last bottle was almost certainly the best! If this sounds like you, use four or six halves and four or three standard bottles. Drink the halves first and then you may be able to keep the standard bottles long enough for the wine to become fully mature!

Cleaning the bottles

Outside: Before use, bottles that have previously contained wine should be soaked for a period in warm water to soften the gum with which the labels were stuck to them. Do not remove labels with a sharp knife in case the glass gets scratched. If the outer surface of the glass is damaged the bottle is weakened and any unusual pressure from within could cause it to crack.

Inside: The inside should be washed with a solution of Chempro and given a once-over with a bottle brush unless there are obvious signs of sediment or staining. In these circumstances leave the bottles for 24 hours, full to the brim with a solution of Chempro. This not only

removes the stain but also sterilizes the bottle. After using Chempro, wash the bottle out three or four times with fresh cold water.
Clean bottles: These need only be sterilized with a sulphite solution and drained. Do not rinse them as the minute traces of sulphite are beneficial rather than harmful to the wine.

Softening the corks

● Having selected your bottles, choose your cylindrical corks; those for half-size bottles are often smaller than those for standard bottles.
● The corks must be new and need to be softened as well as sterilized. This can be done by soaking them for several hours in a sulphite solution, making sure that they are weighted down and kept beneath the surface.
● A less desirable method is to soak them for a shorter period, say 15 minutes, in hot water at 60°C (140°F).

Soften and sterilize your corks by soaking them for several hours in a sulphite solution, keeping them well below the surface. The two corking tools shown are both suitable for use with well-softened corks.

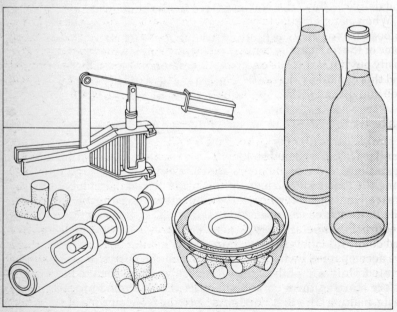

Check your corking tool
- Get out your corking tool and check it. Lever machines benefit from a spot of lubricating oil on their joints.
- A wooden plunger-style tool needs a mallet or the like.
- When all is ready, stand the jar of wine to be bottled on a suitable work surface and the sterilized and drained bottles to be filled on the floor beneath.

Filling the bottles
- Remove the bung from the jar and place a sterilized siphon in the wine.
- Fill the siphon as described for racking (see pages 91–93), and place the end in one bottle after another until all are filled.
- The wine should reach a point in the neck that is about 2 cm ($\frac{3}{4}$ in) from where the bottom of the cork will be situated when it is fully inserted.

Fitting the corks
- Shake any surplus moisture off each cork as it is placed in the tool and deliver it into the bottle so that the cork is flush with the rim.
- When using a mallet to drive down the piston on top of the cork, it is a good idea to stand the bottle on a sponge or a folded towel to absorb some of the force. If the cork is sufficiently soft it slides into the bottle easily but if it is not quite soft enough, a harder blow may be required and this can break the bottle – as I know to my cost! To be on the safe side stand the bottle on a sponge or pad in a large bowl.

Labelling
A simple tag: After corking comes labelling. The most basic label is a small price tag on a cotton loop. These can be bought by the hundred in stationers. Write the name and date of the wine on the label and hang the loop over the neck of the bottle. This kind of label has one great advantage: it can be read without disturbing a bottle lying on its side in a rack or carton.

Decorative labels: Many winemakers prefer to use the decorative and colourful labels that are now widely available. Sometimes these are accompanied by neck labels on which the year of vintage can be printed. Only a few labels are self-adhesive; most need to be gummed before sticking them on to the bottles. Be sparing with the gum or paste, making sure that none gets on to the front surface of the label.

102 · WINEMAKING

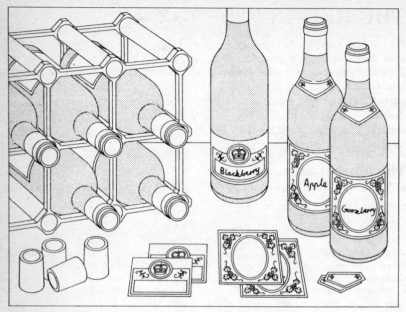

Finished bottles, attractively labelled, awaiting final storage. Store bottles on their side in a wine rack.

Positioning the label: Place the bottle on its side, feel for its two seams and place the label equidistant between the seams and with any embossed code number at the back of the bottle. The label should be nearer the bottom rather than the top of the bottle so as not to give a top-heavy appearance. If the bottle has sloping shoulders – for example, Burgundy and Hock bottles – affix the label to the body of the bottle. Wipe off any surplus gum or paste, leaving the bottle and label neat and clean.

Capsules: The final touch is to cover the mouth and neck of the bottle with a foil or plastic capsule. The latter are usually kept in a moist condition and cling tightly to the bottle as they dry out.

Don't drink the wine yet

Finally, put the bottles back into store again. The wine will benefit from a few months' bottle age. A wine rack in a cool, dark position is ideal; a carton or two under the stairs is better than nothing!

THE BAG-IN-THE-BOX

Having become increasingly popular for everyday commercial wines, this method is now being used for home-made wines. Despite its ingenious construction and adaptability, remember that a bag-in-the-box is only suitable for finished wines ready for drinking; it is not suitable for long storage of newly-made wine nor for high-quality and dessert wines, both of which need proper maturation before being served. The wine is unlikely to improve, although it won't deteriorate in the box, at least for several months.

The advantages
● The great merit of the bag-in-the-box is that anything from a single glass to a carafe-full of wine can be withdrawn. Being pliable the bag

Wine boxes are becoming increasingly popular. The box is made up from a cardboard outer carton, a laminated bag which fits inside it and a tap (*left*). To fill: place the bag in the box and seal it, then siphon the wine into the bag, shaking the box from time to time to help the wine open the bag (*right*). When the bag is full, fit the tap securely.

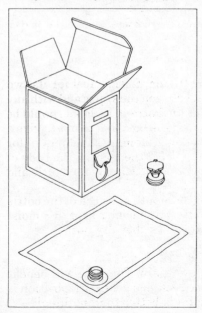
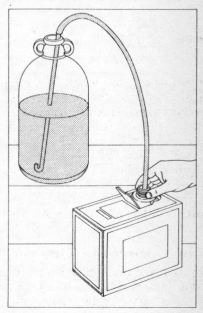

collapses on to the wine and air is therefore excluded. As a result the wine does not deteriorate as it would if left in a partly-filled bottle. It is, therefore, ideal for dispensing everyday table wine.
- The bag-in-the-box also saves bottling wine that will be consumed within a short period of time. The equivalent of one bottle a day between two people is regarded as the ideal by doctors. This involves quite a lot of bottle washing, corking, labelling and putting away – six times as much, in fact, as using a bag-in-the-box because it takes no longer to wash and fill the bag than it does to wash and fill a bottle.

Filling the bag

Boxes and bags are available from specialist home-brew shops.
1 Follow the instructions supplied for forming the flattened cardboard into a box and inserting the bag so that the opening and tap fit through the hole in one side of the box.
2 Remove the cap, sterilize the bag with 50 parts per million sulphite solution and shake out the surplus drops.
3 Siphon in the wine as you would for racking but give the box a gentle shake or two from time to time to assist the bag to open up.
4 When the bag is full fit the cap. Place a box of white wine inside the refrigerator and a box of red wine outside.

Re-using the bag

When the first box of wine has been consumed, remove the tap, wash out and sterilize the bag, shake out the surplus sulphite and refill the bag. It can be used many times, although the cardboard box steadily deteriorates and becomes unsightly.

A better box

- The Bulgarians have just introduced a plastic barrel containing a 3-litre ($5\frac{1}{4}$-pint) bag of wine. This container seems to have a much longer life than the cardboard carton. I have been pressing manufacturers for several years to produce such a pack for home winemakers and one may yet appear.
- The commercial taps are harder to remove than the rubber taps supplied on the bags for the home winemaker. They can be removed, however, with the aid of a short, blunt but thin blade. You first have to penetrate the blade between the tap and its holder and then slowly edge it out by moving your blade all round the tap, twisting the blade as you do so. The joining surfaces will be dented but not harmed by this.

- With the tap removed the bag is washed, sterilized, shaken and filled as before.
- Soften the tap in hot water for a few minutes before inserting it into the bag and support the rim of the fitment as you push the tap home. The task seems almost impossible at first but it can be done and after one or two successes becomes quite easy.

Winemaking summary
1. Sterilize all equipment.
2. Use only the best quality ingredients.
3. Wash and clean fruits, removing stalks and stones.
4. Check for natural sugar and acid.
5. Use pre-activated yeast.
6. Ferment in temperature range 15–21°C (60–70°F).
7. Rack and store in bulk until bright.
8. Rack again and keep for a further period to mature.

Winemaking Problems: Causes and Cures

STUCK FERMENTS

At some stage most people experience a fermentation that stops before all the sugar is converted. There are a number of causes.

Sugar
- You may have miscalculated the quantity of sugar and the yeast has reached its level of tolerance to alcohol. Check your records and ensure that you allowed for the natural sugar in the ingredients and that you have not added too much.
- You may have added all the sugar at once in the making of a strong wine and the weight of the sugar has killed the yeast (see page 59).

Remedy: For both these stoppages you need to dilute. Make up a similar must without added sugar, mix the two together and stir in a newly activated yeast.

Temperature
- The fermentation vessel may have become so cold, especially during the night in winter, that the yeast has become inhibited.

Remedy: Move the jar to a warmer place.

- The fermentation vessel may have become so hot, especially during the middle of the day in a heatwave, that the yeast has become inhibited.

Remedy: Move the jar to a cooler place or stand it in a bucket of cold water.

In both cases fermentation may not start again for several days.

Nitrogen/acid deficiency
- Yeast cannot survive without nitrogen. Some base ingredients have little or none and without the addition of a nutrient tablet or a spoonful of ammonium salts the yeast cells will die. Check that you included some nutrient in the must.

- Yeast also needs an acid solution in which to flourish. Some ingredients contain no acid at all and this must always be added in the form of lemon juice or 10–15 ml (2–3 teaspoons) citric, malic or tartaric acid.

Remedy: In both cases it is difficult to restart the fermentation. Add acid or nutrient and if the fermentation doesn't start of its own accord, then a new yeast must be added as described below.

Bacteria

- It is possible that due to a lack of hygiene, especially in the early stages, the must has become infected by spoilage organisms. This is particularly likely to occur when you use a recipe that relies on the wild yeasts present on the surface of the ingredient to ferment the sugar.
- Wild yeasts can ferment only up to 4% alcohol before they become inhibited. They will be competing with millions of other organisms for the available nitrogen and acid. Some spoilage organisms such as *Bretanomyces* live on malic acid and the ethyl alcohol formed by the yeast. Such a must is likely to have an unpleasant odour.

Remedy: If this is the cause of the stoppage mix in 100 parts per million of sulphite – 2 crushed Campden tablets per 1 gallon – and leave the must in a cool place for 48 hours. If a sediment is deposited, rack the must and mix in a freshly activated wine yeast.

Stale yeast

- It is a waste of ingredients and time if you do not use a good wine yeast bought from a reputable source. Dried yeast cells do not live forever, especially if the container has been opened. Old and poorly packeted dried yeast, or yeast cells from a drum that has been opened several times and kept, maybe, for two or three years, will not be able to reproduce themselves properly and will quickly die off, causing a stuck ferment.

Remedy:
1 If this is the problem, activate a fresh wine yeast and add it to 280 ml ($\frac{1}{2}$ pint) diluted grape juice.
2 When this is fermenting vigorously, mix in 280 ml ($\frac{1}{2}$ pint) of stuck must – no more.
3 When this is fermenting well, mix in a further 560 ml (1 pint) of stuck must and when this is fermenting, mix in 1.1 litres (2 pints).

4 Finally, mix in the remainder when this quantity is fermenting well.

This is by far the best way of restarting a ferment. Adding an activated yeast to a stuck must is rarely effective. Adding a stuck must to an activated yeast in the manner indicated rarely fails.

ABSENCE OF BOUQUET

● This is a fairly common fault in commercial as well as home-made wines and it is usually due to a lack of acid during the fermentation.
● Only a few base ingredients have sufficient acid and these are often diluted because of overpowering flavour. Unless otherwise recommended always include sufficient acid in your must and thus prevent this problem.
● Stale and over-ripe ingredients can also be the cause. It is cheapest in the long run only to use the best-quality ingredients.

Remedy: Blend the wine with another rather sharp wine. The addition of a little tartaric acid to a finished wine is sometimes effective but not always. Blending is the preferred remedy.

UNPLEASANT-SMELLING WINE

Worse than an absence of bouquet are wines that give off an unpleasant odour. Most of these awful smells are caused by bacterial infection and many can be readily identified.

Vinegarish

● This can be caused by an excess of acetic acid. A small quantity is produced during fermentation, which enhances the bouquet when it combines with alcohols. Excessive quantities of the acid can be caused by the presence of bacteria that convert alcohol to acetic acid. These could have been on or in the fruit and can enter the must from the air if it has been uncovered.
● A vinegarish taint can also be picked up by a must or wine if it is in a room where chutney, piccalilli, pickled onions or red cabbage is being prepared. If there is a strong odour of vinegar in a room and a must is uncovered while being stirred, strained or pressed, or if a wine is racked or bottled in the room, then the must or wine will pick up the vinegar odour and become tainted.

Remedy: This problem is far easier to prevent than cure. If the odour is not too bad the wine can be used in cooking. If it is severe, then convert the wine into vinegar as described on page 356.

Mousy
- A mousy odour can develop in a wine. It is similar to that which also emanates from dogs and horses.
- The cause is thought to be the cells of a fungus called *Bretanomyces*, but lactobacillus cells can also contribute.

Remedy: There is no known remedy and if the odour is off-putting, discard the wine and thoroughly sterilize all your equipment, not just the container in which the wine was stored. The invisible cells may be anywhere!

Rotting vegetation
- This appalling odour is caused by leaving a wine on its deposit of decaying yeast cells, particles of pulp and other debris, after fermentation has finished.

Remedy: It can easily be prevented but cannot be cured. Discard the wine and sterilize the container.

Nail varnish
- This odour will develop if there is insufficient nutrient in a must, particularly vitamin B_1. The living yeast cells then use substances in the dead yeast cells to maintain viability. An excess of amyl alcohol is formed and this combines with acetic acid to form amyl acetate, which is the cause of the odour.

Remedy: There is no known remedy but the odour can be prevented by including some grape in every must or at least some vitamin B_1. One 3 mg Benerva tablet per 1 gallon is more than enough.

Bitter almond
- This odour is caused by fermenting a must containing fruit stones, some of which have become cracked or damaged. The acids get into the kernel of the stone and form prussic acid which creates the odour.

Remedy: Again, prevention is easy but there is no known cure. Discard all fruit stones prior to fermentation and scrape away the flesh immediately surrounding peach stones. If the wine is strongly tainted, pour it down a drain and thoroughly sterilize the container.

Bad egg

- The well-known odour of hydrogen sulphide is usually caused by certain strains of yeast, hence the need to use a good wine yeast from a reputable source.

Remedy: The odour can be dissipated with a few drops of a 10% copper sulphate solution. This should be added a drop at a time, the wine stirred and inhaled between the addition of each drop until you can no longer smell the odour. Unless the wine is particularly precious, however, or the taint only slight, it might be as well to discard it. Change your yeast next time you make wine.

Sulphur

- Many people think they can detect the smell of sulphur in a wine. This is only likely if too much sulphite was used immediately before bottling. Whilst it is highly desirable to add sulphite at the rate of 50 parts per million to the first racking at the end of fermentation, only half this quantity need be added at the second racking. There is no need to add sulphite prior to bottling.

Remedy: If there is a sulphur odour in the wine, a gentle stirring will soon dissipate it.

UNPLEASANT-TASTING WINE

Bitterness

- This can be caused by using under-ripe fruit or including too much stalk, especially with flower wines; by the inclusion of the white pith of citrus fruits; by fermenting at too high a temperature; and by fermenting-on-the-pulp for too long.

Remedy: Blend this otherwise sound wine with another wine that lacks 'bite'. If the cause is due to a simple excess of tannin through the accidental addition of too much grape tannin or to the skins of too many pears, etc. all is not lost. Mix in a gelatine solution, stir well and leave the wine in a cool place while the tannin is deposited. Instructions on how to use the gelatine are given on the packet.

Astringency

- If the must contains too much acid and tannin an astringent taste will develop that causes a tingling on the gums and cheeks when the wine is drunk.

Remedy: Here again, an otherwise sound wine can be improved by blending it with one that is a bit short of both acid and tannin. Alternatively, some acid can be removed with potassium carbonate and some tannin with gelatine.

ROPINESS

- Very occasionally a jar of wine, especially white wine, will develop an oily appearance and will seem thicker than normal when poured.
- This is due to an infection by a lactobacillus that hangs together in long ropes. (The lactobacillus family contains many different bacteria that thrive in the presence of lactic acid.) Although they are too small to be seen with the naked eye, the massive collection of the cells imparts this oily and thicker appearance.

Remedy: This is simple.
1 Pour the wine into a bin, mix in 2 crushed Campden tablets per 1 gallon, or a sulphite solution at the rate of 100 parts per million, and beat the wine with a plastic or wooden spoon. The beating breaks up the 'ropes' and the sulphite kills the bacteria.
2 Return the wine to its container, seal it and leave it in a cold place for a few days. A deposit of dead cells will be seen on the bottom of the jar.
3 Rack the clear wine into a sterilized container. It is perfectly safe to drink.

HAZES

- Most wines clear naturally, some even during fermentation, and are crystal clear at the first racking.

Remedy: If there is a haze, however, racking and the addition of sulphite at the rate of 50 parts per million (1 Campden tablet per 1 gallon) stimulates clarification, especially if the wine is left in a cool place where the suspended particles will not be prevented from settling out because of the internal thermal movements.

Suspended particles
- Occasionally, however, the wine does not clear quickly. The most common cause is the polarization of the electrical charges on the suspended particles which all become the same and repel each other.

As a result they fail to associate together and become heavy enough to settle out.

Remedy: The addition of a proprietary brand of fining agent, used as directed by the manufacturer, is usually effective. Mix the recommended quantity of fining agent in a small quantity of wine and, when this is completely dispersed, stir it into the hazy wine. Again, the wine should be left in a cool place for a few days and then racked.

Other fining agents

- Bentonite, isinglass, gelatine, finely crushed eggshells, beaten egg white and milk are other fining agents. The beaten white of one egg is enough for 45 litres (10 gallons) of wine!
- 15 ml (1 tbsp) of milk often precipitates the suspended protein in an apple wine.
- Animal blood has been used to clear red wines.
- A proprietary brand of fining agent is preferable to all other agents.
- Casein (milk), gelatine and isinglass all carry a positive electrical charge and so will combine with negatively-charged particles which cause haze.
- Bentonite, kieselguhr and silicic acid all carry a negative electrical charge and so combine with positively-charged particles.
- A haze that does not clear after fining with an agent from one section may well clear readily with an agent from the other section.

Pectin

The pectin in fruits and vegetables will not succumb to a fining agent so it is often best to check the cause of haze before trying to remove it.

To test for pectin: Mix 5 ml (1 tsp) wine into 4 measures of methylated spirits, shake it well and leave for up to an hour. If dots or threads appear in the methylated spirits, the cause is pectin.

Remedy: Dissolve pectolitic enzyme in a little of the wine and then thoroughly stir it into the bulk. Leave the wine in a warm place for 24 hours and then move it to a cool place for a few days before racking. Rohament P is often more effective than other pectic enzymes in these circumstances.

Starch

- A rarer haze is one caused by starch found in cereal and some vegetable wines.

To test for starch: One or two drops of tincture of iodine in a saucer of wine will cause the wine to turn blue or to darken if starch is present.

Remedy: Fungal amylase used in the same way as a pectic enzyme.

BLOOM

- Wine made from plums sometimes develops an appearance of a bloom. It is more noticeable in the jar or bottle than in the glass.
- It is thought to be due to the waxy substance with which plums are often coated and especially to the little pieces of gum that they sometimes exude.

Remedy: There is no cure for this, although it can be prevented by washing the plums in hot water (60°C/140°F) containing a handful of washing soda for a minute or two. They should then be rinsed in cold water before use.

BROWNING

All wines tend to brown a bit with age.
In red wines the youthful blue gives way to some tawny.
In white wines the pale gold darkens slightly with age.
Other factors can also hasten these changes and even cause a deterioration of bouquet and flavour.

Light

Wines left in bright light tend to go brown. If there is no other storage place for them, at least keep them in earthenware jars, brown coloured glass jars, or cover them with some material that excludes the light.

Heat

- Cooking fruit to extract the colour and flavour is another cause of browning.
- Dried elderberries, prunes, figs, dates and rosehips, as well as muscatels, raisins and some sultanas, cause a brown colour in wine.
- Old concentrated grape juice is likely to be brown in the container and will cause browning in the wine. All are due to caramelization of the sugar.

There are several ways of preventing browning while you are making the wine.

1 Pouring hot water on to fruit to extract colour will avoid browning, especially if the temperature of the water is 80°C (176°F) rather than boiling point.

2 Use light-coloured sultanas in light-coloured wines and save darker sultanas and raisins for sherry, Madeira and heavy dessert wines.

3 Purchase concentrated grape juice only as required and then from a shop known to have a fast turnover. Avoid cheap offers of old stock. If you cannot use a complete containerful immediately after opening it, seal it with a plastic cover and store it in a refrigerator until required.

4 Wines left to mature in a warm place also tend to go brown quickly. The ideal storage temperature is a constant 10°C (50°F). Very few amateur winemakers can achieve this leal and instead have to make do as best they can. Earthenware jars are very effective in keeping the temperature of wines steady because the thickness of the earthenware acts as insulation. The space under the roof is a place to avoid – at least in a summer heatwave!

Air

The admixture of too much air through stirring during pulp fermentation, racking or filtering can also cause browning. Care should be taken to prevent this by:

1 Pressing down the fruit cap gently during pulp fermentation.

2 Keeping the outlet of the siphon tube beneath the surface of the clear wine during racking and filtering.

3 Keeping containers full at all times.

Remedy: The remedy for wine which suffers from browning is uncertain but there are several things you can try.

- If the bouquet and flavour of the wine are not too badly affected drink the wine as soon as you can.
- If there is a noticeable, sherry-like bouquet and flavour in a strong wine you can try to increase the tendency by further maturation in a partially-filled container plugged with cotton wool (see also page 194).
- If the problem occurs with a light table wine, mix it with a *fermenting must* of a similar type. There is a good chance that the oxidation (browning) may be converted into alcohol and carbon dioxide by the active yeast in the fermenting must.

THE COMMONEST PROBLEM

The most common problem is lack of taste.

Remedy: The recommended remedy is blending.
- If you have no other wines with which to blend one that is too thin, too dry, too bland etc., you might get yourself out of a difficulty by adding 6 crushed raspberries or loganberries to a 1 gallon of wine. The raspberries' colour hardly shows in a white wine but can lift a dull flavour dramatically.
- 15 ml (1 tbsp) of glycerine can add just a little substance to a wine.
- A little sorbitol or sweetex can soften the hardness of a wine that is too dry and mask some of the acid.
- Unless a wine is positively bad, do not throw it away. It can always be used in the kitchen and in winter in spiced and sweetened mulls.

A general tip
All the problems just mentioned can occur at any time but you will probably avoid them completely if you:
- pay proper attention to sound winemaking methods.
- maintain absolute cleanliness.
- use high-quality ingredients.

Wines from Kits

BEST FOR THE BEGINNER

If you have never made wine before I do recommend that you make a few wines from kits before attempting other wines. They are not only easy to make and mature quickly, but will also give you an introduction to the procedures of sterilizing, fermenting and racking.

WHAT YOU WILL NEED

A wine kit consists of a container of a concentrated grape juice compound and a sachet of wine yeast. You have only to supply some sugar and water. You will need in addition:
- at least one, and preferably two, demijohns.
- an airlock fitted into a bored bung.
- a siphon.
- wine bottles and stoppers.
- Campden tablets for sterilizing the equipment and adding to the finished wine.

THE CHOICE OF KIT

First of all, choose your wine kit. There is an immense range available as a visit to a good, specialist home-brew shop will prove. Apart from the many different manufacturers and wine styles, the wine kits can be classified in the following way:

High-quality kits

Naturally these are the most expensive but they consist exclusively of concentrated, good-quality wine grape juice without adulteration. No additional sugar is required, only water. The resulting wine is of a high standard. There is a limited choice of styles but the most important ones are covered.

Standard kits

These consist of concentrated grape juice with various flavourings added. Some additional sugar is required as well as water. The quality is good and there is a very wide choice of styles.

Budget kits
These are skilfully prepared from a mixture of concentrated fruit juices, including grape, various sugars and appropriate flavourings. Additional sugar is required as well as water. The kits are inexpensive and produce good, everyday wines.

Express kits
These produce an acceptable wine in as short a time as possible. The fruit juice compound requires additional sugar but a number of chemicals are provided to ferment and stabilize the wine with the minimum of delay. Because these are quaffable wines rather than ones for sipping, they are marketed in a format to produce 22.5 litres (5 gallons) of wine at a time.

WHAT TO DO
Standard kits
Detailed instructions for making the wine are supplied with every kit. When you make a kit for the first time you should follow them meticulously. In general the instructions are much as follows:

1 Having sterilized all the equipment, pour some cold water into a demijohn, add the concentrate and wash out its container so as not to waste any juice.
2 Activate the yeast and add it to the must.
3 Fit an airlock and label the jar. Ferment in an atmospheric temperature of 24°C (75°F).
4 After a few days remove some must, dissolve the sugar in it and return the sweetened must to the jar.
5 Top up with cold water.
6 When fermentation finishes, rack into a clean jar, top up, add 1 Campden tablet, seal and store until bright, then bottle.

118 · WINEMAKING

> ### Variations on the standard kit
> When you are experienced you can consider making one of the following variations:
> - Adding 5 ml (1 tsp) tartaric acid to the must to sharpen the flavour.
> - Reducing the water a little to increase the body.
> - Fermenting the white wines at a lower temperature to improve the bouquet and flavour.
> - Keeping the wine for several months or longer to mature rather than drinking it as soon as it is clear.

Express kits

1 Express kits usually require the sugar to be added at the outset and for some pectolytic enzyme and wine finings to be included at the same time, before the activated yeast.

2 Fermentation in a constantly warm place is essential. If this is not possible, use a thermal belt or heating tray. Fermentation is usually complete within 14 days.

3 Next, move the wine to a cold place and mix in more finings. Shake the vessel thoroughly to release the entrained carbon dioxide.

4 The shaking process should be repeated several times over three days and the wine then left in the cold to clear. It is usually bright within three days and ready for bottling.

5 Although the wine is now ready for drinking it improves a little if kept for two or three months. Both the red and the white wines are light in texture and flavour and taste best when served cool and fresh. Neither benefits from long storage and both are at their best while still young.

Opposite
To make wine from a kit: **(1)** Empty the concentrate into a demijohn part filled with water, then agitate the jar to dissolve the concentrate. (The jug contains the airlock and bung for the demijohn.) **(2)** Add an activated wine yeast. **(3)** Fit an airlock and label the jar. **(4)** Remove some must from the demijohn and stir in the sugar. **(5)** Return this to the jar and ferment out. **(6)** When the wine is clear, siphon it into bottles, then cork and label.

THE ADVANTAGES

- Kits take up little room and need the minimum of equipment. They have particular advantages for people with limited facilities, especially those living in small flats or whose home allows little spare space for hobbies.
- The wine is both easy and quick to make and needs no day-to-day attention.
- As the wines mature quite quickly, they require little storage space.
- The concentrates are widely available, often from large supermarkets. You could buy a kit with your groceries each week and, after a few weeks, be able to enjoy a bottle a day! Better still, rack into a bag-in-a-box and save bottling altogether.
- For those who want to explore country wines, a few kit wines produce some palatable drinking while the others mature. Making kit wines first helps you to make even better country wines later.

Traditional Country Wines

The distinguishing feature of country wines is that they are made from a single flavour ingredient and are sweeter than table wines. Later in the chapter I give some traditional recipes, but first it is worthwhile mentioning how modern methods and equipment have affected our approach to this old-established craft.

More than a gallon
Traditionally, country wine recipes are based on 1 gallon of water which always produces more than 1 gallon of wine. This is useful as the excess can be used for topping-up after racking.
In the past: Fresh baker's yeast was most commonly used. As it does not settle firmly on the bottom of a fermentation vessel, there was quite a lot of wastage due to racking. The end result was probably no more than a gallon of wine.
Today: Modern wine yeast not only ferments more efficiently than baker's yeast but it settles more firmly. It is easier, therefore, to rack all the wine from the sediment with the minimum of wastage. The same recipes today produce more than a gallon of wine.

Sugar
- Single flavour ingredient recipes inevitably have a stronger and more individual aroma and flavour than those made by a mixutre of different flavour ingredients. The pronounced aroma and flavour do need to be balanced by sufficient sweetness to make them as appealing and enjoyable as they can be.
- The traditional measure of sugar was 4 lb to the gallon of water (1.8 kg to 4.5 litres). This quantity of sugar increases the volume of 1 gallon of water by 2 pints (1.1 litres), i.e. from 8 to 10 pints (4.5–5.6 litres). Add to this any juice extracted from the fruit (this can be up to three-quarters of its weight) and the quantity of sugar becomes less excessive than it might at first seem, especially in the making of a sweet wine.
- A lesser quantity, usually from 3 to $3\frac{1}{2}$ lb (1.35–1.64 kg), was used when the sugar was added to a gallon of water and juice.

Acid
- A weakness of some of the old recipes, especially those for flower and vegetable ingredients, was the lack of acid. The fruit recipes usually just get by without it, but even these could be improved with 5 or 10 ml (1 or 2 tsp) citric or tartaric acid.
- Acid crystals were not available to our forebears and they had to use lemons and oranges instead. The juice of a large lemon is roughly equal to 5 ml (1 tsp) citric acid.
- As flowers and vegetables contain no natural acid, the juice of four lemons is really required. Perhaps it was thought that so many lemons would affect the flavour, for old recipes rarely call for more than two, and often only one.
- Yeast needs an acid solution in which to thrive, so always include lemon juice or acid crystals.

Pectic enzyme
- Most fruits contain enzymes which break down the pectin surrounding their juice molecules, but these are destroyed by boiling water. Hazy wines are not uncommon if boiling water is poured on to fruit and pectic enzyme is not added when the water is cool.
- The traditionalist is loath to add chemicals to a must and pectic enzyme has, therefore, been omitted from the recipes. All the fruit recipes would benefit, however, from 5 ml (1 tsp) pectic enzyme, both to assist in juice extraction and in the prevention of haze.

Campden tablets
- The same advice applies to Campden tablets which were rarely, if ever, used in winemaking until the 1950s.
- Some of the traditional country wines contained sufficient alcohol (13 or 14%) to protect them from most infections, especially if the bottles were well sealed. Nonetheless, knowing as much as we do about the problems that can be caused by the spoilage organisms invisible to the naked eye, it is a wise precaution to protect the wines with Campden tablets as an additional insurance.

The demijohn and airlock
In days gone by, winemakers used large earthenware crocks covered with a cloth for pulp fermentation and, subsequently, earthenware jars covered with a teacup; or for large quantities, wooden casks, the bung hole of which was covered with a pebble.

- The demijohn and airlock are too precious not to be used today and it is taken for granted that the present-day maker of traditional country wines will use all the modern equipment available.

'Boiling over'

Warning: Watch out for 'boiling over', especially in hot weather and when fermenting in the traditional 'warm' place specified by old recipes. If the jar is too full of sweet must, a tumultuous ferment might push particles of pulp through the lock and down the side of the jar. This not only makes a mess but also attracts tiny fruit flies and spoilage organisms. Leave some space in the jar for the first few days and then top up when the fermentation steadies.

> ### Keys to success
> - Use sufficient sugar to balance the aroma and flavour.
> - Always include lemon juice or acid crystals.
> - It is wise to use pectic enzyme and Campden tablets.
> - Take advantage of the demijohn and airlock.

THE RECIPES

These recipes are traditional ones which have been followed for some 300 years or so. Indeed, they have been used since sugar became cheaply available, until the modern development of recipes to make wines for a purpose which originated in the early 1960s.
- Follow these recipes or experiment with other countryside berries and flowers.
- People with easy access to hedgerow fruits and flowers sometimes prefer these simple wines to the more complex wine styles. Country wines are rich in the aroma and flavour of the ingredients from which they are made. For that reason they are best finished sweet rather than dry. Indeed, they are best served as 'social' wines.

> ### A word of warning!
> People with a great love of and feel for the countryside seem to know instinctively the plants that are safe to use for making wine. If you are at all unsure please consult the list of plants, vegetables and fruit known to be poisonous on page 46.

APPLE WINE

6 kg (13 lb 5 oz) mixed windfall apples
4.5 litres (1 gallon) cold water
2 kg (4½ lb) white sugar
Wine yeast

Wash and cut up the apples into thin slices; include the skin and core but exclude any brown or damaged portions and any maggot caves. As you cut them, drop the apple slices into a bin containing the water, a quarter of the sugar, well dissolved, and the activated yeast.

Cover the bin and leave for seven to ten days, pressing down the fruit twice a day and keeping the bin covered in the meantime.

Strain out the liquor, press dry and discard the apples and stir in the rest of the sugar. Pour the must into demijohns, fit airlocks and finish the fermentation. Sweeten to taste with saccharin if required. Rack and mature for at least one year.

This recipe makes about 9 litres (2 gallons) of medium-sweet wine, depending on the juiciness of the apples and how hard they are pressed.

Quick tips
- Include plenty of eating apples as well as some cooking apples. The John Downie crab apple may be used alone but the Bramley cooking apple is not suitable by itself.
- Today, we would drop the apples into water containing pectic enzyme and 1 Campden tablet. The yeast would not be added until 24 hours later.

BEETROOT WINE

2 kg (4½ lb) beetroot
4.5 litres (1 gallon) water
1.5 kg (3½ lb) sugar
2 lemons
Wine yeast

Use beetroot the size of tennis balls, freshly dug in the late summer. Cut off the tops close to the beet and discard them. Scrub the beets free of all traces of earth and then cut them into thin slices. Place in a large pan, add the water and boil, uncovered, until tender.

Strain the liquor into a bin, discard the beets, stir in the sugar – making sure that it is completely dissolved – cover and leave to cool.

Thinly pare and chop the lemon skins, express and strain the juice, then add the skins, juice and activated yeast to the beetroot liquor.

Cover and ferment for two days, then pour the must into a demijohn and the surplus into a wine bottle. Fit an airlock to the jar and a plug of cotton wool to the bottle. Ferment in a warm place. Rack and mature for at least two years. This recipe makes six to seven bottles.

Variations

- A large piece of crushed ginger and a dozen cloves can help to improve the flavour.
- 250 g (9 oz) raisins may be washed, chopped and added with the yeast to improve the fermentation and flavour.
- To make a Madeira-style wine use any brown sugar instead of white.
- 10 ml (2 tsp) tartaric acid would be beneficial added at the same time as the lemons.

BEGGARMAN'S WINE

3.25 kg (7¼ lb) mixed ingredients
4.5 litres (1 gallon) boiling water
1.5 kg (3½ lb) white sugar
Wine yeast

Collect together small quantities of as many summer fruits as you can: apples; black, red and white currants; cherries; apricots; gooseberries; loganberries; raspberries; strawberries; sultanas – indeed you could also include fresh pea pods, boiled rice, crystallized jams, and crusts of bread. Whatever is available in fact!

Clean, stone and wash all the ingredients as necessary, chop them up, put into a fermentation bin and pour on boiling water, stir well, then cover and leave to cool.

Leave for three days, stirring occasionally.

Strain out the liquor, press the pulp and discard. Stir in the sugar and an activated yeast into the must, pour the must into a demijohn and a jumbo bottle, fit airlocks and ferment to a finish.

Rack and store for six months.

Quick tip
Today we would recommend adding 5 ml (1 tsp) of pectic enzyme and 1 crushed Campden tablet to the must.

BLACKBERRY 'PORT'

4 kg (9 lb) hedgerow blackberries
1 Campden tablet
1.35 kg (3 lb) sugar
Wine yeast

Clean the blackberries and wash them in water containing 1 crushed Campden tablet. Crush the berries with a potato masher, mix in an activated yeast and layer them in a bin alternately with layers of sugar. Cover the bin and leave it in a warm place for four days.

Strain off the juice through a nylon straining bag and squeeze well until no more juice can be extracted. Pour the must into a demijohn and fit an airlock. After four days top up with water if necessary, or better still mix in 56 g (2 oz) washed and well-chopped raisins.

When fermentation is finished, rack the wine into a storage jar, top up with cold boiled water or vodka and mature for eighteen months, racking whenever a deposit is formed.

BLACKBERRY TABLE WINE

3 kg (6½ lb) cultivated blackberries
2.8 litres (5 pints) boiling water
1 kg (2¼ lb) sugar
Wine yeast

Clean and wash the blackberries, crush them with a potato masher, place them in a bin, pour boiling water over them and leave them well covered for two days, stirring twice each day.

Strain and press the fruit dry, stir the sugar into the liquor, add the activated wine yeast, pour the must into a demijohn and ferment out.

CHERRY WINE

2.75 kg (6 lb) morello cherries
4.5 litres (1 gallon) hot water
1.8 kg (4 lb) sugar
Wine yeast

Stalk and wash the black-ripe cherries, place in a fermentation bin, pour 3.4 litres (6 pints) hot water over them, cover and leave to cool. Dissolve the sugar in the rest of the water and leave to cool.

Open up the cherries by squeezing them between your fingers. Cover the bin and leave for three days, stirring twice each day to extract colour and juice.

Strain out and gently squeeze the pulp to extract as much juice as possible. Mix in half the sugar syrup and the activated yeast and ferment in a closely covered bin for one week. Keep the remainder of the syrup well covered in the refrigerator. Mix in half the remaining syrup and the rest one week later.

Pour into fermentation jars, fit airlocks and ferment to a finish. Rack and mature for at least one year. You should end up with ten bottles of a strong, sweet wine with a delightful and distinctive flavour.

> **Quick tip**
> As with damsons, take care not to break any stones when you squeeze the cherries and the pulp.

DAMSON WINE

3.25 kg (7¼ lb) black, ripe damsons
4.5 litres (1 gallon) hot water
2 kg (4½ lb) sugar
Wine yeast

Stalk and wash the damsons, put into a fermentation bin, pour 3.4 litres (6 pints) hot water over them, cover and leave to cool.

Crush the damsons with your hands, taking care not to break any stones, cover and leave for four days, stirring twice each day.

Dissolve the sugar in 1.1 litres (2 pints) hot water and leave to cool.

Strain out the damsons and press the pulp dry. Mix in half the sugar syrup and the activated yeast, and ferment under a close-fitting cover. Keep the remainder of the syrup well covered in the refrigerator.

After one week, mix in half the remaining syrup and the rest one week later. Pour the must into demijohns, fit airlocks and ferment to a finish.

This recipe should produce ten bottles of a strong, sweet wine that needs eighteen months' maturation.

DATE WINE

2 kg (4½ lb) dates
4.5 litres (1 gallon) water
4 lemons
250 g (9 oz) brown sugar
Sherry wine yeast

Chop the dates into small pieces and place them in a preserving pan, together with half a dozen of their stones and all the water.

Thinly pare the lemons, chop up the rinds and add these to the pan together with the juice of 1 lemon.

Mix in the brown sugar, bring the must to the boil and simmer steadily in a covered pan for 30 minutes, stirring from time to time. Leave to cool.

Strain out the juice and gently press the dates or roll them around in a nylon straining bag.

Mix in the rest of the lemon juice and an activated sherry wine yeast; pour the must into a demijohn, fit an airlock and ferment out.

Rack and mature this wine in a vessel not quite full and plugged with cotton wool for at least one year.

Historical note
This is an interesting adaptation of an old recipe. The original one used baker's yeast and was matured in a sealed container.

ELDERBERRY WINE

2 kg (4½ lb) black-ripe berries
1 lemon
4.5 litres (1 gallon) water
500 g (18 oz) chopped raisins
1.8 kg (4 lb) sugar
Wine yeast

Clean the elderberries from every bit of stalk, cap stem and unripe berries, wash the sound berries in running cold water, drain and place them in a preserving pan, together with the thinly pared and chopped lemon rind.

Add the water, bring to the boil and then simmer the berries in the water until they are all dimpled. Strain off the liquor on to the washed and chopped raisins and half the sugar. Stir well to dissolve the sugar and press the berries gently against the straining bag to extract any more juice. Do not press too hard in case you extract too much bitterness. Discard the elderberries.

When cool, add the activated yeast and expressed and strained juice of the lemon and ferment in a covered bin, pressing down the floating raisins twice daily.

Mix in the remaining sugar in 4 equal portions every ten days.

When fermentation is finished, strain out the raisins, leave the wine in a cold place to settle, then siphon into jars or bottles and mature for eighteen months.

Variation
Some old recipes also include a large piece of well-bruised root ginger and a dozen or so cloves, but this is a matter of personal taste.

ELDERFLOWER WINE

2 litres (3½ pints) elderflowers
4.5 litres (1 gallon) water
2 lemons
250 g (9 oz) chopped sultanas
1.5 kg (3½ lb) sugar
Wine yeast

Clean the freshly picked florets from every trace of green leaf, stalk and stem, and measure them in a jug. Tap the jug on to a table to shake the florets down but do not press them. Empty them into a pan, add the water and the thinly-pared and chopped lemon rinds. Bring to the boil and simmer in a covered pan for 15 minutes.

Strain the liquor on to the washed and well-chopped sultanas and the sugar, stir well, then leave to cool.

Mix in the expressed and strained lemon juice and activated yeast. Ferment in a warm place, rack and mature for at least six months.

GOOSEBERRY WINE

2.75 kg (6 lb) green gooseberries
4.5 litres (1 gallon) hot water
1.5 kg (3½ lb) sugar
Wine yeast

Make this wine from green gooseberries that are only just ripe. Top, tail and wash them, place in a bin and pour hot water over them.

When cool, crush the berries between your fingers and leave them in a covered vessel for two days, stirring occasionally.

Strain out, press dry and discard the pulp. Stir in the sugar, add the activated yeast and pour into a demijohn and a jumbo-sized (magnum) wine bottle. Fit airlocks and ferment out. Rack and store for one year or more.

ORANGE WINE

12 Seville oranges
4.5 litres (1 gallon) hot water
1.5 kg (3½ lb) white sugar
Wine yeast

Wash the oranges and thinly pare and chop the rinds, avoiding all white pith. Pour hot water over the rinds and leave to cool.

Halve the oranges, express and strain the juice and add this to the bin of water and rinds. Cover and leave for three days, stirring occasionally.

Strain out the parings, stir in the sugar and mix in an activated wine yeast. Pour into a demijohn and jumbo bottle, fit airlocks and ferment to a finish.

Rack, add 280 ml (½ pint) of gin and store for one year.

Mature in containers, not quite full and plugged with cotton wool, for at least one year.

Variation
You can use a sherry yeast and omit the gin and add the sugar in small portions to build up the alcohol tolerance of the yeast.

PARSNIP WINE

2 kg (4½ lb) frosted parsnips
4.5 litres (1 gallon) water
2 Seville oranges
2 large lemons
1.36 kg (3 lb) sugar
Wine yeast

Make this wine from parsnips freshly dug in late January. Cut out the crowns and scrub the parsnips clean from every trace of soil. Cut them into thin rings, place in a large pan and add the water. Bring to the boil, covered and simmer them with the thinly pared rinds of the oranges and lemons until they are soft but not mushy.

Strain off the liquor on to the sugar and stir well until it is dissolved, then cover and leave to cool.

Mix in the expressed and strained juice of the oranges and lemons and an activated wine yeast. Pour the must into a demijohn and a wine bottle, fit an airlock to the jar and a plug of cotton wool to the bottle and ferment out. Rack and store this medium-sweet wine for one year.

Variations

- A stronger and sweeter version can be made by pouring the hot liquor on to 250 g (9 oz) washed and chopped sultanas, as well as the sugar. 5 ml (1 tsp) tartaric acid would also improve this old recipe.
- Another 250 g (9 oz) sugar added during the fermentation would make the wine even stronger.

PLUM WINE

2 kg (4½ lb) plums, any sort
4.5 litres (1 gallon) hot water
1.36 kg (3 lb) sugar
Wine yeast

Stalk, wash and stone the plums, place them in a fermentation bin, pour on hot water, stir in half the sugar, cover and leave to cool.

Mix in the activated wine yeast and ferment-on-the-pulp for four days. Keep the bin covered but press down the floating fruit twice each day.

Strain out, press dry and discard the pulp, stir in the rest of the sugar, pour the must into a demijohn and a wine bottle; fit an airlock to the jar and plug the bottle with cotton wool. Ferment to a finish, rack and store this medium-sweet wine for one year.

Plum varieties
Greengages and **yellow plums** make a golden wine.
Early River plums make a splendid rosé.
Prolific plums make a medium red wine.
Victoria plums make a good sherry-type wine.
To make a sherry-style wine: Use a sherry yeast and feed the fermentation with another 250 g (9 oz) sugar. Finish the wine fairly dry.

Quick tip
If you cannot remove the plum stones easily to begin with, wait until the hot water has softened them. It is inadvisable to ferment any of these plum wines in the presence of their stones.

ROSE PETAL WINE

1.1 litres (2 pints) scented red rose petals
4 litres (7 pints) hot water
500 g (18 oz) sultanas
10 ml (2 tsp) citric acid
Sauternes wine yeast
1 kg (2¼ lb) sugar

Place the rose petals in a bin and pour on half the water – hot but not boiling, around 80°C (176°F). Rub the petals against the side of the bin with the back of a wooden or plastic spoon to squeeze out the colour and perfume. Repeat this several times during the day, keeping the bin covered in between.

Next day strain off all the liquor on to the washed and chopped sultanas and mix in the citric acid. Pour the remaining water, also hot, over the petals and give them another day of rubbing against the bin.

Strain this liquor on to the sultanas and squeeze out all the essence from the rose petals. Mix in the activated yeast and ferment-on-the-pulp for one week, pressing down the sultanas twice each day.

Strain out, press dry and discard the sultanas. Stir in the sugar, pour the must into a demijohn, fit an airlock and finish the fermentation.

Rack into a storage jar and bottle the wine as soon as it is bright. After six months serve the wine cold with sweet biscuits.

Variation
The same quantity of concentrated rosé grape juice may be used instead of sultanas. This avoids the period of fermentation-on-the-pulp.

SLOE WINE

2 kg (4½ lb) black, ripe sloes
4.5 litre (1 gallon) boiling water
1.36 kg (3 lb) sugar
Wine yeast

Stalk and wash the sloes, place them in a fermentation bin, pour on boiling water, cover and leave to cool. Break up the sloes with your hand, then leave them covered for three days, stirring occasionally to extract the colour and other constituents.

Strain out the liquor, press dry and discard the fruit. Mix the sugar into the must, and when it is completely dissolved add the activated yeast.

Pour into a fermentation jar and a jumbo bottle. Fit an airlock to the jar and plug the bottle with cotton wool.

Ferment in a warm place, rack and store for one year at least.

Variation

Another sloe wine recipe requires an additional 1 kg (2¼ lb) sloes and another 454 g (1 lb) sugar. Feed this into the fermentation in two portions, the first two weeks after the start and the second one week later.

Rack into a storage jar containing 280 ml (½ pint) of gin and keep for two years to make a superb dessert wine.

Modern Table Wines

A PURPOSE-MADE WINE

The distinguishing feature of these wines is that they are made from several flavour ingredients that harmonize with the specific yeast recommended to produce a wine suitable to accompany certain foods. It is often impossible to identify these ingredients by smelling and tasting the wines.

Bouquet and flavour: These are vinous in character and the wines are sometimes reminiscent of those from the area from which the yeast originates. Some winemakers try to make a wine similar in style to a specific commercial wine.

Alcohol content

The alcohol content must be carefully balanced with the flavour and texture. Since the wine is to be drunk with a meal it is important not to make it too strong.

Red table wines: These may vary from 11.5 to 12.5% alcohol in harmony with the fullness of the wine. A stronger and fuller-bodied wine would be served with rump steak, for example, and one with less alcohol and a little less fullness with roast lamb.

White and rosé wines: These may vary from 10 to 11.5% alcohol, depending on both their fullness and sweetness. The lower alcohol would balance a less full and less sweet wine. But a firm and full dry white could be as high as 11.5% or a shade more to accompany poached salmon.

Controlling the alcohol content: This is done by using only sufficient sugar to produce the quantity of alcohol required.

- Record the likely sugar content in the fruits and grape concentrate or sultanas (see the table on page 75), as well as the sugar you have.
- Take specific gravity readings as necessary to corroborate your calculations.
- Note the finishing gravity to ensure that the right ending has been achieved.

Sweetness

Red table wines: These must be free from any taste of sweetness and have a finishing specific gravity of 0.996 or lower.

Light white and rosé wines: A hint of sweetness may be tasted in some of these.
Fuller bodied and sweeter white wines: These are drunk during the dessert course of the meal and could have a finishing specific gravity of 1.016.
• These Sauternes-style wines are best made full-bodied, fermented out to dryness, then sweetened at the bottling stage with the addition of potassium sorbate and sulphite to prevent re-fermentation.
• Alternatively, terminate the fermentation by racking at the required level of sweetness and adding sorbate and sulphite or a proprietary brand of a stabilizing agent. It is, however, harder to be sure of the alcohol level in this way.

Grape

Although you will rarely be able to use grapes exclusively to make these wines, they nearly all contain grape in one form or another. Sometimes it is fresh grapes grown by the winemaker, sometimes sultanas, but more often it is concentrated grape juice.
What the grape contains: In addition to some sugar and tartaric acid, the grape contains mineral salts and vitamins essential to a good fermentation. Black grapes also contain tannin, an essential ingredient of red wines.
Sultanas: These are dehydrated grapes which have lost three-quarters of their weight in the process. Thus 1 kg ($2\frac{1}{4}$ lb) grapes makes only 250 g (9 oz) of sultanas. The ratio of fresh grape juice to concentrated grape juice is about the same i.e. 4 to 1; 250 g (9 oz) of sultanas is roughly the same as 250 g (9 oz) of concentrated grape juice.

A general tip
Although liquid, concentrated grape juice is usually measured by weight because of its high sugar content.

How much to use: This is a matter of opinion, but I always use between 200 g and 250 g (7 and 9 oz) concentratred grape juice per 1 gallon of wine. Some winemakers use only half this quantity, others use something in between. Good winemakers always include some grape in their musts.

Freshness for quality
Whether you use sultanas or concentrated grape juice, the advantages to the finished wine seem to be the same as long as both are fairly fresh. Old stock of either ingredient is likely to impart a tawny hint to the wine.

Water
If you use concentrated grape juice, use a little less water. The quantity of water given in the recipes is likely to be the maximum required. It is always best to use up to 560 ml (1 pint) less at first. The fruit may be juicier than expected or the extraction rate better than average. You can always top up the demijohn after the sugar has been mixed in and the tumultuous ferment has finished.

Yeast and nutrient
- Do use the wine yeast recommended as this contributes to the style of wine being made.
- Always activate the yeast beforehand as directed on the sachet or phial.
- Do include some nutrient with it. A single nutrient tablet, or up to 5 ml (1 tsp) diammonium phosphate, is adequate to ensure fermentation to dryness.

Acidity
- To obtain the right balance between all the different ingredients you should ensure that the must has a starting acidity of between 4 and 5 parts per thousand. Many fruits contain sufficient acid when used in the quantity recommended in the recipes (see page 45).
- Provided you use a good wine yeast, ferment in a moderate to low atmospheric temperature, (20–15°C/68–59°F), and do not stir up the must too much, you will achieve a fermentation that increases the acidity by $1\frac{1}{2}$ to 2 parts per thousand, so that the wine contains between 5 and 7 parts per thousand overall.

Tannin
- One of the notable features of some home-made red table wines is their lack of tannin compared with commercial wines. Few ingredients contain sufficient when the must is prepared. Furthermore, fining a wine often reduces the tannin content because tannin combines with many fining agents and is precipitated with the sediment.

- It is essential to add extra tannin after fining a wine. In any case the must should be started with sufficient tannin. 5 ml (1 tsp) of grape tannin powder is recommended for red wines. Liquid tannin seems to be much less effective than the reddish-brown powder.

Fining/Filtering
- Fining and filtering should rarely be necessary. If you have made the wine from good-quality ingredients, and included sufficient pectic enzyme at the start, most table wines will clear readily, given a cool storage space and sufficient time.
- The besetting sin of most winemakers is impatience! It is essential to give all table wines adequate time to clear and mature, especially red wines with their higher tannin content.

Keys to success
- Control the alcohol content carefully.
- Always ensure that the sultanas or concentrated grape juice are fresh.
- Use the wine yeast recommended in the recipe and include some nutrient with it.
- Ferment at the temperatures recommended.
- Add extra tannin to red wines after fining.

APPLE AND ELDERBERRY WINE

500 g (18 oz) ripe elderberries
100 g (3½ oz) raspberries
2 litres (3½ pints) hot water
Pectic enzyme
1 Campden tablet
3 kg (6½ lb) mixed eating apples
250 g (9 oz) concentrated red grape juice
Bordeaux wine yeast and nutrient
680 g (1½ lb) sugar

Stalk, wash and crush the elderberries and raspberries, place in a fermentation bin and pour 2 litres (3½ pints) hot water (80°C/176°F) over them. Cover and leave to cool.

Add the pectic enzyme and 1 crushed Campden tablet, then wash the apples and crush them as finely as you can, dropping them into the elderberry must as you do so. Cover and leave for 24 hours in a warm place.

Mix in the concentrated grape juice, the activated yeast and nutrient. Ferment-on-the-pulp for six days, keeping the fruit submerged with a weighted plate.

Strain out, press dry and discard the pulp. Stir the sugar into the must as gently as you can, pour into a demijohn, fit an airlock and ferment to specific gravity 0.996 at room temperature.

Rack into a storage jar, top up, seal and keep in a cold place until the wine is bright. Then rack again and keep for at least one year in bulk and another six months in bottle.

Serve at room temperature with red meats and cheese.

APRICOT WINE

2 kg (4½ lb) fresh apricots
250 g (9 oz) sultanas
2.8 litres (5 pints) cold water
Pectic enzyme
1 Campden tablet
1 ml (¼ tsp) grape tannin
Chablis wine yeast and nutrient
680 g (1½ lb) sugar

Stalk, wash, stone and crush the apricots; wash and chop the sultanas and place them both in a bin containing the cold water, pectic enzyme and 1 crushed Campden tablet. Stir well, cover and leave for 24 hours.

Stir in the tannin, activated yeast and nutrient and ferment-on-the-pulp for five days, keeping the fruit submerged and the bin covered.

Strain out, press dry and discard the fruit. Stir the sugar into the must, pour the must into a demijohn, fit an airlock and ferment out. Rack and store for one year.

Serve cold with poached smoked haddock, baked or grilled fish, roast pork or roast poultry.

BLACKBERRY AND APPLE WINE

Pectic enzyme
1 Campden tablet
2 litres (3½ pints) cold water
3 kg (6½ lb) mixed eating apples
1 kg (2¼ lb) ripe blackberries
Bordeaux wine yeast and nutrient
5 ml (1 tsp) grape tannin
250 g (9 oz) concentrated grape juice
454 g (1 lb) white sugar

Mix the pectic enzyme and 1 crushed Campden tablet into the water and pour into a fermentation bin. Wash and crush the eating apples and drop them into it as crushed; stalk, wash and crush the blackberries, stir them in, cover and leave for 24 hours.

Add the activated yeast and nutrient and ferment-on-the-pulp for five days, keeping the fruit submerged and the bin covered.

Strain out, press dry and discard the fruit. Mix the tannin, concentrated grape juice and sugar into the must; pour the must into a demijohn, fit an airlock and ferment out.

Rack and store for at least one year, preferably two.

Serve free from chill with steak, casseroled beef and similar chunky beef dishes.

BLACKBERRY AND ELDERBERRY WINE

1.36 kg (3 lb) blackberries
454 g (1 lb) elderberries
200 g (7 oz) sultanas
2 ripe bananas
2.8 litres (5 pints) boiling water
Pectic enzyme
1 Campden tablet
Bordeaux wine yeast and nutrient
725 g (1 lb 9½ oz) sugar

Stalk, wash and crush the blackberries and elderberries; wash and chop the sultanas; peel and mash the bananas. Place the fruit in a bin and pour boiling water over them. Cover and leave to cool.

Stir in the pectic enzyme and 1 crushed Campden tablet, cover and leave for 24 hours.

Mix the activated yeast and nutrient into the must and ferment-on-the-pulp for five days, keeping the fruit submerged and the bin covered.

Strain out, press dry and discard the fruit. Stir the sugar into the must, pour the must into a demijohn, fit an airlock and ferment to dryness.

Rack and store for at least one year, preferably two.

Serve free from chill with roast meats and cheese dishes.

CHERRY WINE

2.5 kg (5½ lb) cooking cherries
2.27 litres (4 pints) cold water
5 ml (1 tsp) tartaric acid
Pectic enzyme
2 Campden tablets
250 g (9 oz) concentrated grape juice
Sauternes wine yeast and nutrient
800 g (1¾ lb) sugar

Stalk and wash the cherries and, if possible, remove all the stones. Drop them into a bin containing the water, acid, pectic enzyme and 1 crushed Campden tablet, then cover and leave for 24 hours.

If the stones cannot be removed, place the cherries in a bin and pour hot water over them, cover and leave to cool. The stones can now be removed and the pectic enzyme, acid and Campden tablet added.

Mix in the concentrated grape juice, activated yeast and nutrient, and ferment-on-the-pulp for four days, keeping the pulp submerged or pressed down twice each day.

Strain out, press dry and discard the pulp. Gently stir in the sugar and pour the must into a demijohn. Top up, fit an airlock and ferment out at 16°C (61°F).

Rack into a storage jar, top up and add 1 Campden tablet. Seal and keep until the wine is bright and then rack again.

Mature this white table wine for about one year. It has marginal sweetness.

Serve the wine cold with poultry or pork.

DAMSON WINE

1.36 kg (3 lb) ripe damsons
2 bananas
200 g (7 oz) raspberries
250 g (9 oz) sultanas
3.4 litres (6 pints) hot water
Pectic enzyme
1 Campden tablet
5 ml (1 tsp) grape tannin
Bordeaux wine yeast and nutrient
750 g (1 lb 10½ oz) sugar

Stalk, wash, stone and crush the damsons; peel and mash the bananas; stalk, wash and crush the raspberries; wash and chop the sultanas. Place all these in a bin and pour on 2.27 litres (4 pints) hot water (80°C/176°F). Cover and leave to cool. Stir in the pectic enzyme and crushed Campden tablet. Cover and leave for 24 hours.

Mix in the tannin, activated yeast and nutrient, and ferment-on-the-pulp for four days, keeping the fruit submerged.

Strain out, press dry and discard the pulp. Dissolve the sugar in 560 ml (1 pint) hot water and when cool add it to the must and pour it into a demijohn. Top up with cold water, if required, fit an airlock and ferment to specific gravity 0.996.

Rack into a storage jar, top up, seal and store until bright, then rack again. Keep for a minimum of one year in bulk and another year in bottle.

This is a wine of some character that takes time to mature, but has a superb flavour. Serve at room temperature with roast meats, game and cheese.

GREENGAGE WINE

2 kg (4½ lb) greengages
250 g (9 oz) sultanas
2.8 litres (5 pints) cold water
Pectic enzyme
1 Campden tablet
1 ml (¼ tsp) grape tannin
Chablis wine yeast and nutrient
680 g (1½ lb) sugar

Stalk, wash, stone and crush the greengages. Wash and chop the sultanas. Place the fruit in a bin containing cold water, pectic enzyme and 1 crushed Campden tablet. Stir well, cover and leave for 24 hours.

Mix the tannin, nutrient and an activated yeast into the must and ferment-on-the-pulp for five days, keeping the fruit submerged and the bin covered. Strain out, press dry and discard the fruit. Stir in the sugar into the must, pour the must into a demijohn, fit an airlock and ferment out.

Rack and store for one year.

Serve cold with poached salmon, baked and grilled fish, roast pork and poultry.

MIXED SOFT FRUIT WINE

250 g (9 oz) blackberries
200 g (7 oz) blackcurrants
250 g (9 oz) cherries
250 g (9 oz) gooseberries
200 g (7 oz) loganberries
200 g (7 oz) raspberries
250 g (9 oz) strawberries
454 g (1 lb) seedless grapes
2.8 litres (5 pints) cold water
Pectic enzyme
2 Campden tablets
Sauternes wine yeast and nutrient
908 g (2 lb) sugar

Stalk, wash, stone and crush the fruit, pour on 2.27 litres (4 pints) cold water and stir in the pectic enzyme and 1 crushed Campden tablet. Cover and leave for 24 hours.

Mix in an activated yeast and nutrient, and ferment-on-the-pulp for four days, keeping the fruit submerged.

Strain out, press dry and discard the pulp. Dissolve the sugar in 560 ml (1 pint) hot water and when cool add it to the must. Then pour this into a demijohn. Fit an airlock and ferment out at around 17°C (63°F).

Rack into a storage jar, top up and add 1 Campden tablet. Seal and store until the wine is bright, then rack again and keep for one year.

This is an attractively flavoured rosé table wine just off complete dryness. Serve it cool with veal or lamb.

Variation
The fruits mentioned are only examples and indicate the quantity of each that is desirable. Use as many different fruits as you have available.

PEACH WINE

2 kg (4½ lb) ripe peaches
2 ripe bananas
250 g (9 oz) sultanas
2.8 litres (5 pints) cold water
Pectic enzyme
2 Campden tablets
Sauternes wine yeast and nutrient
1 kg (2¼ lb) sugar
1 ml (¼ tsp) potassium sorbate

Peel, stone and mash up the peaches; peel and mash the bananas; wash and chop the sultanas. Stir these into a bin containing cold water, pectic enzyme and 1 crushed Campden tablet. Cover and leave for 24 hours.

Mix in the yeast and nutrient and ferment-on-the-pulp for five days, keeping the fruit submerged and the bin covered.

Strain out, press dry and discard the fruit. Stir the sugar into the must, pour the must into a demijohn, fit an airlock and ferment down to a specific gravity of 1.016.

Stir in the potassium sorbate and 1 crushed Campden tablet, or the recommended measure of a proprietary brand of stabilizing tablets or powder, and move the jar to a cold place for a few days while the sediment settles.

Rack into a storage jar and keep for one year.

Serve cold with the dessert course of a meal.

PINEAPPLE WINE

2 kg (4½ lb) fresh pineapple
2.8 litres (5 pints) cold water
Pectic enzyme
2 Campden tablets
250 g (9 oz) concentrated grape juice
4 ml (¾ tsp) grape tannin
Chablis wine yeast and nutrient
680 g (1½ lb) sugar
5 ml (1 tsp) tartaric acid

Top and tail the pineapple but do not peel it. Crush it finely, or cut it up into very thin slices, collecting the juice as you do so. Place in a fermentation bin and pour on 2.27 litres (4 pints) cold water. Stir in the pectic enzyme and 1 crushed Campden tablet. Cover and leave for 24 hours.

Stir in the concentrated grape juice, the tannin, activated yeast and nutrient, and ferment-on-the-pulp for four days, keeping the pulp submerged.

Strain out, press dry and discard the pulp. Boil the sugar, acid and 560 ml (1 pint) water for 20 minutes and, when cool, mix it into the must and pour this into a demijohn. Fit an airlock and ferment out at 16°C (61°F).

Rack into a storage jar, top up and add 1 Campden tablet. Seal, store until the wine is bright and then rack again. Keep this wine for one year and serve it cold, as a dry white wine with roast pork or poultry.

PLUM WINE

2 kg (4½ lb) Prolific plums
2.8 litres (5 pints) hot water
250 g (9 oz) sultanas
Pectic enzyme
1 Campden tablet
5 ml (1 tsp) grape tannin
Beaujolais wine yeast and nutrient
680 g (1½ lb) sugar

Stalk and wash the plums in hot water to remove the waxy bloom. Drain and dry them. Then remove the stones, mash the fruit and place in a fermentation bin. Pour on the hot water. Add the washed and chopped sultanas and leave to cool.

Stir in the pectic enzyme and crushed Campden tablet, cover and leave for 24 hours.

Mix in the tannin, activated yeast and nutrient and ferment-on-the-pulp for five days, keeping the fruit submerged and the bin covered.

Strain out, press dry and discard the pulp. Stir in the sugar, pour the must into a demijohn, fit an airlock and ferment to dryness.

Rack and store for one year.

Serve this light red table wine just below room temperature with cold meats, and for lunch rather than for dinner.

PLUM AND APPLE WINE

1 kg (2¼ lb) black plums
100 g (3½ oz) loganberries
250 g (9 oz) sultanas
2 litres (3½ pints) hot water
Pectic enzyme
2 Campden tablets
3 kg (6½ lb) eating apples
Sauternes wine yeast and nutrient
570 g (1¼ lb) sugar

Stalk, wash, stone and crush the plums. Wash and crush the loganberries; wash and chop up the sultanas. Place them all in a bin and pour hot water (80°C/176°F) over them. Cover and leave to cool.

Stir in the pectic enzyme and 1 crushed Campden tablet, then wash the apples and crush them as finely as you can, dropping them into the bin and mixing them in as you do so. Cover and leave for 24 hours.

Stir in the activated yeast and nutrient, then ferment-on-the-pulp for six days, keeping the fruit submerged with a weighted plate.

Strain out, press dry and discard the fruit. Gently stir in the sugar, pour the must into a demijohn and ferment out at room temperature.

Rack into a storage jar, top up and add 1 Campden tablet. Seal, keep until bright and then rack again.

Keep for one year, then bottle and, if necessary, marginally sweeten this rosé wine with saccharin. Serve it cold at parties and picnics and with supper snacks.

RHUBARB WINE

2 kg (4½ lb) 'Champagne' rhubarb
1 sweet orange
2 ripe bananas
250 g (9 oz) sultanas
2.5 litres (4½ pints) cold water
Pectic enzyme
2 Campden tablets
2.5 ml (½ tsp) grape tannin
Chablis wine yeast and nutrient
800 g (1¾ lb) sugar

Top and tail the rhubarb and wipe the stalks with a clean cloth dipped in a sulphite solution. Wipe over the orange with the same cloth. Chop and liquidize, or mince, the rhubarb; thinly pare and chop up the orange skin (avoid all white pith); peel and mash the bananas; wash, chop, liquidize or mince the sultanas. Place all these ingredients in a bin, pour on 2.27 litres (4 pints) cold water, stir in the pectic enzyme and 1 crushed Campden tablet. Cover and leave for 24 hours.

Mix in the tannin, activated yeast, nutrient and the expressed and strained juice of the orange. Ferment-on-the-pulp for four days, keeping the fruit submerged.

Strain out, press dry and discard the pulp. Dissolve the sugar in 280 ml (½ pint) hot water. When cool, mix the syrup with the must and pour it into a demijohn. Fit an airlock and ferment out to specific gravity 0.996 in a temperature of 16°C (61°F).

Rack into a storage jar and add 1 Campden tablet. Seal, keep until bright and then rack again. Keep this wine for one year before bottling, and then for a further three months. Serve it chilled with roast poultry or pork.

Second-Run Wines

These wines are not for beginners or for those who make only a gallon of wine at a time, or who have limited facilities. Rather, they are for the winemaker who makes his wines in larger batches and has some large bins and a press.

A DEFINITION

- A second-run wine is essentially a second wine made from the ingredients used for the first run. The idea possibly came from the French who often make one wine from the free-run juice of the crushed grapes and then a second wine from the juice extracted by pressing the grapes.
- The first wine usually has a finer flavour and commands a higher price than the second which the *vigneron* might even keep for the use of his family and workers.

Press gently
When a 45-litre (10-gallon) batch of wine is made at home, a fine wine can be made from a light pressing of the fruit. Possibly only 40.5 litres (9 gallons) of must will be produced, the remaining gallon being left in the pulp together with some acids, mineral salts and a little sugar. Some additional water, sugar, acid and concentrated grape juice could easily produce a second-run wine of quite fair quality.

Orchard and autumn harvest = rosé
- I first made this wine in the late autumn of 1970 when large batches of an orchard wine were made from apples, pears and quinces and an autumn harvest wine was made from blackberries, damsons and elderberries. 1970 was a particularly good season and the fruit used was of a very high quality. After a light pressing both the pulps seemed too good to throw away and were mixed together.
- Concentrated white grape juice was used in the orchard wine and red in the autumn harvest. A rosé was therefore used in the mixture, together with some water, a little extra acid and nutrient and some sugar. No yeast was necessary because there was a fine mixture of champagne and burgundy wine yeasts in the pulp.

- From the two batches of pulp a further 22.5 litres (5 gallons) of a rosé wine was produced of a remarkably high quality. It was Christmas by the time the second-run wine was racked and so it was called Christmas Rosé.

The quantity to make
- About 50 kg (112 lb) of orchard fruits and 2 kg (4½ lb) of concentrated grape juice were used to make the 45 litres (10 gallons) of the white wine and some 20 kg (45 lb) of fruit with 2 kg (4½ lb) of concentrated grape juice to make the same quantity of red wine.
- To the mixed pulp was added: 1 kg (2¼ lb) of concentrated rosé grape juice, 56 g (2 oz) tartaric acid, 20 ml (4 tsp) yeast nutrient, and 11.25 litres (2½ gallons) of cold water.
- Fermentation was continued on the pulp for four days, giving the pulp a gentle mix twice each day. It was then firmly pressed until some 8 litres (4 gallons) of must had been produced.
- While fermentation-on-the-pulp was proceeding, 4 kg (9 lb) sugar was mixed with 2 litres (3½ pints) of water and 5 ml (1 tsp) citric acid.
- This was boiled for 20 minutes and cooled before being stirred into the liquid must. The resulting 22.5 litres (5 gallons) was fermented under an airlock and racked in the usual way.

Four to make one
- Other mixtures of pulp can also be used to make second-run wines, but use the same proportions. It may be possible to make as much as 31.5 litres or even 45 litres (7 or 10 gallons) of wine from the mixed pulps, but the wine is likely to be light in flavour and thin in body.
- Smaller quantities of pulp may be used. The pulp residue from two 9-litre (2-gallons), or four 4.5-litre (1-gallon) batches, would make 4.5 litres (1 gallon) of second-run wine. Batches of pulp can also be frozen until it is convenient to use them with other pulps.
- Pulps that contain sultanas or raisins are especially suitable for second-run wines as some goodness certainly remains in dried fruits after a single pulp fermentation.

Blended pulps are best
- A significant quantity of a single pulp can be used to make a second run of the same wine but the flavour would be much diluted. I think it is better to blend different pulps that will produce a different flavour.
- Sweeten the wines slightly with saccharin and serve them cold with picnics and snacks when fine wines are not required.

Social Wines

AN INDIVIDUAL STYLE

Commercially there is no comparison with this style which home winemakers have made their own. The German *Tafelweins* drunk in beer gardens during the summer evenings are much lighter in texture and flavour and contain less alcohol than a social wine. The Austrian *Heurige* drawn from the cask is more akin to the German wine, being young and light but dry enough to drink with cold meats and crusty bread.

The ingredients and alcohol content

- These wines are often made by those fairly new to winemaking. As a result they are usually fairly strong, 13–14% alcohol, and sweetish. They are frequently made from a single ingredient or as the result of an experiment – not necessarily one that 'went wrong'.
- Social wines need not be strong, although many are. Some of the most delightful ones can be made from elderflowers, rose petals and so on. These wines need to be sweetish to harmonize with the sweetness of their fragrant aroma.
- Folly wines come into a similar category, as do some vegetable wines. Fruit juices, canned fruit and jam all contribute to these attractive wines.

When to drink them

Social wines are drunk not with a meal but when sitting back in an armchair while enjoying the company and conversation of friends. Cheesy biscuits, crisps or salted peanuts may accompany the wines if you wish, but rarely anything more.

A general hint
Social wines are essentially talking points, positive and with a distinctive flavour and satisfaction of their own.

CARROT AND ORANGE WINE

2 kg (4½ lb) freshly dug carrots
4 litres (7 pints) water
3 large oranges
250 g (9 oz) sultanas or raisins
Sauternes wine yeast
1.25 kg (2¾ lb) sugar

Remove the leaves and crowns of the carrots, scrub them clean, cut them into thin rings and boil in the water until tender.

Thinly pare the oranges, chop them up, mix with the washed and chopped sultanas or raisins. Place in a fermentation bin and pour the hot carrot water over them. Cover and leave to cool.

Express and strain the orange juice and mix this in with the activated yeast. Ferment-on-the-pulp for five days, then strain out, press dry and discard the pulp. Stir in the sugar, pour the must into a demijohn, fit an airlock and ferment to a finish.

Rack and store for one year, then bottle and sweeten further if necessary.

GINGER WINE (1)

85 g (3 oz) root ginger, fresh or dried
3 large lemons
2.5 ml ($\frac{1}{2}$ tsp) cayenne pepper
4 litres (7 pints) water
500 g (18 oz) large raisins
Sauternes wine yeast
1.25 kg ($2\frac{3}{4}$ lb) sugar

Grate the fresh ginger or bruise the dried roots well; thinly pare the lemons and chop them up; place in a pan, add the cayenne pepper and water and boil, covered, for 20 minutes.

Leave for 15 minutes while the solids settle, then slowly strain through a fine nylon sieve, leaving the pepper and solids behind in the pan if you can. Add the washed and chopped raisins, stir well, then cover and leave to cool.

Mix in the expressed and strained lemon juice and activated yeast and ferment-on-the-pulp for five days, pressing down the raisins twice each day. Keep the pan well covered in the meantime.

Strain out, press dry and discard the raisins. Mix in the sugar, pour the must into a demijohn, fit an airlock and ferment out.

Rack and store for one year.

GINGER WINE (2)

1 kg ($2\frac{1}{4}$ lb) concentrated sweet white grape juice
20 ml ($\frac{3}{4}$ fl oz) liquid ginger essence
5 ml (1 tsp) capsicum tincture
Approx 3.4 litres (6 pints) water
Sauternes wine yeast
250 g (9 oz) sugar

Make up the kit of grape juice compound as directed on the container. Add the ginger essence and capsicum tincture at the outset.

Adjust with additional essence and/or tincture and/or saccharin at the bottling stage.

LEMON BALM WINE

2.25 litres (4 pints) lemon balm leaves
4 litres (7 pints) water
500 g (18 oz) sultanas
Sauternes wine yeast and nutrient
10 ml (2 tsp) citric acid
900 g (2 lb) sugar
1 Campden tablet

Pick the lemon balm in the spring while the leaves are still young and fresh. Discard the stems and measure the leaves. Wash the leaves, shake off the surplus water and boil them in the water for 15 minutes in a covered pan.

Strain through a nylon bag into a bin containing the washed and chopped or liquidized sultanas. Cover and leave to cool.

Mix in the activated yeast, nutrient and citric acid and ferment-on-the-pulp for six days, keeping the sultanas well submerged.

Strain out, press dry and discard the pulp. Stir in the sugar, pour the must into a demijohn, fit an airlock and ferment to a finish.

Rack into a storage jar and add the Campden tablet. Top up, seal and store until bright. Then rack again.

Keep for nine months, then bottle and keep for another three. Sweeten further if you wish and serve the wine cold with sweet biscuits.

MARROW AND GINGER WINE

2.5 kg (5½ lb) ripe marrow
250 g (9 oz) sultanas
28 g (1 oz) root ginger
2.8 litres (5 pints) boiling water
15 ml (3 tsp) citric acid
Sauternes wine yeast and nutrient
1.25 kg (2¾ lb) sugar

Wash the marrow and cut it up into thin slices (include the skin and pips but be careful not to cut them). Place the marrow in a bin.

Wash and chop the sultanas and add these to the bin together with root ginger. (Grate the fresh ginger or bruise the dried roots well.)

Pour boiling water over the marrow, sultanas and ginger, cover and leave to cool.

Mix in the acid, activated yeast and nutrient and ferment-on-the-pulp for five days, pressing down the floating pulp each day.

Strain out, lightly press the pulp and discard. Stir in the sugar, pour the must into a demijohn, fit an airlock and ferment to a finish.

Rack and store for one year.

> **Variation**
> Use the same quantity of courgettes or pumpkin instead of marrow.

MINT WINE

1.1 litres (2 pints) mint leaves
4 litres (7 pints) hot water
500 g (18 oz) sultanas
Sauternes wine yeast and nutrient
10 ml (2 tsp) citric acid
900 g (2 lb) sugar
1 Campden tablet

You can use apple mint, peppermint or spearmint leaves as well as the usual garden mint. Pick them early in the season as soon as the plant is fully grown.

Remove the leaves from their stems, measure them in a jug or ½-pint mug and then wash them in cold water. Chop them up, place them in a bin and pour on the hot water (80°C/176°F).

Macerate the leaves against the side of the bin with the back of a strong plastic spoon to extract as much of the flavour as possible. Cover and leave to cool.

Strain through a nylon sieve, again pressing with the back of the spoon until the leaves are fairly dry. Discard them and add the washed and chopped sultanas to the liquor.

Mix in the activated yeast, nutrient and citric acid and ferment-on-the-pulp for six days, keeping the sultanas well submerged.

Strain out, press dry and discard the pulp. Stir in the sugar, pour the must into a demijohn, fit an airlock and ferment to a finish.

Rack into a storage jar and add the Campden tablet. Top up, seal, keep until bright and then rack again.

Store in bulk for nine months and for three in bottle.

Serve cool with savoury biscuits or water biscuits and a mild cheese.

PARSLEY WINE

500 g (18 oz) English parsley leaves
4 litres (7 pints) cold water
2 lemons
340 g (12 oz) sultanas
Hock wine yeast and nutrient
680 g (1½ lb) sugar
1 Campden tablet

Use only young and tender parsley leaves without stems. Wash them in cold water, chop them up and boil them with the thinly pared and chopped rind of the lemons for about 15 minutes.

Strain into a bin through a large nylon sieve, pressing the leaves with the back of a plastic spoon. Add the washed and chopped sultanas, cover and leave to cool.

Mix in the activated yeast, nutrient and the expressed and strained juice of the lemons. Ferment-on-the-pulp for six days, keeping the sultanas well submerged.

Strain out, press dry and discard the pulp. Stir in the sugar, pour the must into a demijohn, fit an airlock and ferment out in a cool place.

Rack into a storage jar and add the Campden tablet. Top up, seal and store until the wine is bright. Rack again and keep for nine months before bottling and then keep for another three.

If necessary, sweeten marginally and serve cold with baked fish or vegetarian dishes.

RICE AND RAISIN WINE

500 g (18 oz) wholemeal rice
500 g (18 oz) raisins
2 large lemons
4 litres (7 pints) boiling water
Cereal yeast and nutrient
1 kg (2¼ lb) sugar

Wash the rice in running water, crush or coarsely grind it and then place it in a bin. Wash and chop the raisins without breaking any pips and add these to the bin. Thinly pare the lemons, chop up the parings and add these to the bin. Pour on the boiling water, cover and leave to cool.

Express and strain the lemon juice and add this to the bin together with the activated yeast and nutrient. Use *Saccharomyces diastaticus* for preference, since this yeast will ferment a little starch as well as sugar.

Ferment-on-the-pulp for a week, then strain out and press the pulp dry. Stir in the sugar, pour the must into a demijohn, fit an airlock and finish the fermentation.

Rack into a storage jar and mature this wine for one year or more, although it is drinkable after three months or so.

Variation
You can use wheat instead of rice but this wine really does need long maturation to become smooth.

TEA WINE

4 litres (7 pints) cold tea
500 g (18 oz) raisins or sultanas
1 large lemon
1 large orange
Sauternes wine yeast
1 kg ($2\frac{1}{4}$ lb) sugar

Although you can save the tea from the pot each day, it is better to use freshly-made tea that is strained off the leaves after 5 minutes' infusion. Pour the tea into a fermentation bin.

Wash and chop up the raisins or sultanas, thinly pare and chop up the orange and lemon skins and add all these to the tea, cover and leave to cool. Mix in the expressed and strained juice of the orange and lemon and an activated yeast.

Ferment-on-the-pulp for one week, pressing down the floating cap twice each day. Strain out, press dry and discard the pulp. Stir in the sugar, pour the must into a demijohn, fit an airlock and ferment to a finish.

Rack into a storage jar and mature this wine for three to four months.

Quick tip
Different tea flavours make different wines and you can also use your favourite teabags.

FLOWER WINES

Although flowers contribute only perfume and flavour to a wine, this can be most fragrant and enjoyable. Indeed, some winemakers enhance the bouquet of their wines by including some dried elderflowers or dried rose petals in their fruit or vegetable musts.

Sweetening

Because of their sweet aroma flower wines need to be finished slightly sweet rather than dry. The wine also needs to be light in alcohol and texture to match the delicacy of the flower fragrance. The easiest way to do this is to use concentrated grape juice as the base, ferment out to dryness and sweeten with saccharin before serving.

BASIC RECIPE

Flower petals as indicated below
3.4 litres (6 pints) hot water
1 kg ($2\frac{1}{4}$ lb) concentrated white grape juice
5 ml (1 tsp) citric acid
Sugar as required
Sauternes wine yeast
1 Campden tablet

Pour half the water on to the flower petals and rub them with the back of a wooden or plastic spoon to extract the essence. Repeat this two or three times during the next 24 hours, covering the container in between.

Strain the flower water through a sieve and funnel into a sterilized demijohn. Mix in the concentrated white grape juice and citric acid. Fit an airlock.

Pour the rest of the hot water over the flowers and repeat the process for a further 24 hours.

Strain the flower water into the demijohn and check the specific gravity with a hydrometer. You need a reading of 1.074–6. Stir in sufficient sugar to raise the gravity to the upper figure (56 g/2 oz increases the gravity by about 5 units).

Mix in the yeast which could have been activated in the traces of concentrate left in the container and mixed with about 140 ml (5 fl oz) of tepid water. Replace the airlock and ferment out.

Rack into a storage jar and add the Campden tablet. Top up and keep in a cool place until bright. Then bottle and sweeten to taste with 2 or 3 saccharin pellets per bottle.

Serve the wine cool with sweet biscuits.

Flowers to use

Agrimony	– 1 medium-sized bunch
Broom	– 2 litres (3½ pints) yellow petals
Carnation	– 1 litre (1¾ pints) white 'garden pinks'
Clover	– 2 litres (3½ pints) purple petals
Coltsfoot	– 2 litres (3½ pints) yellow petals
Dandelion	– 2 litres (3½ pints) yellow petals
Elderflower	– 0.5 litre (1 pint) cream florets
Hawthorn blossom	– 2 litres (3½ pints) white petals
Marigold	– 2 litres (3½ pints) orange petals
Primrose	– 2 litres (3½ pints) yellow petals
Rose petal	– 2 litres (3½ pints) scented petals

Keys to success
- Remember that petals only may be used. Discard every trace of green leaf, stem or seed box.
- It is unwise to experiment with other flowers (see page 46).
- Instead of concentrated grape juice, you can use sultanas as indicated in the recipes for elderflower and rose petal wines on pages 132 and 136.

Easy Wines from Juices, Jams and Canned Fruits

JUICES
The advantages
Fruit juice wines are excellent for people who have limited facilities, whether in the form of space or equipment. As it is an all-liquid must that can be mixed in the demijohn if necessary, it can also be made by the very elderly, the chairbound or the blind.

The ingredients
- A wide range of differently flavoured wines can be made from the fruit juices available in the shops. The most popular are apple, grape, grapefruit, orange and pineapple juice but there is also a cocktail of several of these and a 'tropical' fruit juice.
- In addition passion fruit, rosehip, apricot and redcurrant syrups can sometimes be bought as well as blackcurrant juice.
- The quality and quantity of the fruit juices vary from one manufacturer to another as does the price.
- In addition the different fruit juice combinations are almost endless. You can also change the flavour by including a small quantity of honey in the must.
- Do avoid tomato juice. It does not make an attractive wine. It is best mixed with vodka or Worcestershire sauce or drunk on its own.

Preparing the must
Diluting the fruit juice: It is not necessary to make the wine entirely from juice – indeed blackcurrant, orange and grapefruit juice wines in particular would be far too acid. The fruit flavour would also be far too pronounced; some dilution is therefore essential. A rough guide is as follows:
Apple juice – dilute with an equal quantity of water.
Grapefruit juice – dilute with 3 parts water to 1 grapefruit.
Orange juice – dilute with 3 parts water to 2 orange.
Pineapple juice – dilute with an equal quantity of water.
As an economy measure, however, some winemakers use only 1 litre of

juice per gallon of wine, or a little more if the container holds 39 fl oz (approx 1.1 litres), as many do.
Use unsweetened fruit juice: This is important in case the sweetened version contains saccharin. Most fruit juices contain about 10% fermentable sugar but this is best measured after blending and dilution and before the addition of sugar. This is particularly important with the syrups or nectars, as they are sometimes called.
Pectic enzyme: Most of the juices contain pectin that must be reduced with a pectic enzyme to obtain a clear wine.
Acid and nutrient: The additional dilution of the acid often needs to be redressed by the inclusion in the must of 5–10 ml (1–2 tsp) of tartaric acid. 5 ml (1 tsp) of nutrient is also required.
Wine yeast: Canned and cartoned fruit juices produce excellent, fast-maturing, light wines for social drinking, particularly in warmer and sunnier weather when heavier wines lose their appeal. A German wine yeast is usually best. Aim for an alcohol content of 10 or 11%.

Fermentation
1 When all the ingredients have been mixed together, leave a little space in the demijohn in case of frothing. If none appears with the start of fermentation, or if there is frothing, then as soon as it dies down, top up with cold, boiled water.
2 Leave the jar in an atmospheric temperature of 15–16°C (59–61°F) until fermentation is complete.

Maturation and storage
1 Rack the clearing wine into another jar, add some wine finings and 1 Campden tablet. Top up, seal and store in a cold place until the wine is clear.
2 Siphon the wine into bottles, sweetening marginally with saccharin if you so wish.
3 Seal, label and store the bottles for three months. Then serve the wine freshly chilled.

Key to success
- Always use unsweetened fruit juice.

ORANGE APERITIF

1 litre (1¾ pints) orange juice
½ litre (18 fl oz) grapefruit juice
125 g (4½ oz) concentrated grape juice
2.5 litres (4½ pints) water
Pectic enzyme
1 Campden tablet
1 kg (2¼ lb) sugar
Sherry wine yeast and nutrient

Mix together the orange and grapefruit juices, concentrated grape juice, water, pectic enzyme and crushed Campden tablet. Cover and leave for 24 hours. Stir in half the sugar and add the yeast and nutrient. Pour the must into a demijohn, fit an airlock and ferment at room temperature for one week.

Remove some of the must, stir the rest of the sugar into it and return the must to the demijohn. Replace the airlock and ferment out.

Rack into a storage jar, top up, seal and store for six months.

PINEAPPLE AND ORANGE WINE

1 litre (1¾ pints) pineapple juice
1 litre (1¾ pints) orange juice
125 g (4½ oz) concentrated grape juice
2 litres (3½ pints) water
Pectic enzyme
2 Campden tablets
908 g (2 lb) sugar
Sauternes wine yeast and nutrient

Mix together the pineapple and orange juices, concentrated grape juice, water, pectic enzyme and 1 crushed Campden tablet. Cover and leave for 24 hours. Stir in the sugar and, when it is well dissolved, add the yeast and nutrient. Pour the must into a demijohn, fit an airlock and ferment out in a cool room.

Rack into a storage jar, add 1 Campden tablet and store in a cool place until the wine is bright.

Siphon into bottles and keep until the wine is six months old.

PINEAPPLE AND HONEY WINE

2 litres (3½ pints) pineapple juice
2 litres (3½ pints) water
250 g (9 oz) light honey
750 g (1 lb 10½ oz) sugar
5 ml (1 tsp) tartaric acid
Hock wine yeast and nutrient
1 Campden tablet
Saccharin pellets

Mix all the ingredients listed down to the nutrient together, pour the must into a demijohn, fit an airlock and ferment out at room temperature (20°C/68°F).

Rack into a storage jar, add the Campden tablet and keep until the wine is six months old. Then bottle and sweeten with 1 saccharin pellet per standard size bottle.

Quick tip
Do not use more honey than recommended and select a thin mixed flower honey for preference.

JAMS

The ingredients
- For wine-making purposes jams include bramble, cranberry, quince and redcurrant jelly as well as preserves of all kinds, whether made commercially or at home. Marmalades, too, can be used. They make a slightly bitter aperitif.
- When buying jams from the grocer or supermarket look for brands that do not contain setting agents, added pectin or preservatives. Good jam consists only of fruit, sugar and water and this is best for winemaking.
- Like juice wines, jam wines are also fast-maturing. They are ideal light wines for warm days and are particularly acceptable at picnics and parties.

Preparing the must
Three 454 g (1 lb) jars of jam are needed to make 1 gallon of wine, although a somewhat fuller wine can be made with four.
Pectic enzyme: By its very nature jam contains a great deal of pectin so include a double dose of whatever pectic enzyme you use in your must.
Acid and sugar: Additional acid is also needed. But use much less sugar than in other wines, since between 50 and 60% of the jam consists of fermentable sugar.

Method
1 Dissolve the jam in warm water and when cool enough (25°C/77°F), mix in the pectic enzyme, cover and leave overnight.
2 Next day mix in some concentrated grape juice and adjust the sugar and acid. Stir in an activated Bordeaux wine yeast for red jams and a Sauternes wine yeast for golden jams.

Fermentation
1 Since there is so little pulp you can ferment the must in a demijohn under the safety of an airlock. Keep the jar in a coolish atmospheric temperature.
2 Strain out the few solid particles after a week. This is best done by removing the airlock and bung, then slowly pouring the wine out of the jar, through a fine nylon sieve placed over a polythene funnel fitted into another demijohn. If you pour carefully, you will avoid

large bubbles of air forcing their way through the wine into the jar, with consequent splashing.
3 When there is only a cupful or so of wine left, give the jar a swirl so that all the sediment is carried over, for this will include much of the yeast colony. Press the small amount of pulp in the sieve with the back of a wooden spoon and then discard it.
4 If necessary, top up the jar with cold boiled water, fit the airlock again and continue fermentation to the finish.

Maturation and storage
1 Rack the clearing wine from its sediment, add 1 Campden tablet, top up, seal, label and store until the wine is bright. It usually clears quickly and easily. If it doesn't, then add some more pectic enzyme.
2 As soon as the wine is bright, bottle, seal, label and store until it is six or eight months old.

Serving
Fruit juice and jam wines are a pleasant accompaniment to a lunch of quiche, cold meats or fish and lightly-flavoured cheeses. They should be served chilled, but not ice cold.

Keys to success
- Do not use jam which contains setting agents, additional pectin or preservatives.
- Always include a double dose of pectic enzyme when making wines from jam.
- Home-made jams and jellies are ideal and may be mixed if you have insufficient of one variety.
- Always use 1.36 kg (3 lb) jam.
- Always use an appropriate concentrated grape juice.

STRAWBERRY ROSÉ

1.36 kg (3 lb) strawberry jam
3.4 litres (6 pints) warm water
250 g (9 oz) concentrated grape juice
5 ml (1 tsp) tartaric acid
Pectic enzyme (double quantity)
Sauternes wine yeast and nutrient
250 g (9 oz) sugar
1 Campden tablet

Dissolve the jam in the water and leave to cool. Stir in the grape juice, acid and pectic enzyme. Cover and leave for at least 24 hours.

Add the yeast and nutrient, pour the must into a demijohn, fit an airlock and ferment at 20°C (68°F) for two weeks.

Remove some of the must, gently stir the sugar into it and return this to the jar. Replace the airlock and ferment to a finish.

Rack into a storage jar, add the Campden tablet, top up and keep for six months before bottling.

This makes a very attractive rosé wine for parties and picnics. Serve the wine cold.

Quick tips
- For preference use a rosé concentrated grape juice, but a red or white may also be used.
- The jam should be free from preservative and additional pectin. Jam made only from fruit, sugar and water is best.

REDCURRANT JELLY WINE

Make with similar other ingredients and in the same way as Strawberry Rosé.

BRAMBLE JELLY WINE

Use a concentrated red grape juice and a Bordeaux or Burgundy wine yeast. Otherwise, use similar ingredients and quantities as in Strawberry Rosé. Serve at room temperature.

DAMSON AND PLUM JAM WINES

Use similar other ingredients and quantities as recommended for Bramble Jelly Wine and make in the same way.

APRICOT, GREENGAGE AND OTHER GOLDEN-COLOURED JAM WINES

Use a concentrated white grape juice and a Chablis or Burgundy wine yeast. Otherwise use similar ingredients and quantities as in Strawberry Rosé. Serve cold.

GOLDEN SHRED MARMALADE APERITIF

1.36 kg (3 lb) Golden Shred marmalade
3.4 litres (6 pints) warm water
250 g (9 oz) concentrated grape juice
5 ml (1 tsp) tartaric acid
Pectic enzyme (double quantity)
Dry sherry yeast and nutrient
450 g (1 lb) sugar

Dissolve the marmalade in the warm water and when cool mix in the concentrated grape juice, tartaric acid and a double quantity of pectic enzyme. Cover and leave for at least 24 hours.

Mix in the activated sherry yeast and nutrient, pour the must into a demijohn, fit an airlock and ferment at room temperature.

After two weeks, remove some must, gently stir in half the sugar and return to the jar. One week later repeat the process with half the remaining sugar, and one week later mix in the rest.

When fermentation finishes, move the wine to a cold place to clear and, if need be, mix in 5 ml (1 tsp) chitosan finings.

Rack into a storage jar, leaving some air space, and plug the neck of the jar with loose cotton wool. Leave at room temperature for at least six months and preferably longer.

Serve this wine cool as an aperitif.

Quick tips
- Use only Golden Shred marmalades. Coarse-cut, thick-cut and dark marmalades are too bitter for winemaking.
- If possible, use a dry sherry concentrate, or at least a white concentrate.

CANNED FRUITS

A good range of light wines, both red and white, can be made from the wide variety of canned fruits available in most supermarkets. The fruit is usually canned in a light sugar syrup that is fully fermentable. Some brands are sugar-free and may be used for making wine as long as they do not contain a preservative. Preservatives inhibit fermentation. The precise size of the can is not critical as long as the total quantity used is about 1.35 kg (3 lb). The best results seem to come from a mixture of fruits, although canned apricots and gooseberries both make fine wines on their own.

CANNED FRUIT WINE (1)

1.35 kg (3 lb) canned apricot pieces
10 ml (2 tsp) tartaric acid
Pectic enzyme
2 Campden tablets
Approx 3.4 litres (6 pints) cold water
680 g (1½ lb) sugar
Hock wine yeast and nutrient
250 g (9 oz) concentrated grape juice
Saccharin pellets

Drain off and save the syrup, then empty the apricot pieces into a bin. Add the tartaric acid, pectic enzyme, 1 crushed Campden tablet and 2.2 litres (4 pints) water. Cover and leave in a warm place for 24 hours.

Stir in the sugar and when it is dissolved add the activated yeast and nutrient. Ferment-on-the-pulp for three days; keeping the fruit cap submerged or gently pressed down twice each day.

Strain out, press dry and discard the pulp. Mix in the concentrated grape juice, pour the must into a demijohn and top up with cold water. Fit an airlock and ferment out in a cool temperature (16°C/61°F).

When fermentation is finished and the wine begins to clear, rack into a storage jar, top up and add 1 Campden tablet. Seal and store until the wine is bright. Siphon into bottles, adding 1 saccharin pellet to each.

Leave for three to four months and serve this light wine cold at lunch.

Variations
- Canned gooseberries may be used instead of the apricots to make a wine remarkably similar to a Moselle.
- Three 440 g (15½ oz) cans may be used, or a catering pack.
- Both these wines are well worth making in double quantities for summer drinking.

CANNED FRUIT WINE (2)

440 g (approx 15½ oz) canned golden plums
440 g (approx 15½ oz) canned gooseberries
440 g (approx 15½ oz) canned peaches
10 ml (2 tsp) tartaric acid
Pectic enzyme
2 Campden tablets
2.8 litres (5 pints) cold water
750 g (1 lb 10½ oz) sugar
200 g (7 oz) concentrated grape juice
Hock wine yeast and nutrient

Drain off and save the syrups, discard the plum stones and then crush or liquidize the fruit. Place the fruit in a bin and add the acid, pectic enzyme, 1 crushed Campden tablet and 2.27 litres (4 pints) water. Cover and leave in a warm place for 24 hours.

Dissolve the sugar in 560 ml (1 pint) warm water and, when cool, add it to the syrup and set it aside in a refrigerator.

Add the concentrated grape juice to the pulp and mix in the activated yeast and the nutrient. Ferment-on-the-pulp for three days, keeping the fruit cap submerged.

Strain out the pulp through a fine-meshed sieve or nylon bag, roll it around but do not press it, and then discard it.

Mix in the syrup, pour the must into a demijohn and, if necessary, top up with cold water. Fit an airlock and ferment out in a cool temperature, 16°C (61°F).

Rack into a storage jar, add 1 Campden tablet and top up. Seal and store until the wine is bright. Then bottle and keep until the wine is four months old. Serve this light wine cold at lunch.

The peaches give a Hock-like taste to this wine.

CANNED FRUIT WINE (3)

440 g (approx 15½ oz) canned blackberries
440 g (approx 15½ oz) canned black cherries
312 g (approx 7½ oz) canned blackcurrants
440 g (approx 15½ oz) canned damsons
2.8 litres (5 pints) cold water
Pectic enzyme
1 Campden tablet
10 ml (2 tsp) tartaric acid
200 g (7 oz) concentrated grape juice
5 ml (1 tsp) grape tannin
Bordeaux wine yeast and nutrient
800 g (1¾ lb) sugar

Drain off and save the syrup, discard the fruit stones, and crush or liquidize the fruit. Place the fruit in a bin containing 2.27 litres (4 pints) water, the pectic enzyme, 1 crushed Campden tablet and 5 ml (1 tsp) tartaric acid. Cover and leave for 24 hours.

Add the concentrated grape juice, tannin, activated yeast and nutrient. Ferment-on-the-pulp for four days, keeping the fruit cap submerged.

Boil the sugar, the remaining acid and 560 ml (1 pint) water for 20 minutes and leave to cool.

Strain out the fruit, press it gently and discard it. Mix in the fruit syrup and sugar syrup and pour the must into a demijohn. Top up if necessary, fit an airlock and ferment out at room temperature, 20°C (68°F).

Rack into a storage jar and top up. Seal and store until bright; then bottle and keep until the wine is eight months old.

Serve the wine at room temperature with red meats and cheese.

CANNED FRUIT WINE (4)

908 g (2 lb) bottled bilberries
440 g (approx 15½ oz) canned blackberries
213 g (approx 7½ oz) canned prunes
2.8 litres (5 pints) cold water
Pectic enzyme
10 ml (2 tsp) tartaric acid
1 Campden tablet
250 g (9 oz) concentrated grape juice
5 ml (1 tsp) grape tannin
Burgundy wine yeast and nutrient
800 g (1¾ lb) sugar

Strain the light syrup from the fruit and set it aside. Discard the prune stones and crush or liquidize all the fruit. Place the fruit in a bin, pour on 2.27 litres (4 pints) water and stir in the pectic enzyme, 5 ml (1 tsp) acid and 1 crushed Campden tablet. Cover and leave for 24 hours.

Mix in the concentrated grape juice, tannin, activated yeast and the nutrient. Ferment-on-the-pulp for four days, keeping the fruit submerged.

Strain out the liquor and lightly press the fruit, then discard it. Mix the fruit syrup into the must. Boil the sugar with the rest of the acid and 560 ml (1 pint) water for 20 minutes. When this is cool, mix it into the must and pour it into a demijohn. Top up if necessary, fit an airlock and ferment out at 20°C (68°F).

Rack into a storage jar, top up, seal and store until the wine is bright. Then bottle and keep the wine for a further four months.

Serve this more robust wine with red meats and cheese.

CANNED FRUIT WINE (5)

425 g (approx 15 oz) canned red cherries
440 g (approx 15½ oz) canned red plums
385 g (approx 13½ oz) canned raspberries
2.8 litres (5 pints) cold water
Pectic enzyme
10 ml (2 tsp) tartaric acid
2 Campden tablets
200 g (7 oz) rosé concentrated grape juice
Sauternes wine yeast and nutrient
2.5 ml (½ tsp) grape tannin
680 g (1½ lb) sugar

Strain off and save the fruit syrup, discard the fruit stones and crush or liquidize the fruit. Place the fruit in a bin containing 2.27 litres (4 pints) water, the pectic enzyme, 5 ml (1 tsp) acid and 1 crushed Campden tablet. Cover and leave for 24 hours.

Add the concentrated grape juice, fruit syrup, activated yeast, nutrient and grape tannin. Ferment-on-the-pulp for three days, keeping the fruit submerged.

Strain out, press dry and discard the pulp. Boil the sugar and remaining acid in 560 ml (1 pint) water for 20 minutes and, when cool, mix it into the must. Pour this into a demijohn, fit an airlock and ferment out.

Rack into a storage jar, top up, add 1 Campden tablet, seal and store until the wine is bright. Siphon into bottles and, if you wish, marginally sweeten with saccharin.

Serve this rosé cold at parties, picnics, lunches and with supper snacks.

Sparkling Wines

CHOICE OF METHOD

- A large number of people now make and enjoy their own sparkling wine at home and it is relatively simple to make.
- The best method is the traditional one of a secondary fermentation in the bottle. This is the method by which Champagne is made in France. Some factors are critical, however, and put off the fainthearted.
- The other method is merely to carbonate a suitable still wine in a Soda Stream jug. For parties a larger quantity can be carbonated with CO_2 in a small beer keg.

The ingredients

- It is rarely suitable to sparkle a wine which has been made for another purpose. The best sparkling wine is made from the right choice of ingredients. Of these pear, gooseberry, rhubarb and white currants are the most popular but apple may also be used. A delicious sparkling rosé can be made from Early River plums and just a few raspberries.
- It is important that the flavour of the base ingredients is not too strong. Otherwise it will mask the yeast flavour and the effect of the carbon dioxide.

Preparing the must

Make the wine as for a dry wine, controlling the total sugar to about 11% alcohol. A must specific gravity of 1.078 is about right – total sugar 200 g per litre (32 oz per gallon). This is the first critical figure. Too much sugar and the wine will be too strong to sparkle.

Fermentation

Ferment the wine with a Champagne yeast in a cool atmosphere around 13°C (55°F) and make sure that it ferments right out. The final specific gravity should be 0.996 or below but no higher.

Maturation and storage

Rack the wine, adding no more than 1 Campden tablet per gallon; then store it for at least six months in a cool place.

Putting in the sparkle

1 Bring the wine into the kitchen and prepare a clean and sterile demijohn, an airlock and bored bung and a siphon. You will also need to activate another sachet of Champagne yeast.
2 While this is happening, carefully measure out 70 g (2½ oz) sugar. This is called the priming sugar. This is another critical figure, as more than this per gallon of wine will cause exceptional gushing, and less will prevent the wine from sparkling adequately. Dissolve the sugar in a little wine and pour it into the empty demijohn.
3 As soon as the yeast is activated, pour it into the demijohn. Finally, siphon the bulk of the wine into the demijohn and when it is full fit the airlock.
4 Place the jar in a warm position (24°C/75°F) for a few hours.

Filling the bottles

1 Meanwhile prepare six standard champagne bottles. These are all made from heavy, dark-green glass. Soak them in warm water to remove the labels, being careful not to scratch the glass. Wash the bottles out with a cleansing sterilizer such as Chempro, then rinse them three or four times with fresh cold water. Up-end to drain dry.
2 Prepare six hollow-domed plastic stoppers of a size that fits the bottles tightly, and six wire cages to fasten the stoppers to the bottles. Place the stoppers in a bowl of hot water to soften them. Instead of using this type of stopper you can also use a special stopper with a pliable teat above it obtainable from specialist home-brew shops. Use in the same way.
3 As soon as the wine in the jar starts to ferment and the first bubbles begin to pass through the airlock, siphon it into the prepared bottles, filling each one to within 5 cm (2 in) of the top. It is essential to leave this gap for the gas to collect.

Fitting the stoppers

If the stopper and cage are not properly fitted, the pressure of the gas from the secondary fermentation will ease out the stopper sufficiently for it to escape into the atmosphere, leaving the wine flat. The bottle might also leak, wasting not only the wine but also all your effort. This is the correct procedure:
1 Shake the stoppers free of the water and push them into the bottles, pressing them right home so that the bottom of the dome is in contact with the bottle. If necessary hit the dome with the heel of your hand.

Do not hit it with a mallet, or anything that might damage it.
2 Cover the dome of the stopper with the wire cage, making sure that the lower wire nestles neatly under the lip of the bottle. Twist the surplus wire several times to tighten the grip so that the wire under the lip cannot move.

Labelling
- Fit some sort of label to the bottle indicating the date the wine was made, the date it was sparkled and, if you wish, the name of the main ingredient. A tie-on neck label is the most suitable as it can be read easily without disturbing the bottle.
- You can also cover the stopper and the neck of the bottle with a foil and fasten it with some glue. A quick glance at the foil from time to time will tell you if all is well – or not!

Fermentation and storage
1 For the next five or six days leave the bottles in a warm place while the yeast enzymes ferment the added sugar. Lie the bottles on their side; *do not stand them up*. The shape of the vessel plays a significant part in fermentation and a more complete fermentation is obtained in this position.
2 Then store the bottles on their sides in a cool place for at least six months, longer if possible. Sparkling wine develops the best flavour in this position.

Moving the sediment into the stopper
During the period of storage, the sediment – consisting mainly of dead yeast cells from the secondary fermentation in the bottle – will have settled all along the lower side of the bottle. The next process is to move this sediment into the hollow dome of the stopper.
1 Lift the bottles out of their store and place them, stopper first, into a bottle carton.
2 Prop up the carton at an angle of 45° and give each bottle a little shake and a slight twist. Do this every day or so, gradually turning the bottle in a full circle during the course of a week.
3 Increase the angle to about 60° and repeat the process.
4 Finally, stand the carton upright with the bottles resting on their stoppers and repeat the process once more. By the end of this period the wine should be perfectly bright and all the sediment should be in the stopper.

Removing the sediment

There are various ways of doing this, depending on which sort of stopper you have used. But in each case first stand the bottle upside down in a cold refrigerator for several hours. This thoroughly chills the wine and inhibits the release of the carbon dioxide. Then wrap the body of the bottle in several layers of newspaper to prevent the wine

To remove sediment from sparkling wines: (1) Twist and shake the bottles head down until the sediment has moved from the side of the bottle into the hollow stopper. (2) Freeze the wine in the stopper by standing the bottle upside down in a mixture of crushed ice and salt in a cold refrigerator. (3) Remove the wire cage and stopper containing the frozen wine and sediment and fit with a clean and softened stopper.

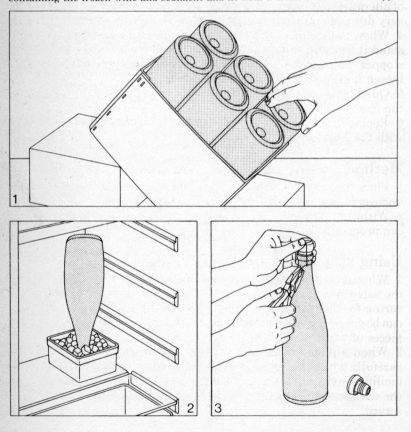

from warming up or getting too cold, depending on your choice of the next process.

Method 1 using hollow-domed plastic stoppers

1 Crush a tray of ice cubes with a mallet, steak hammer or rolling pin, place them in a basin and mix in 30 ml (2 tbsp) of cooking salt.
2 Stand the neck of one of the bottles of sparkling wine in the mixture and leave it there for about 10 minutes. This is usually long enough for the wine in the stopper to freeze and encapsulate the sediment. If you place the basin in a corner position in the refrigerator the bottle can be supported by the angle of the walls.
3 Place a clean stopper in hot water to soften it and have ready a pair of pliers and one or two saccharin or sweetener pellets. One takes the very dry edge off the wine, two makes it slightly sweet.
4 When the ice has formed in the stopper, take the bottle out and stand it upright; undo the wire, remove the cage and ease out the stopper. You may have to twist the stopper slightly with the pliers to loosen it enough to remove with your fingers.
5 Quickly remove the ice-full stopper, pop in the saccharin and push the freshly softened stopper home.
6 Replace the wire cage and put the bottle on one side while you deal with the next bottle.

Method 2 using hollow-domed plastic stoppers

1 Place the wrapped-up bottle upside down in a home freezer with the uncovered stopper surrounded by frozen packages.
2 Within 30–40 minutes the wine in the stopper will be frozen and you can proceed as above.

Using stoppers with pliable teats

1 When it is time to remove the sediment, treat the bottles in exactly the same way as described above but make provision in the wine carton for the pliable teat in which the sediment is to collect. Holes can be cut in the bottom of the carton which can then be supported on pieces of wood.
2 When all the sediment has collected in the teat, bend it over carefully while the bottle is still upside down and fasten it with the facility provided. This avoids the necessity of freezing and removing the encapsulated sediment and the wine need only be chilled and served.

Adding sweetener

As every grain of sugar should have been fermented, wines made by this method are exceedingly dry unless sweetened with saccharin at the bottling stage. Only a small quantity of saccharin is required. Sorbitol or a liquid sweetener can also be used.

Carbonation method

- This is simply the carbonating, i.e. addition of carbon dioxide, of a still wine to impregnate it with bubbles. Again, it is better to make a suitable wine for this purpose or at least to choose a suitable wine from your stock.
- Dessert and social wines are not suitable for carbonating because they contain too much alcohol and body. Choose dry light wines that you can sweeten marginally with saccharin.
- The wines can be carbonated in a soda siphon or in a Soda Stream system. Follow the instructions precisely for the use of the equipment.
- Do not try to carbonate your wine in a wine bottle, but only in the much stronger container provided.
- The wine will have a pleasant and attractive tingle but unfortunately the bubbles do not last very long.

1 A 10-litre ($2\frac{1}{4}$-gallon) plastic beer keg may also be used. Fill the keg with marginally sweetened mature wine to within 3 cm ($1\frac{1}{4}$ in) of the top. Screw down the lid, fit the CO_2 injector, give a squirt of gas to the wine and place the keg in a refrigerator for several hours.

2 Withdraw the wine by opening the tap as you would if the contents were beer. From time to time additional squirts of gas will be required to maintain the pressure. Some kegs are fitted with graduated pressure valves. If you have such a keg, a pressure of between 15 and 17 kg (35 and 40 lb) per 6.45 sq cm (1 sq in) is about right. This is below the pressure created inside champagne bottles during the secondary fermentation but is recommended for safety.

Serving

- Always serve sparkling wine in tall, narrow glasses to maintain the sparkle as long as possible. For the same reason, also ensure that the wine is thoroughly chilled.
- Sparkling wine can be used to accompany picnic or party fare but can also be enjoyed with just a sweet biscuit or cake. By itself it makes a splendid aperitif before meals.

SPARKLING WINES · 189

> **Keys to success**
> - Check the specific gravity of the must very carefully. If there is too much sugar the wine will not sparkle.
> - Make sure you add exactly 70 g (2½ oz) sugar per gallon when putting in the sparkle.
> - Leave a gap when filling the bottles for the gas to collect.
> - Always fit the stopper and cage correctly.

SPARKLING APPLE WINE

1.4 litres (2¼ pints) cold water
5 ml (1 tsp) tartaric acid
1 Campden tablet
Pectic enzyme
200 g (7 oz) sultanas
4 kg (9 lb) eating apples
2 sachets Champagne wine yeast and nutrient
500 g (18 oz) sugar
70 g (2½ oz) priming sugar
Saccharin pellets

Pour the water into a bin, dissolve the acid, Campden tablet and pectic enzyme in it and add the washed and chopped sultanas. Then wash and crush the apples, drop them into the water as crushed, stir well, cover and leave for 24 hours.

Activate one sachet of yeast, mix into the must plus the nutrient and ferment-on-the-pulp for six days, keeping the floating fruit submerged.

Strain out, press dry and discard the pulp. Mix in the sugar, pour the must into a demijohn, fit an airlock and ferment out.

Rack and store for six months, then prime and continue as described on pages 184–188.

SPARKLING FRUIT JUICE WINE

1 litre (1¾ pints) apple juice
1 litre (1¾ pints) grapefruit juice
600 ml (21 fl oz) white grape juice
1.7 litres (3 pints) cold water
Pectic enzyme and 1 Campden tablet
500 g (18 oz) sugar
Champagne wine yeast and nutrient
70 g (2½ oz) priming sugar
Saccharin pellets

Mix together the three juices, water, pectic enzyme and 1 crushed Campden tablet. Seal and leave for 24 hours.

Stir in the sugar and check that the specific gravity is around 1.076–1.080. Adjust if necessary. Activate one sachet of yeast, mix into the must plus the nutrient and ferment to dryness.

Rack and store for six months, then prime and continue as described on pages 184–188.

SPARKLING GOOSEBERRY WINE

1.36 kg (3 lb) Careless gooseberries
200 g (7 oz) sultanas
3.4 litres (6 pints) water
Pectic enzyme and 1 Campden tablet
2 sachets of Champagne wine yeast and nutrient
800 g (1¾ lb) sugar
70 g (2½ oz) priming sugar
Saccharin pellets

Top, tail, wash and crush the gooseberries, wash and chop the sultanas, pour on hot water and leave to cool. Add the pectic enzyme and 1 crushed Campden tablet, cover and leave for 24 hours.

Activate one sachet of yeast, mix into the must plus the nutrient and ferment-on-the-pulp for three days, keeping the fruit submerged.

Strain out, press and discard the fruit. Stir in the sugar, pour the must into a demijohn, fit an airlock and ferment out.

Rack and store for six months, then prime and continue as described on pages 184–188.

SPARKLING STRAWBERRY ROSÉ WINE

1.36 kg (3 lb) strawberry jam
3.4 litres (6 pints) water
Pectic enzyme
5 ml (1 tsp) citric acid
1 Campden tablet
200 g (7 oz) concentrated grape juice
125 g (4½ oz) sugar
2 sachets of Champagne wine yeast and nutrient
70 g (2½ oz) priming sugar
Saccharin pellets

Dissolve the jam in warm water, cover and leave to cool. Add a double quantity of pectic enzyme, the acid and 1 crushed Campden tablet, cover and leave for 24 hours.

Strain out the strawberry pulp and roll it round a sieve rather than pressing it.

Mix the concentrate and sugar into the liquor and check the specific gravity. If necessary adjust to between 1.076 and 1.080.

Activate one sachet of yeast, mix into the must plus the nutrient and ferment to dryness.

Rack and store for six months, then prime and continue as described on pages 184–188.

Variation
You can use apricot jam in the same way.

SPARKLING WHITECURRANT WINE

1.36 kg (3 lb) whitecurrants
200 g (7 oz) sultanas
Pectic enzyme
1 Campden tablet
3.4 litres (6 pints) cold water
Champagne wine yeast and nutrient
800 g (1¾ lb) sugar
70 g (2½ oz) priming sugar
Saccharin pellets

Stalk, wash and crush the whitecurrants and wash and chop the sultanas. Add them to a bin containing the water, pectic enzyme and 1 crushed Campden tablet; cover and leave for 24 hours.

Add the activated yeast and ferment-on-the-pulp for five days, keeping the fruit submerged and the bin covered.

Strain out, press dry and discard the pulp. Gently stir in the sugar, pour the must into a fermentation jar, fit an airlock and ferment to dryness.

Rack and store for six months, then prime and continue as described on pages 184–188.

Variation
You can also use redcurrants to make an attractive sparkling rosé wine.

Sherry-style Wines

REAL SHERRY
Commercial sherry is made from a blend of wines from successive years and then fortified. It is made in a variety of forms. The three best known are:
Fino – a pale dry wine.
Amontillado – a tawny, medium-dry/sweet wine.
Oloroso – brown sweet wine.
The system of blending wines is known as a **solera** and can be reasonably well imitated in the home.

The commercial solera
- In simplified terms the commercial sherrymaker lays down a row of casks, not quite full, of a given season's wine. In the second year he mounts another row of casks of similar wine on top of the first. In the third and fourth years he repeats the process.
- In the fifth year he withdraws some wine from each of the first-year casks and sells it, usually to another producer. The quantity withdrawn from each cask on the bottom row is replaced with an equal quantity from the second row. These are replenished from the third row which is in turn replenished from the fourth row. These casks are topped up with the new season's wine.
- This happens again the following year, the sherrymaker selling off no more than a third of the wine in each of the lowest casks and replenishing the casks from the row above.

SHERRY-STYLE WINE
The ingredients
You can make some good wines similar in style to sherry at home. Begin with suitable base ingredients as indicated in the following recipes. These have all been tested and are known to be successful. Seville orange is particularly good for pale dry wines; parsnip and rosehip, parsnip and fig, rosehip and fig are also good; date and lemon work well for the darker sherry style; prunes make an excellent base.

Preparing the must
Do this in the usual way, remembering to include some sherry-style concentrated grape juice or sultanas. Start with a fairly low specific gravity and add sugar in small doses over a period of some weeks.

Fermentation
- Ferment the must in a steady atmospheric temperature of around 21°C (70°F), with a sherry yeast and plenty of nutrient.
- Begin by making up 1 gallon of a sherry-style recipe. It is most important to use a good sherry yeast. An ordinary general-purpose wine yeast is not suitable.
- It is also very important to feed the fermentation with small additions of sugar every week until the maximum alcohol content has been reached.

Maturation and storage
1 When fermentation is finished and the wine begins to clear, rack five-sixths of it into a clean demijohn.
2 Siphon the remaining sixth into a 1-litre (1¾-pint) bottle which will only be partially filled.
3 Plug the demijohn and the bottle with cotton wool and set both aside in a cool place while the wine matures.

Maturing a sherry-style wine in a demijohn. Note the airspace above the wine and the plug of cotton wool.

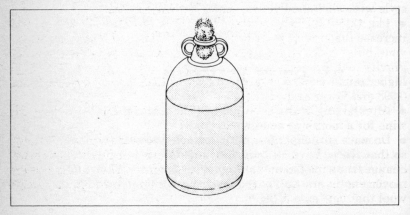

More wine

- As soon as you can, make up another gallon of wine from either the same or a similar recipe. Try to keep to the same colour – pale, tawny or dark – and to the same kind of body. At this stage it is better to make the wines dry or nearly dry.
- Mature the second wine as just described and, as soon as you can, make a third and then a fourth. Overall, this may take up to a year to complete.

A home-made solera

1 If possible acquire an ex-sherry 25-litre plastic cube in a cardboard carton. These can sometimes be obtained from off-licences at a modest price. Cyprus sherry is imported in them and sold to restaurants.
2 Empty 18 litres (4 gallons) of your home-made sherry-style wines into the freshly cleaned and sterilized container and, if you can afford it, add 1 litre ($1\frac{3}{4}$ pints) of Spanish sherry of a similar style to yours.
3 Screw on the cap of the cube, open the tap in the cap and plug the spout lightly with cotton wool.
4 A further period of storage of at least three months and, if possible longer, is now necessary for the wines to homogenize.
5 When you draw off wine from the solera, always replace it with new wine.

Sweetening

- If you wish to sweeten sherry-style wine, add some good-quality concentrated grape juice of a variety adjusted to produce a sherry-style wine similar to yours – pale, medium or dark.
- 1 kg ($2\frac{1}{4}$ lb) of concentrate in 18 litres (4 gallons) of wine will increase the gravity by 12 to 15 points. Depending on the gravity of your bulk wine, add only sufficient concentrate to increase the gravity to the sweetness of your choice. A specific gravity of 1.012 or higher might well be regarded as sweet, 1.004–1.006 as medium and 0.998 and lower as dry.
- After mixing in any additional concentrated grape juice leave the wine for a month or so longer.
- Do make sure that there is an airspace above the wine at all times, so that the wine can oxidize properly. With marginal temperature changes the wine expands and contracts slightly. This causes a subtle movement, in and out, of the air above the wine through the cotton wool that acts as a filter.

Keep the solera going
- When your sherry-style solera is established, you should make more sherry-style wine regularly to equal the quantity you want to drink. For example, if you wish to consume a bottle each week then you will need to make a fresh gallon of a similar wine every six weeks. If one bottle every two weeks is sufficient for your needs you need only make 1 gallon every twelve weeks.
- Before drawing off your first bottle of wine to drink, it is desirable to have a gallon of wine maturing. This can be added a bottle at a time. As you draw off one bottle add another bottle of new wine. In this way the quality and flavour of your solera wine will not change. The older wine confers its mature flavour on to the young wine, which in turn refreshes the older wine.

Flavourings
Artificial sherry flavouring: Try not to succumb to the temptation to add sherry flavouring. It usually imparts an artificial taste that is not pleasing. If you use sensible ingredients, a good sherry yeast, ferment to the maximum and mature for as long as possible in jars with a large air gap and plugged with cotton wool, you will get a well-flavoured wine.
Commercial sherry: The addition of the occasional bottle of Spanish sherry is advantageous.
Vodka: Fortification with vodka is rarely necessary. Properly fermented wine should reach 16% alcohol and this is quite adequate for home use, particularly with the dry, sherry-style wine.
Glycerine and vodka: If you prefer the fuller, richer and sweeter style then you could add 20–25 ml (4–5 tsp) BP glycerine together with one bottle of vodka to every gallon of the wine. This enriches the wine and increases the alcohol content to between 19 and 20%.

Serving
Keep any bottle of wine withdrawn from the cube or jar in the refrigerator, preferably in a screw-capped sherry bottle, as this is easier to seal and unseal. There is no need to draw off more than one bottle at a time. This allows the bulk of the wine longer to mature in its entirety and thus develop the attractive sherry flavour more fully.
Cold, dry sherry-style wine: This is very refreshing before a meal or before going out in the evening. It sometimes accompanies a soup, especially a cold soup or a consommé rather than a hot cream soup.

Medium sherry-style wine: This can be enjoyed not only before a meal but also at any time of the day with visitors.
Sweet sherry-style wine: The richer version can be enjoyed after a meal instead of a dessert wine, or served at bedtime with a sweet biscuit. The high alcohol content and sugar relaxes the nervous system and encourages a good night's sleep.

Keys to success
- Use a good sherry-variety yeast.
- Ferment to the maximum.
- Mature for as long as possible in jars with a large air gap plugged with cotton wool.

DRY SHERRY

454 g (1 lb) ripe bananas
3.4 litres (6 pints) water
454 g (1 lb) mature carrots
454 g (1 lb) frosted parsnips
500 g (18 oz) concentrated grape juice (dry sherry style)
10 ml (2 tsp) citric acid
Pectic enzyme
5 ml (1 tsp) nutrient
3 mg (1 tablet) vitamin B_1
Sherry yeast
1 kg (2¼ lb) sugar

Peel and thinly slice the bananas, place the rings in a saucepan containing 560 ml (1 pint) of water, bring to the boil and simmer, covered, for 30 minutes.

Scrub and thinly slice the carrots and parsnips, place them in a saucepan with 2.27 litres (4 pints) of water, bring to the boil and simmer, covered, for 30 minutes.

Strain off the liquor and discard the banana rings. Strain off the carrot and parsnip rings. Eat them as vegetables or discard them.

Mix both liquors together and when cool mix in the concentrated grape juice, half the acid, the pectic enzyme, nutrient, vitamin and activated yeast. Pour the must into a demijohn, fit an airlock and leave for one week.

Boil the sugar and remaining portion of acid in 560 ml (1 pint) of water for 20 minutes and, when cool, pour one third of the syrup into the must. A week later add half the remainder and one week later still add the final portion. Keep the syrup meanwhile in a corked bottle in the refrigerator.

When fermentation is finished, rack the wine and mature it in containers not quite full and plugged with cotton wool.

MEDIUM SHERRY

2.8 litres (5 pints) cold water
Pectic enzyme
1 Campden tablet
1.5 kg (3½ lb) eating apples
1 kg (2¼ lb) seedless raisins
125 g (4½ oz) dried figs
450 g (1 lb) ripe bananas
Sherry yeast
5 ml (1 tsp) nutrient
3 mg (1 tablet) vitamin B_1
560 g (20 oz) white sugar

Measure the water into a bin and add the pectic enzyme and 1 crushed Campden tablet.

Wash, core and finely slice the apples and then drop them into the water. Wash and chop the raisins, break up the figs and add these to the apples.

Peel and thinly slice the bananas and mix them in. Cover the bin and leave for 24 hours in a warm place.

Stir in the activated sherry yeast, nutrient and vitamin and ferment-on-the-pulp for seven days, keeping the fruit cap submerged.

Strain out, press dry and discard the pulp. Stir in one third of the sugar, pour the must into a fermentation jar, fit an airlock and leave for one week.

Stir in half the remaining sugar and add the remainder one week later.

Leave to ferment to dryness, then rack and mature in vessels not quite full and plugged with cotton wool.

SWEET SHERRY

2 lemons
1 orange
4 litres (7 pints) water
1 kg (2¼ lb) stoned dates
2 bananas
500 g (18 oz) seedless raisins
Pectic enzyme
5 ml (1 tsp) nutrient
3 mg (1 tablet) vitamin B_1
Sherry yeast
600 g (21 oz) sugar

Thinly pare the lemons and orange, chop the parings and place them in a preserving pan containing 3.4 litres (6 pints) of water and the well chopped-up dates.

Peel and thinly slice the bananas and add to the dates. Bring to the boil and simmer, covered, for 30 minutes.

Strain the hot liquor onto the washed and chopped raisins and, when cool, add the expressed and strained juice of the lemons and orange, the pectic enzyme, nutrient, vitamin and activated yeast.

Ferment-on-the-pulp for seven days, then strain out, press dry and discard the raisins.

Mix one third of a syrup made by dissolving the sugar in 560 ml (1 pint) of hot water into the must and allow to cool; fit an airlock and leave in a warm position.

After ten days mix in half the remaining syrup and ten days later still, add the rest.

Ferment to the finish, rack and mature in vessels not quite full and plugged with cotton wool.

ORANGE 'FINO SHERRY'

4 Seville oranges
4 sweet oranges
2 mandarin oranges
3.4 litres (6 pints) water
Pectic enzyme
5 ml (1 tsp) sulphate
250 g (9 oz) concentrated grape juice
Fino sherry wine yeast and nutrient
1.25 kg (2¾ lb) sugar

Wash the oranges and mandarins and thinly pare the skin, avoiding all the white pith. Cut the parings into small pieces, place them in a bin and pour on 2.8 litres (5 pints) hot water (80°C/176°F). Cover and leave to cool.

Add the pectic enzyme, the expressed and strained juice of the fruit, the sulphate, concentrated grape juice, activated yeast and the nutrient. Ferment for three days, covered in the meantime, gently stirring twice each day.

Dissolve the sugar in the remaining 560 ml (1 pint) hot water and leave to cool.

Strain out the solids. Mix in half the sugar syrup and pour the must into a demijohn. Fit an airlock and ferment at room temperature (20°C/68°F). Store the syrup in a sealed bottle in the refrigerator.

After two weeks, mix in half the remaining syrup, one week later half the remainder again, and one week later still, the final portion.

Ferment to a finish, move the jar to a cold place for a few days and then rack into a storage jar, leaving an airspace. Plug the neck of the jar with loose cotton wool and store for at least one year, racking when necessary to remove the sediment. Long storage of this wine under cotton wool improves the flavour (see page 194). Bottle ageing is not necessary.

Serve the sherry cool as an aperitif.

> **Quick tip**
> You can use calcium or magnesium sulphate or the hardening salt used for beer.

RAISIN, PRUNE AND FIG 'SHERRY'

1 kg (2¼ lb) raisins
250 g (9 oz) stoned prunes
125 g (4½ oz) figs
3.7 litres (6½ pints) water
Pectic enzyme
1 Campden tablet
Sherry yeast and nutrient
1 kg (2¼ lb) sugar
5 ml (1 tsp) citric acid

Liquidize the fruit in 2.8 litres (5 pints) of cold water, add the pectic enzyme and one crushed Campden tablet. Cover and leave for 24 hours.

Mix in the activated yeast and nutrient, and ferment-on-the-pulp for four days, keeping the pulp well mixed into the juice.

Boil the sugar, acid, and the remaining water for 20 minutes. Leave to cool, then store in a sealed bottle and set aside in the refrigerator until required.

Strain out the pulp and roll it round and round a nylon straining bag before discarding it or adding it to another must.

Mix one sixth of the sugar syrup into the must, pour it into a demijohn, fit an airlock and continue the fermentation.

After ten days, add one fifth of the remaining syrup and the rest in four more portions at intervals of seven days. Ferment to a finish.

Rack and mature in a vessel not quite full and plugged with cotton wool.

ROSEHIP AND FIG 'SHERRY'

1.36 kg (3 lb) freshly gathered rosehips
250 g (9 oz) raisins with pips
125 g (4½ oz) figs
3.7 litres (6½ pints) water
Pectic enzyme
10 ml (2 tsp) tartaric acid
1 Campden tablet
Sherry yeast
5 ml (1 tsp) nutrient
1 kg (2¼ lb) sugar
250 g (9 oz) concentrated 'sherry' grape juice

Top, tail, wash and crush the rosehips without breaking the pips. Wash and chop the raisins without breaking the pips. Break up the figs.

Place all three ingredients in a bin, pour on 2.8 litres (5 pints) boiling water, stir well, cover and leave to cool.

Mix in the pectic enzyme, half the acid and 1 crushed Campden tablet, cover and leave for 24 hours.

Add the activated yeast and nutrient and ferment-on-the-pulp for five days, keeping the fruit submerged.

Boil the sugar and remaining acid in the rest of the water for 20 minutes. Leave to cool and then store in a sealed bottle and set aside in the refrigerator until required.

Strain out, press dry and discard the pulp. Stir the sherry-style concentrated grape juice and one quarter of the sugar syrup into the must. Pour the must into a demijohn, fit an airlock and ferment for ten days.

Add the rest of the syrup in four equal portions at intervals of seven days and ferment to a finish.

Rack and mature in a container not quite full and plugged with cotton wool.

Dessert Wines

PORT-STYLE WINES

These are probably the hardest wines for the country winemaker to emulate. It is essential that the home-made, port-style wine should contain a high fruit content to produce sufficient body and flavour but a relatively low acid content should be coupled with this.

The ingredients
- It is far easier to obtain a high-sugar/low-acid ratio in grapes than in other fruits. Elderberries, blackberries, bilberries, blackcurrants and damsons might seem to be ideal ingredients but all have high acid levels that diminish their suitability.
- You can overcome this problem by blending these fruits with low-acid/low-flavour fruits such as bananas, eating apples, pears and peaches. No additional acid is needed.
- Port wine has a higher alcohol content than can be achieved by fermentation alone. Indeed, when the wine is being made in Portugal grape spirit is added in large quantities. In making home-made port-style wine it is essential, therefore, that:
1 The must contains plenty of yeast nutrient.
2 Yeast with a high alcohol tolerance is used.
3 The fermentation is fed with small doses of sugar to obtain the maximum alcohol content.
- As long maturation is required to obtain a quality wine, two years should be regarded as the minimum.

Preparing the must
Aim for a fruit content of around 2.5 kg ($5\frac{1}{2}$ lb) per gallon, bearing in mind the acid content of the ingredients. The total acid content of the must ought to be about 3.5 parts per thousand when first prepared. This will be reduced to about 3 parts per thousand after the pulp has been removed, the sugar added and the must topped up. During fermentation other acids will be produced that will increase this figure to a sufficient level to balance the alcohol, sugar and flavour.
Enhancing the bouquet: In addition to the fruit mixture, which should always contain some fresh grapes, concentrated grape juice or sultanas, it is also beneficial to include some bananas for additional

body, and rose petals or elderflowers to enhance the bouquet.
Pectic enzyme: This should always be used to ensure maximum juice extraction from the fruit.

Preparing the fruit
- The colour may be extracted by any of the methods described on pages 64–70. If pulp fermentation is used, take care not to extract too much tannin from **grapes**, **elderberries**, **bilberries** and **pears**. Indeed, the pears should be thinly peeled and cored to reduce their tannin content.
- Remove the cap stems from all berries and also from **blackcurrants**. Discard any unripe fruit. **Blackberries** should be treated similarly and only the ripest berries used. **Damsons** and **black plums** should be stalked and any traces of gum removed.
- Before crushing all fruit wash it in plenty of cold water containing a little sulphite. Take care not to break or damage any stones or pips or leave them in the must. If possible, remove and discard the stones.
- If **sultanas** are used, wash and then chop or liquidize them.
- **Bananas** with brown/black skins should be peeled, crushed and added to the must, together with any flower petals to be used.

Method
1 Pour hot water over the fruit and flowers and leave to cool under a cover. Stir in pectic enzyme and sulphite and leave the must covered for two or three days, stirring occasionally.
2 By this time, sufficient colour and other ingredients will be extracted from the pulp, which you can now strain and press. Use a fine-gauge nylon straining bag and squeeze it to obtain as much juice as possible without extracting fine particles of pulp.
3 You can add the residue of pulp to another must as it will still contain some colour and other ingredients.

Fermentation
- Some winemakers recommend using a port wine yeast but this is not very tolerant to a high-alcohol content, since port wine is always fortified. Madeira and Tokay yeast strains are more alcohol-tolerant.
- Alternatively, begin the fermentation with a port wine yeast so that the right yeast flavours are given to the must. When fermentation is coming to an end, mix in a fresh Madeira or Tokay yeast to carry the fermentation on for another few degrees of alcohol.

1 During fermentation try to maintain an even atmospheric temperature of 21°C (70°F).
2 Ensure that the yeast has an adequate supply of nitrogen and vitamin B_1 and be careful to add the sugar in small doses. Do this by removing about 560 ml (1 pint) of must and gently stirring in about 125 g ($4\frac{1}{2}$ oz) sugar until it is dissolved. Return the must to the jar slowly to avoid foaming.
3 Repeat this process as often as possible at five- or six-day intervals.
4 Alternatively, save about 560 ml (1 pint) of the water, heat it and dissolve the sugar in it so that doses of syrup can be added to the must. This avoids stirring, with possible loss of alcohol and esters.

Maturation and storage

1 When the wine has become still and begins to clear, siphon it into another jar and top it up with a similar wine or, preferably, with vodka. Even better than vodka is the colourless grape spirit called 'eau de vie pour les fruits' that you can buy in French wine shops and supermarkets.
2 Seal the jar and leave it in a cool place to clear to a ruby brilliance, then rack and top up again. There is no need to add sulphite at either racking since the high alcohol content will protect the wine.
3 A long period of bulk storage – at least two years and from three to five years – is necessary if you want the best results. This is the kind of wine to put away in a dark corner and forget about! But don't forget to label the jar with full details of its contents, the dates and specific gravities.
4 When sealing wines to be stored for long periods, leave a small air gap of about 2.5 cm (1 in) in the neck of the jar beneath the cork. When fitting the softened cork slip a piece of string or plastic-coated wire into the neck of the jar with the cork. When the cork has been pushed well in, pull out the string and with it the small amount of air that would otherwise be under pressure. If there are minute changes in the volume of the wine due to temperature variations, the wine will now be able to expand without pushing out, or loosening the cork. A tight seal keeps out air that might contain spoilage organisms.

Bottling

● After several years' bulk storage, the wine should be bottled and given a further rest of some months, if not a year or so. When bottling the wine, consider your needs; perhaps use some half-size as well as standard bottles.

● During maturation many chemical changes take place in this style of wine. Some of the different acids combine with the different alcohols and form fragrant esters. The overall acid level falls, tannins, proteins and other substances are deposited, and the wine develops a smooth and very complex bouquet and flavour.

Decanting
1 Carefully remove the bottle from its rack and lay it in a cradle basket without disturbing the sediment. Then remove the foil and steadily pull out the cork.
2 Pour the clear wine carefully into a decanter, leaving the sediment behind in the bottle.
3 Alternatively, stand the bottle upright for a couple of days so that the loose sediment falls to the bottom of the bottle and then siphon out the clear wine.

Serving
● Pour the wine into glasses that look like a shortened version of the tulip.
● Port-style wine accompanies good cheese, shortbread, walnuts and crystallized fruits superbly.
● Serve it after a meal and consume it leisurely to taste it at its best. To drink it hurriedly is to insult the years of care and patience that have gone into its making.

Keys to success
● The high fruit content must be balanced by a low acid content.
● Feed the fermentation with sugar to obtain the maximum alcohol content.

PORT-STYLE WINE (1)

2.8 litres (5 pints) hot water
1 kg (2¼ lb) elderberries (black ripe)
125 g (4½ oz) raspberries or loganberries
1 kg (2¼ lb) bananas (brown skins)
1 cupful rose petals (red scented)
Pectic enzyme
1 Campden tablet
500 g (18 oz) concentrated grape juice
Port wine yeast and nutrient
1 kg (2¼ lb) white sugar
Tokay wine yeast

Pour the water over the crushed berries, peeled bananas, and rose petals. Cover and leave to cool.

Mix in the pectic enzyme and Campden tablet, cover and leave for two days, stirring occasionally. Strain out and lightly squeeze the solids. Mix the grape juice and activated port wine yeast and nutrient into the must.

Pour into a fermentation jar, fit an airlock and leave in a warm, dark place.

After seven days dissolve the sugar in 620 ml (22 fl oz) hot water. When cool pour in 250 ml (9 fl oz) of it into the must. Repeat this every seven days until all the sugar syrup has been added. Keep the remaining syrup in a sealed bottle in the refrigerator.

After twenty-one days from the start of fermentation add a freshly activated Tokay yeast.

Continue fermentation to the end, then rack and store as described on page 206.

PORT-STYLE WINE (2)

2 kg (4½ lb) black stoned cherries
500 g (18 oz) blackberries
250 g (9 oz) bananas
250 g (9 oz) bilberries (fresh or bottled)
250 g (9 oz) sultanas
15 ml (1 tbsp) dried elderflowers
2.8 litres (5 pints) boiling water
Pectic enzyme
Port wine yeast and nutrient
1 kg (2¼ lb) white sugar

Crush the cleaned cherries, blackberries, bilberries and peeled bananas. Liquidize the sultanas and place all the fruit in a fermentation bin. Sprinkle on the elderflowers, pour on the water and stir well. Cover and leave to cool.

Mix in the pectic enzyme, activated yeast and nutrient, cover again and ferment-on-the-pulp for four days, keeping the fruit cap submerged.

Strain out and press dry. Pour the must into a demijohn, fit an airlock and ferment in a warm, dark place.

After four days dissolve the sugar in 620 ml (22 fl oz) hot water and when cool pour 255 ml (9 fl oz) of the sugar syrup into the must.

Repeat this process every week until all the syrup has been used, top up the jar and ferment to a finish.

Siphon into a clean jar, top up and store.

BILBERRY AND ELDERBERRY 'RUBY PORT'

908 g (2 lb) ripe elderberries
908 g (2 lb) bottled bilberries
4 bananas
250 g (9 oz) sultanas
2.5 litres (4½ pints) water
Pectic enzyme
1 Campden tablet
2.5 ml (½ tsp) grape tannin
Port wine yeast
2.5 ml (½ tsp) nutrient
1.25 kg (2¾ lb) sugar

Stalk, wash and crush the elderberries and place them in a bin. Strain off the bilberry syrup and put to one side; crush the bilberries and add them to the bin. Peel and mash the bananas; wash and chop the sultanas and add them to the bin. Pour on 2 litres (3½ pints) hot water, cover and leave to cool. Mix in the pectic enzyme and 1 crushed Campden tablet, stir well, cover and leave for 24 hours.

Add the bilberry syrup, grape tannin, activated yeast and nutrient and ferment-on-the-pulp for five days.

Strain out through a fine-mesh nylon bag and press lightly to extract as much juice as possible without carrying over any pulp.

Dissolve the sugar in 560 ml (1 pint) hot water and leave to cool. Mix one third of the syrup into the must and store the rest in a sterilized sealed bottle in the refrigerator until required.

Pour the must into a sterilized demijohn, fit an airlock and ferment in an atmospheric temperature around 20°C (68°F).

After ten days, add one quarter of the remaining syrup, seven days later adding another quarter. Repeat this process each week until all the syrup has been added and the jar is full. If necessary top up with cold boiled water. Alternatively, wait until fermentation has finished and top up with some vodka after racking.

Store in a cold place, racking when a further deposit appears and the wine falls bright.

Mature this wine for two years before bottling and at least another one year in bottle. The longer this wine is kept the more it will improve. The bilberries impart a delightful aroma and flavour.

BILBERRY AND ELDERBERRY 'TAWNY PORT'

125 g (4½ oz) dried bilberries
250 g (9 oz) dried elderberries
250 g (9 oz) large raisins
4 bananas and 1 lemon
4 litres (7 pints) water
Pectic enzyme and 1 Campden tablet
2.5 ml (½ tsp) grape tannin
Port wine yeast
2.5 ml (½ tsp) nutrient
1.25 kg (2¾ lb) sugar

Wash the dried bilberries and elderberries in a sulphite solution to kill the micro-organisms that tend to settle on these dried fruits; also to remove dust and any cap stems. Put the cleaned fruit, washed and chopped raisins, peeled and mashed bananas and the thinly pared and chopped rind of the lemon in a bin and pour on 3.4 litres (6 pints) hot water. Cover and leave to cool.

Mix in the pectic enzyme, 1 crushed Campden tablet and the expressed and strained juice of the lemon. Cover and leave for 24 hours. Stir in the grape tannin, activated yeast and nutrient and then ferment-on-the-pulp for five days.

Strain out through a fine-mesh nylon bag and press lightly to extract as much juice as possible without carrying over any pulp.

Dissolve the sugar in 560 ml (1 pint) hot water and leave to cool. Mix one third of the syrup into the must and store the rest in a sterilized sealed bottle in the refrigerator until required.

Pour the must into a sterilized demijohn, fit an airlock and ferment in an atmospheric temperature around 20°C (68°F).

After ten days, add one quarter of the remaining syrup, seven days later adding another quarter. Repeat this process each week until all the syrup has been added and the jar is full. If necessary top up with cold boiled water. Alternatively, wait until fermentation has finished and top up with some vodka after racking.

Store in a cold place, racking when a further deposit appears and the wine falls bright. Mature this wine for two years before bottling and at least another one year in bottle. The longer this wine is kept the more it will improve.

BLACKBERRY 'PORT' WINE

2.5 kg (5½ lb) ripe blackberries
250 g (9 oz) raisins
4 bananas
85 g (3 oz) blackcurrants
2 litres (3½ pints) water
Pectic enzyme
1 Campden tablet
2.5 ml (½ tsp) grape tannin
Port wine yeast
2.5 ml (½ tsp) nutrient
1.25 kg (2¾ lb) white sugar

Stalk, wash and crush the blackberries; wash and chop the raisins; peel and mash the bananas; stalk, wash and crush the blackcurrants. Place all the fruit in a bin and pour on 1.4 litres (2½ pints) hot water (80°C/176°F). Cover and leave to cool.

Mix in the pectic enzyme and 1 crushed Campden tablet, stir well, cover and leave in a warm place for 24 hours.

Add the grape tannin, an activated yeast and nutrient, and ferment-on-the-pulp for five days, keeping the pulp submerged or gently pressed down twice a day and the bin covered.

Strain out through a fine-mesh nylon bag and press lightly to extract as much juice as possible without carrying over any pulp.

Dissolve the sugar in 560 ml (1 pint) hot water and leave to cool. Mix one third of the syrup into the must and store the rest in a sterilized sealed bottle in the refrigerator until required.

Pour the must into a sterilized demijohn, fit an airlock and ferment in an atmospheric temperature around 20°C (68°F).

After ten days, add one quarter of the remaining syrup, seven days later adding another quarter. Repeat this process each week until all the syrup has been added and the jar is full. If necessary top up with cold boiled water. Alternatively, wait until fermentation has finished and top up with some vodka after racking.

Store in a cold place, racking when a further deposit appears and the wine falls bright.

Mature this wine for two years before bottling and at least another one year in bottle. The longer this wine is kept the more it will improve.

MADEIRA-STYLE WINES

The once much-loved wines from the island of Madeira are less popular now than they were in Victorian days. They were then so much in vogue that a sponge cake of the same name was developed to accompany the wine. A similar-style wine is not too difficult to make at home but it does take a long while to mature. There are, in fact, four styles of wine from this Atlantic island:

Sercial – a full-bodied, well-flavoured dry aperitif.
Verdelho – a golden-coloured wine, not quite dry, and sometimes served as an accompaniment to soup.
Boal or **Bual** – an amber-coloured, full-bodied sweet wine that accompanies rich and sweet desserts.
Malmsey – a luscious, dark sweet wine normally drunk after meals. Most people think of Malmsey when Madeira wine is mentioned, but when you get to know the other three you will find them equally good.

The ingredients

- The four wines are named after the four different grapes from which they are made, each growing at a different level on the slopes of this mountainous island. The country winemaker must do the best possible with a limited range of base ingredients that include bananas, beetroots, blackberries, golden plums, dessert gooseberries, parsnips, grapes, peaches and raisins.
- Low acid and long fermentation with a Madeira wine yeast are important.
- Madeira's caramellized flavour is its distinguishing feature. The use of brown sugar or golden syrup and a period of storage in a warm place rather than a cool one is therefore necessary.

Preparing the must

Beetroots and parsnips: Scrub these clean, cut into thin rings and boil until tender. The hot juice can be poured over other ingredients or allowed to cool, covered. Beetroot liquor has a splendid red robe at first but during maturation this fades to a dark tawny colour, especially if the wine is stored in a colourless glass jar in a light place.
Blackberries: These are also suitable ingredients as the wine tends to fade in similar circumstances.
Bananas: These should have brown-speckled skins and feel slightly soft. Remove the skin, slice the bananas, boil in some water for half an hour and strain out the solids without pressing them. This liquor

makes a suitable ingredient. Alternatively, mash up the ripe bananas.
Peaches: These should be fully ripe but undamaged. Peel and stone them before crushing.
Golden plums: These must also be fully ripe and the stones removed and discarded before use.
Gooseberries: These should be large and golden and, again, fully ripe. Top and tail them before washing and crushing them.
Dessert white grapes: Varieties such as Almeria and muscatel may also be used. Raisins should be large and contain seeds or pips. These are more suitable than the Thompson seedless variety.
Sugar: Light brown sugar imparts a better flavour than white sugar. It can be mixed with some golden syrup or treacle, but not black treacle.
Honey: A small quantity of honey adds to the complexity of flavour but use it sparingly, 100 g ($3\frac{1}{2}$ oz) per gallon may be enough.
Acid: When beetroot or parsnip are used, some additional acid may be required; use tartaric for preference.
Pectic enzyme: Include this in the must when fruits are used.
Wine yeast: Always use a Madeira wine yeast with a good supply of nutrients to ensure a high alcohol content.

Fermentation
- The island of Madeira enjoys an even and comfortably warm temperature all the year round; it rarely has highs and lows. Get your fermentation started in an atmospheric temperature around 21°C (70°F) but as soon as the must is fermenting well and steadily, move the container to a somewhat cooler place where the surrounding temperature is around 18°C (64°F). A long, slow fermentation helps to build-up a high alcohol content.
- Adding the sugar in small doses will also help here. Made into a syrup it is easier to add to the must and avoids the stirring that can dissipate alcohol.

Maturation and storage
- After racking and clearing, store the new wine in a warm place for quite a long while. Try to find somewhere with a constant temperature between 40 and 60°C (104 and 140°F). The lower end of the range is best. Leave the wine there for about ten months. The higher end of the range effects a quicker action and three months is long enough. Although the jar should be full, leave a little space for the expansion of the wine.

- After this essential storage a further period of maturation is desirable at a temperature nearer to 15°C (59°F). Altogether, the wine needs at least two years in bulk (preferably three or four) before bottling. It should then rest for a further year. All too often the last bottle proves to be the best. These wines, when carefully made by experienced winemakers, are so rewarding that they are well worth waiting for.

Serving

- Serve all Madeira wines in port wine-type glasses, cool rather than cold, and certainly not icy, with appropriate food as already suggested for the commercial variety on page 213.
- This wine has a distinction not possessed by any other wine. The process by which it is made enables it to remain in good condition even after it has been opened for a few weeks. When mature and ready for drinking you can use a cork stopper to seal the bottle after the cylindrical cork has been withdrawn.
- Keep the opened bottle in a cool place or a larder refrigerator at 10°C (50°F) and, if you can resist drinking it, even a half-empty bottle will keep for weeks.

Keys to success
- A low acid content and long fermentation produce the best results.
- Store in a warm place for a few months, then in a cool one for as long as your patience allows!

BEETROOT 'MADEIRA'

2 kg (4½ lb) freshly dug beetroots
3.7 litres (6½ pints) water
3 large lemons
500 g (18 oz) raisins
Madeira wine yeast and nutrient
1.36 kg (3 lb) brown sugar

Trim the beets, scrub them clean, cut them into thin slices. Place in a large pan, add the water, cover and boil in the water until tender.

Thinly pare the lemons, chop the parings up and place in a bin with the washed and chopped raisins. Pour the hot beet liquor over the fruit, stir well, then cover and leave to cool.

Express and strain the lemon juice and add this to the bin with the activated yeast and nutrient. Ferment-on-the-pulp for five days, keeping the raisins submerged and the bin covered.

Strain out, press dry and discard the pulp. Stir in one third of the sugar, pour the must into a demijohn, fit an airlock and continue the fermentation.

After one week remove some must, stir in a quarter of the sugar, return the must to the jar, replace the airlock and continue the fermentation.

Repeat this process at weekly intervals until the last quarter of the sugar has been stirred in, then finish the fermentation.

This process can be made easier by reserving 560 ml (1 pint) water, heating it and dissolving 908 g (2 lb) sugar in it. This makes 1.1 litres (2 pints) of syrup that can be poured through a funnel into the demijohn in the same proportions – approximately one quarter at weekly intervals.

When fermentation is finished, rack into a storage jar and leave it in a cool place to clear.

As soon as the wine is bright, store it in a warm place as described on page 214. Keep for at least two years and preferably for three to five.

PRUNE 'MADEIRA'

3 kg (4½ lb) large prunes
3.7 litres (6½ pints) water
500 g (18 oz) large raisins
4 ripe bananas
Pectic enzyme
1 Campden tablet
10 ml (2 tsp) citric acid
Madeira wine yeast and nutrient
1.25 kg (2¾ lb) brown sugar

Wash the prunes and place them in a bin. Pour 2.8 litres (5 pints) hot water over them, cover and leave to cool.

Remove the stones and add the washed and chopped raisins and the peeled and mashed bananas.

Mix in the pectic enzyme, 1 crushed Campden tablet and half the citric acid. Cover and leave for 24 hours. Add the activated yeast and nutrient and ferment-on-the-pulp for five days, keeping the bin covered.

Then boil the brown sugar and the rest of the acid in 850 ml (1½ pints) hot water, simmer for 20 minutes and leave to cool.

Strain out, press dry and discard the pulp. Mix in approximately one sixth of the sugar syrup, pour the must into a demijohn, fit an airlock and continue the fermentation.

After five days mix in another sixth of the syrup and repeat this every five days until all six portions have been added. Finish the ferment to the end.

Rack into a storage jar and leave it in a cool place to clear. As soon as the wine is bright, store it in a warm place as described on page 214. Keep for at least two years and preferably for three to five.

Fortified Wines

Why fortify wine?
In the past poorly fermented sweet country wines were often fortified with brandy to make them more palatable. Today, with a better understanding of the technique of fermenting a must into wine (by adding sugar in small quantities, using better yeast and nutrients and the invention of the airlock, for example), there is fortunately less need for fortifying wine. But our improved skills still encourage some winemakers to try to emulate the more difficult commercial fortified wines, notably port, sherry and Madeira.

Vodka is best
- Spirits, such as brandy, gin, rum and whisky, all have distinct flavours that overwhelm any wine to which they are added. Only vodka, the colourless and tasteless spirit, is suitable for fortifying wines made in the home as it increases the alcohol content without affecting the flavour in any way.
- The only problem experienced by the home winemaker is knowing how much to add to a wine to increase its alcohol to a particular level.

OTHER SPIRITS
In France a colourless brandy, *eau de vie pour les fruits*, is used in the production of apricot, peach and similar fruit brandies. This is ideal to add to a port-style wine, so do bring some back if you visit France. Vodka or Polish spirit is best, however, for sherry and Madeira styles.

The maximum alcohol tolerance
- Continue fermentation to the maximum alcohol tolerance of the yeast. Frequent hydrometer readings of the specific gravity, especially before and after the addition of sugar, will enable you to calculate accurately enough the total number of units that have been fermented.
- Consider the temperature at which the must was fermented and remember that a fast fermentation may well have caused some alcohol to be dissipated with the carbon dioxide. Frequent stirring of the must would have a similar effect. Bear this in mind and, if necessary, reduce

the total number of points by 2, 4 or 6 as you consider appropriate.
- Clearly, a slow fermentation with little stirring will have retained all but a point or so.
- From all this and by reference to the hydrometer readings, you can ascertain approximately, yet fairly accurately, the quantity of alcohol you have obtained in your wine.
- This is the starting point of fortification. Unless you know the existing alcohol content of your wine, you cannot calculate the quantity of spirit that you will need to add to increase the level to the right degree.

Monitoring the alcohol content
- As with most other wine styles it is always best to start off with a clear idea of what you want to achieve. In particular, you need to monitor closely the alcohol content of your wine, so calculate the total amount of sugar fermented as accurately as you can.
- Remember that there is natural sugar in most base ingredients, particularly in fruit, and that this must be included, not forgetting any concentrated grape juice, sultanas and so on.

Which vodka to choose
- Two kinds of vodka are used to fortify wines. The first has a proof spirit of 65.5° equal to 37.35% of alcohol. The second, known as Polish spirit, has a proof of 140°, equal to 79.8% alcohol.
- Naturally, the weaker vodka is about half the price of the stronger one. Remember that it contains twice as much water, which will dilute the flavour and other ingredients of your wine. The brand of vodka that you use is entirely a matter of choice.

The 5-points calculation
The formula used to calculate the additional spirit needed is known as Pearson's Square and is set out as:

$$\begin{array}{ccc} A & & B \\ & C & \\ D & & E \end{array}$$

At **A** write the alcohol content of the spirit to be used
At **B** write the alcohol content of your wine
At **C** write the alcohol content required
At **D** write the difference between C and B
At **E** write the difference between A and C

The ratio of D to E is the ratio of spirit to wine necessary to increase the alcohol content of your wine to the level required.

Example 1:
Assume A equals 37.35% alcohol
Assume B equals 15% alcohol
Assume C equals 17.5% alcohol
Then   D equals 17.5 − 15 = 2.5
and   E equals 37.35 − 17.5 = 19.85

You will therefore need 2.5 measures of spirit to increase the alcohol content of 19.85 measures of wine from 15 to $17\frac{1}{2}$% – approximately 1 bottle of vodka to 8 bottles of wine.

Example 2:
Assume A equals 80% alcohol
Assume B equals 16% alcohol
Assume C equals 20% alcohol
Then   D equals 20 − 16 = 4
and   E equals 80 − 20 = 60

You will therefore need 4 measures of Polish spirit to increase the alcohol content of 60 measures of wine from 16 to 20% i.e. a ratio of 1 to 15.

Proof spirit
- Confusion can sometimes arise if the bottle of spirit is marked in degrees proof rather than percentage alcohol. In the UK 100% alcohol is recorded as 175° proof.
- To convert proof to percentage divide the proof by 7 and multiply by 4. Thus to convert 140° proof: 140 ÷ 7 = 20, 20 × 4 = 80% alcohol. In reverse, percentage alcohol can be converted to proof spirit by dividing by 4 and multiplying by 7. Thus to convert 40% alcohol: 40 ÷ 4 = 10, 10 × 7 = 70° proof.
- When fortifying a wine it is important to make your calculations in either degrees proof or percentage, but do not mix the two.

Gay-Lussac notation
On the labels of some bottles of commercially produced wines and spirits the percentage alcohol is printed as 12° or 25°. This is the Gay-Lussac notation and is the same as percentage. (Occasionally the letters G–L are printed beside the figures.) The proof spirit notation is usually followed by the word 'proof', thus 65.5° proof.

When to fortify
- Having decided to make a wine that you will ultimately fortify and having calculated the quantity of spirit to add, you should mix it into the wine as soon as the wine is bright. This could be after the first racking but is more likely to be after the second.
- If the wine is clear, bright, sound and in good condition, it can be racked into a container into which the spirit has already been poured. This thoroughly mixes the wine and spirit, which must now be matured for a couple of years or more.
- The stronger the wine the longer it takes to mature. The spirit needs to be added at an early stage to homogenize fully with the wine. Newly added spirit can often be tasted in a wine.
- When port wine is made commercially, fermentation is terminated by the addition of spirit while some grape sugar still remains in the wine. This, however, requires facilities for measuring the alcohol content that are too expensive for home use. It is better to make your wine and add the spirit later, allowing it adequate time to mature.

Flavour fortification
This is a much more difficult procedure as synthetic flavourings often impart a synthetic taste to the wine. If used at all, add them almost a drop at a time and taste the wine constantly, otherwise it can easily be ruined.
Sherry flavouring: Treat this with caution. It is far more sensible to add a bottle of a good commercial sherry, as the mature sherry imparts its flavour to the young wine if left long enough to mature.
Port: Little improvement is obtained by the addition of a bottle of commercial port wine to a home-made port-style wine. Reasonably inexpensive bottles of port are often not much better than a good home-made port-style wine. The better ports are expensive and too precious not to be enjoyed as they are.
Red wine: A litre of Spanish or Italian red wine can enhance a gallon of home-made red wine but the commercial whites are sometimes not as good as home-made white wines.

A general tip
The major fault with so many home-made wines is that they are never given sufficient time to mature. Patience is the remedy, not fortification.

Wines for the Diabetic

Doctor's orders
It is quite easy for a diabetic to make suitable and enjoyable wines at home. Indeed, the occasional glass of wine is a tonic. Before starting, however, if you know that you suffer from diabetes please consult your doctor. There are now various medications for diabetes, with one of which you should not take alcohol. Once having got clearance from your doctor you can then go on to consider what wines to make.

Sugar and alcohol
- Avoid all sweet wines. These include dessert wines and even medium-sweet social wines.
- Remember that alcohol is a carbohydrate, so if you are on a calorie-controlled diet you must include the alcohol as part of your daily intake. This rules out high-alcohol wines, even if they contain no residual sugar.
- The emphasis then must be on low-alcohol wines that have been fermented out to complete dryness. If properly balanced these will be light in flavour and texture. This excludes the strongly-flavoured fruits such as blackcurrants, elderberries, figs and raspberries and also most vegetable wines, which tend to be full bodied.

The ideal base
Fresh fruits: This group includes apples, blackberries, gooseberries, grapes, oranges, plums and rhubarb.
Fruit juices: These are the ideal base because they are light and easy.
Canned fruits: These can also be used.
Jams: These are suitable, as they need very little extra sugar and this can all be fermented out.
Flowers: These make light wines but should be fermented right out and then sweetened with saccharin.

> ### A general tip
> Any wine can be sweetened with saccharin. Do remember, however, that the wine must be fermented right out and the final specific gravity 0.996 or lower.

Fermenting out

To ensure complete fermentation:
1 Start with a specific gravity between 1.070 and 1.075.
2 Use a good wine yeast with sufficient acid and nutrient, including vitamin B_1.
3 Maintain an even temperature throughout.
4 Always use pectic enzyme or Rohament P to ensure the maximum release of fruit juice.
5 It is a good idea to leave pulped fruit containing pectic enzyme and sulphite for 48 hours rather than for 24. When a sample of pulp is pressed to extract the juice to obtain a specific gravity reading, there is then less likelihood of sugar remaining in the pulp and so increasing the alcohol content during fermentation.

Quick maturation

One of the advantages of all low-alcohol, light-textured wines is that they mature quickly and are frequently ready to drink between three and six months after fermentation has finished. Unfortunately, they often don't keep as well as stronger wines of 12% alcohol. But the intention here is that of making wines for drinking, not keeping. As soon as a wine is ready for drinking it should be enjoyed.

How much to enjoy

This is another matter. The average glass of wine consists of 100 ml ($3\frac{1}{2}$ fl oz). The number of calories present in that quantity depends on the precise alcohol content. If it is around 10% then the number of calories present will be about 80. If you have to count your calories you may not be able to have a second glass. Ask your doctor's advice on this. Some people who are only slightly affected need only avoid the very sweet wines.

A general tip
To be on the safe side, consult your doctor and, if he agrees, make only dry, light wines and consume them in moderation.

GRAPEFRUIT AND APPLE JUICE WINE

1 litre (1¾ pints) grapefruit juice
1 litre (1¾ pints) apple juice
250 g (9 oz) concentrated grape juice
2 litres (3½ pints) cold water
Pectic enzyme
2 Campden tablets
Approx 680 g (1½ lb) sugar
Hock wine yeast and nutrient
Saccharin pellets

Empty the three fruit juices into a sterilized demijohn, together with half the water, the pectic enzyme and 1 crushed Campden tablet. Seal and leave for 48 hours.

Warm the remaining water, dissolve the sugar in it and, when cool, mix it into the fruit juices.

Check the specific gravity and, if necessary, adjust to between 1.070 and 1.075 with water or sugar. (The quantity of natural sugar in the fruit juices varies from one brand to another.) If the specific gravity of the must exceeds 1.075, add a little water to reduce it. If the reading is below 1.070 then add some sugar to increase it. Make sure that the added sugar is completely dissolved before you take the second reading.

When the specific gravity is adjusted, mix in the activated yeast and nutrient, then ferment right out. Rack into a storage jar, add 1 Campden tablet and top up. Seal and store until the wine is bright.

Rack into bottles, sweetening each one with 1 or 2 saccharin pellets to suit your taste.

ORANGE JUICE WINE

1.25 litres (2¼ pints) orange juice
250 g (9 oz) concentrated grape juice
Approx 2.8 litres (5 pints) water
Pectic enzyme
2 Campden tablets
740 g (1 lb 10 oz) sugar
2.5 ml (½ tsp) citric acid
Chablis wine yeast and nutrient

Follow the same method as in Grapefruit and Apple Juice Wine on the facing page.

PINEAPPLE JUICE WINE

1 litre (1¾ pints) pineapple juice
250 g (9 oz) concentrated grape juice
Approx 2.8 litres (5 pints) water
Pectic enzyme
2 Campden tablets
500 g (18 oz) sugar
225 g (8 oz) honey
5 ml (1 tsp) citric acid
Bordeaux wine yeast and nutrient

Follow the same method as in Grapefruit and Apple Juice Wine on the facing page. Include the honey and citric acid with the sugar.

Grape Wines

REAL WINE

Traditionally, the word wine means the product of the fermentation of the juice of freshly-pressed grapes. All other wines should be described as fruit, flower, vegetable wines and so on. For the home winemaker, however, grape is just another fruit – and in the UK not always one that can be obtained at a price that makes the production of wine from its juice worthwhile.

GROWING YOUR OWN VINES

Since the 1960s, and increasingly in the 1970s and 80s, grape vines have been planted in gardens both large and small. Some have fared better than others but many have died only through a lack of understanding of the vine's needs. Happily, knowledge of the varieties and the methods of tending them is becoming more widespread.

Choosing the best site
- Remember that the vine will not flourish in the open on sites in the UK that are 100 metres (300 feet) above sea level.
- The grape also needs 100 days of fair and warm weather from flowering to harvesting, so it is best grown in a sunny position well protected from cold winds. A well-drained soil on a limestone substructure is best. There are many such sites in the southern half of England and Wales and some isolated sites in the Midlands and East Anglia. There are even a few further north.

Protecting the vines
- In less good sites the vines can be protected in greenhouses or in large plastic cloches. Warm, dry air in the last 30 days, when the acid in the fully grown grape is being converted into sugar, is particularly important.
- Even in southern sites some protection during the period from mid-September to mid-October is desirable. This is the period in which the malic acid is converted to sugar. Rain, cold winds and possibly night frosts will cause rot in some grapes and leave them all low in sugar and high in acid.

Grape varieties
The actual varieties of vines to grow depend on your site.
Cooler sites: These need early-ripening varieties and only white grapes are worth growing out of doors and unprotected.
Warmer sites: These, especially ones against a wall, can grow black grapes as well as white.
Recommended white grape varieties: Müller–Thurgau, Kerner, Madeleine Angevine and Seyval.
Recommended black grape varieties: Seibel, Gagarin Blue, Bacco No. 1 and Cabernet Sauvignon.

Early planting
Having chosen a suitable site, buy some appropriate vines in pots and plant them out by early November at the latest before the ground gets too cold. The roots will then get settled in preparation for growth the following spring. Indeed, provided that you use very large ones, vines can be successfully grown in pots!

Pruning
- During the first three years allow only three shoots to develop. Pinch out the sideshoots to produce a strong cane and a good root structure.
- In the fourth and subsequent years, the fruit develops on the previous year's canes like raspberries. After harvesting cut these canes out and replace them with the new canes that will have grown during the summer.
- You can leave only one cane to fruit and nurture a single replacement through the summer. Alternatively, leave two canes to fruit, one on either side of the main stock. Replacement canes must be nurtured for each side.
- Another option is to allow the vines to develop more widely, perhaps over a wall of the house, and prune back only the fruited canes.
- Remember that a piece of ground can only produce a certain quantity of fine wine. The more grapes produced, the lower the quality of the wine produced from them is likely to be.

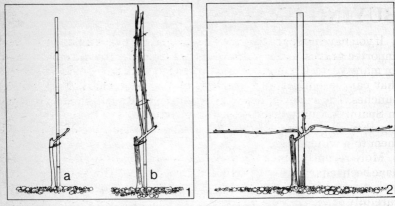

Grape pruning: (**1a**) The vine when planted with three buds only. (**1b**) At the end of the first year the three shoots are tied into a cane. (**2**) As the shoots grow two are tied into the first wire and the remaining shoot is cut back to three buds.

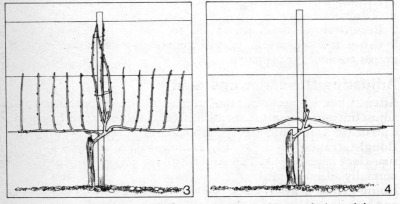

(**3**) During the summer the fruiting shoots are tied into the second wire and three new shoots are tied into the cane. (**4**) In the winter pruning cut out the laterals and fruiting shoots. Tie two new shoots to the first wire and cut back the third shoot to three buds. Continue this procedure every year in January.

BUYING GRAPES

- If you have no space to grow vines, you can always make wine from imported grapes. Little sultana grapes from Cyprus have been used for many years. Greengrocers are often left with boxes of loose grapes that can be bought at a fraction of the price charged for whole bunches. The same applies to grapes from South Africa and Almeria in Spain. A kindly disposed fruiterer will be very happy to collect together all the loose grapes and unsaleable small bunches and sell them to a winemaker.
- More recently, since the middle 1970s in fact, Italian wine grapes have been imported and distributed – at a price – to those interested in making wine from them. These grapes are of good quality and arrive carefully packed in wooden trays, covered with paper to protect them. They have made some good red wine.

MAKING THE WINE

Inspecting and preparing the grapes

1 All grapes need careful inspection, whether home grown or bought in. Throw away any that are mouldy or oxidized.
2 Remove the stalks and wash the grapes well in running water.
3 Crush and sulphite them, add the pectic enzyme and leave the grapes covered for 24 hours.

Adjusting the sugar and acid

After 24 hours, check the sugar and acid content of the juice and adjust this as necessary. An acidity of from 4 to 6 parts per thousand or a pH of 3 to 3.4 is required for both bought-in and home-grown grapes.
Bought grapes: These usually contain sufficient sugar but sometimes lack acid. One 5 ml spoonful (1 tsp) per gallon of tartaric acid is normally adequate.
Home-grown grapes: These are likely to be somewhat low in sugar and high in acid. Increase the specific gravity with granulated sugar or concentrated grape juice to 1.080 for white wines, and 1.090 for red wines. Excess acidity can be removed with potassium carbonate but beware of the frothing.

Fermentation
White grapes: These should now be strained and the pulp pressed dry. Pour the juice into a fermentation vessel, mix in a Hock wine yeast and fit an airlock. Stand the vessel in a cool place as soon as fermentation has started.
Black grapes: These should be left in the bin. Mix in a burgundy wine yeast and ferment the must on the pulp for ten days. Press the fruit down and mix it into the juice twice each day; keep the bin covered and leave it in an atmospheric temperature of 20°C (68°F). When fermentation-on-the-pulp is nearly complete, strain out and press dry the skins and pips. Pour the must into a fermentation vessel and fit an airlock.

Racking and bottling
When fermentation is complete, the wines, both red and white, should be racked, stored and bottled in the same way as any other wine.

Which grape is best?
The wine from white grapes, whether home grown or bought, makes interesting and enjoyable wine, but the same cannot always be said for the red. This wine blends well with other red wines, however, and greatly improves their vinosity.

Serving Wine

One of the great joys of winemaking is the variety of different wines that we can produce. Among the main wine styles we can have countless different flavours from main ingredients or complex ones from a mixture of several. The yeasts, too, make their contribution as do the fermentation and storage temperatures. All these wines accompany some foods, some companions or some occasions better than others. To serve your wines to their best advantage you should consider a number of factors.

MATURITY

Some wines are ready for drinking a few weeks after fermentation finishes; others need several years to grow smooth and mellow.

Check it before you serve it

Before serving any wine make sure that it is bright and clean in sight, smell and taste and that in the mouth it is smooth and free from rough edges caused by a temporary imbalance of acid, tannin or flavour. During storage the acid, tannin and flavour not only become less pronounced but also homogenize to form a perfect whole.

Experience is the best guideline

There are no definite indications of maturity since each wine differs. After tasting a number of wines, however, you will quickly learn which wines are ready for drinking and which need longer storage.

SUITABILITY

The next question to ask yourself is whether the wine is right for the purpose you have in mind. Is it suitable for drinking as an aperitif, as a dry table wine or as a dessert wine after the meal, or is it a wine to share with friends who have called in. Each occasion would be the less enjoyable for serving the wrong wine.

A few examples

- Dessert wines, full bodied, well flavoured, sweet and luscious, just do not accompany meat pie as well as a dry red table wine.

- Conversely, a dry table wine, whether it be red or white, tastes quite unpleasant with apple pie and cream or prunes and custard. This course cries out for a sweet white wine, not too full or strong.
- Matching the right wine with the right food and occasion is something of an art, but one that is soon learned if you care to take the trouble.

YOUR COMPANIONS

- You also need to consider the people with whom you will be drinking your wine. Some people have limited, even prejudiced ideas about wine. Think of their tastes and only offer them the wines that they like. If they only drink white wine do not offer them red. If they only drink sweet wine, do not offer them dry.
- Some people do not like wine at all. It is a waste of a good wine to offer it to them and you might do better to serve tea or coffee instead.

TEMPERATURE

Having chosen a mature wine suitable for the occasion and the company, consider next the temperature of the wine.

White wine: This tastes best when served cold, i.e. around 9°–10°C (48–50°F).

Sparkling wine: This needs to be a bit colder than white wine in order to help retain the bubbles. Around 7°C (45°F) seems to be the best temperature.

Rosé, sherry and Madeira-style wine: This applies especially to the fino and Sercial types. These wines can be served at the same temperature as white wines.

Red and port-style wine: These wines need quite a bit more warmth to soften the harshness of their tannin. Around 18–20°C (64–68°F) seems to be the best temperature.

The proof is in the tasting

- A little experiment will illustrate the value of these suggestions. Empty a bottle of a dry elderberry or similar-style red table wine into two half bottles. Put one of these into the refrigerator for an hour or so and leave the other one in a warm kitchen. Do the same with a bottle of white wine.
- Pour out two glassfuls of red wine – one from each half bottle – and notice the difference. The red wine from the refrigerator will taste

harsh and astringent. The other will taste altogether smoother and more enjoyable.
• The white wine from the refrigerator will taste fresh, crisp and clean while the one from the kitchen will be soft and flabby.

A happy medium
Do not get carried away, however, and serve white, rosé, sparkling and sherry-style wines so freezing cold that they lose their bouquet and flavour and become dumb. In the same way, do not serve red table and port-style wines so warm that they taste half cooked. It is worth checking the temperature of a few wines to make sure that you get them just right.

DECANTERS AND CARAFES

The advantages
1 No matter how attractive the decorative label on the dark green or brown wine bottle, all that can be admired on the table is the bottle and label – the wine will be virtually invisible. Served in a plain, colourless decanter or carafe, however, the wine's hue and clarity will be immediately pleasing to the eye.
2 Pouring the wine into the container will not only aerate it and disperse any carbon dioxide but will also separate the clear wine from any bottle sediment.
3 One to three hours in a decanter improves bouquet and flavour – of young red wines, in particular.

How to decant
1 When decanting older wines that will have almost certainly thrown a sediment, be careful to stand the bottle upright for a day or two before unsealing it. This allows the deposit of fine particles of tannin, salts and general debris to slide down into the bottle.
2 Remove the cork with care, making sure that you do not shake the bottle and create a cloudy swirl, then slowly tilt the bottle towards the mouth of the decanter and pour slowly.
3 Avoid large globules of air from rushing back into the bottle and disturbing the sediment.
4 As the bottle empties, the sediment will creep up the side of the bottle into the shoulder. As soon as it reaches the neck, stop pouring. Use the last tablespoonful or so of wine in the sauce or gravy.

GLASSES

Over the years suitable glasses have been developed for each style of wine.

White wine: This should be served in a glass shaped rather like a **tulip**. The incurved, elongated bowl is supported by a stem firmly attached to a foot. This shape is best for keeping the wine cool and holding the bouquet. The glass should hold about 140 ml (5 fl oz).

Sparkling wines: These are served in tall glasses known as **flutes**. They have an even longer and narrower bowl than a tulip so that the bubbles of carbon dioxide have further to rise and thus please the eye still more with their shining. The shape also helps to keep the wine cold and to slow down the release of the gas. This glass holds about 140 ml (5 fl oz). Saucer-shaped glasses allow the bubbles to disperse too fast and the wine to warm up too quickly through its large surface contact with warm air.

Red wines: These are served in **goblets** more spherical in shape, so that the wine in them is the better able to breathe and to maintain warmth from the atmosphere. The most suitable size contains about 140 ml (5 fl oz).

Dessert and port-style wines: These are served in glasses that are small versions of the **tulip** and hold only 40–55 ml (1½–2 fl oz). Rosé wines are usually served in these glasses.

The correct wine glasses for different wines (*from left to right*): tulip for white wines, goblet for red wines, miniature for liqueurs, copita for aperitifs and dessert wines, flute for sparkling wines.

Aperitif wines: These, especially those in the sherry style, are best served in **copitas**. These glasses are smaller versions of the flute but with more bulbous middles and more incurved mouths. This glass holds from 85 to 100 ml (3–3½ fl oz).

The shape of the glass
- All glasses should be colourless and unembellished. They should be incurved at the mouth to help retain the bouquet. Straight-sided and V-shaped glasses are quite unsuitable for wine since they encourage the dissipation of the aroma and bouquet.
- They should have a stem by which to pick them up and a foot with which to hold them. The glass should be to the wine the same as a frame is to a picture. It simply holds the wine free from distraction so that its beauty can be seen and enjoyed.

Filling the glass
Never fill a glass to more than two-thirds of its total content. More than this not only looks greedy but also leaves insufficient space for the bouquet to gather. Furthermore, handling the glass without spillage then becomes extremely difficult, particularly in a crowded room.

Washing-up
- After use, wash glasses in warm water containing a detergent. This removes the oily glycerine from inside as well as the greasy fingerprints from outside.
- Rinse off the detergent with clean water and turn the glass upside down to drain dry.
- Give the glass a wipe around the rim with a clean cloth and then store it upright in an enclosed cabinet. This protects it from dust and the entrapment of stale air.

Trays
- Trays on which glasses of wine are served should be of mirrored silver or at least stainless steel.
- If this is not possible, cover another tray with a white damask table napkin. The silver reflects the brilliant hues of the wine and the napkin is the next best.
- Avoid all colours since they kill the colour of the wine.
- Similarly, wine served at table shows to its best advantage on a plain white cloth that enhances its colour.

WITH FOOD

- Wine is meant to be the perfect accompaniment to food. In wine-producing countries the gastronomic delights of a region often make a magnificent match with the local wine.
- The tradition of drinking red wine with red meat, game and cheese, and white with poultry, fish and pork is well established and commonly found to be most satisfying. It does not mean, however, that you should never drink wine other than in the traditional way. Indeed, some would say, 'Any wine is better than no wine.'
- Furthermore, there are those who claim that drinking red wine causes them to have headaches, stomach upsets, even migraines. Whilst as yet this has not been proved scientifically, it would be a pity if such a person were denied the opportunity of drinking white wine instead of red.
- Younger and lighter wines taste better when drunk before older, stronger and more full-bodied wines.
- Within the range of red wines, some will be found more suitable for roast beef and others for roast lamb. Less fine wines will accompany everyday casseroles, pies and pastas. Well-flavoured wines match game such as venison and hare but fine and elegant wines are needed for most cheeses. Gorgonzola and Danish Blue are the exceptions. They virtually spoil vinous company, as do pickled onions, walnuts and piccalilli. Avoid the domination of one flavour over another.
- A few wines, notably light white wines, drink well on their own. They taste best when they are just off complete dryness and with only the merest hint of sweetness. Served cold on a warm day in the garden they are delicious, thirst-quenching and palate cleansing. Some splendid wines of this kind can be made from canned fruits.

COOKING WITH WINE

Home winemakers have a wonderful opportunity to enhance their cooking by the judicious addition of wine to their recipes. It is not desirable to use your best wine and experience shows that any sound wine may be used successfully. Home-made wine may be used instead of commercial wine in any recipe that includes wine. One 140-ml (5-fl oz) glass of wine is usually enough.

Ways of using wine in cooking
- Poach fish in wine, herbs and spices.
- Bake ham in apple wine, cider or mead.
- Add red wine to beef casseroles and to lamb goulash.
- Use red or white wine for chicken casseroles.
- Use home-made wines for marinades.
- Add red wines to gravies and white wines to sauces.
- The end of a bottle of port-style wine can be added to the gravy to enrich it.
- Soak sponge cake in sweet wine when making trifles.
- Stew fruit in wine instead of water.
- Pour sweet wine over fruit salads.

> ### A general tip
> Home winemakers have an advantage over others in that they always have wines available for culinary purposes, so do make use of your wines in this way.

APPRECIATING THE WINE

- Now raise your half-filled glass to the light and examine the colour and clarity. Bring the glass to your nose and deeply inhale the aroma and bouquet. Think about it before taking a mouthful of wine. Chew the wine and move it around with your tongue. Consider the degree of acidity, dryness or sweetness, alcoholic strength, flavour, body and texture.
- Swallow the wine slowly and pause for a while. In a few seconds a pleasant taste should develop around your uvula in the back of your throat. This is the **aftertaste** or farewell. It should linger for up to half a minute and is the jewel in the crown of a wine that looks good, smells good and tastes good.

Keeping Records

WHY KEEP RECORDS?

Given the almost infinite variations in the quality of the ingredients that are used to make wines, meads and ciders; the methods that are used and the atmospheric temperatures during fermentation and storage, it is extremely difficult to repeat a success. It is almost impossible to do so without some record of the ingredients used, how and when the beverage was made and what you thought of the result.

- All too often we have access to a particular ingredient one year, such as a glut of a fruit or vegetable, and then not for several years. When it becomes available again we may have forgotten just what else we included and exactly how the wine was made.
- Sometimes we come up against a problem and cannot remember every detail of what we previously used and did, thus making it more difficult to find a remedy.
- By keeping a record of every wine, mead and cider that you make, you will at least have a reminder of all these things.

HOW TO KEEP RECORDS

- Records need not be elaborate, although at first you will find that the more detail you note down the more helpful it will be. You can simply allocate a number to each batch, attaching a small label to the bottle bearing the number. Keep the details in a notebook beside that number.
- Alternatively keep a record card for each batch and attach this to the jar or bin. A simple luggage label will do but you can also buy printed record cards and a ring binder in which to keep them for future reference.

Ingredients

It helps to keep a note not only of the name and quantity of the main ingredients used but also of their quality and from where they came. Record, too, similar details about the minor ingredients. For example: **Acid** – did you use citric, malic or tartaric; as crystals or in the form of citrus or other fruits, or as a mixture?

KEEPING RECORDS · 239

NAME OF WINE/MEAD/CIDER _____

QUANTITY _____ DATE STARTED _____

MAIN INGREDIENTS	DESCRIPTION	QUANTITY
_____	_____	_____
_____	_____	_____
_____	_____	_____
_____	_____	_____

WATER _____
ACIDS _____

TANNIN _____
PECTIC ENZYME _____
SULPHITE _____
YEAST _____
NUTRIENT _____
SUGAR _____
SPECIFIC GRAVITY (S.G.) BEFORE SUGAR ADDED _____
S.G. AFTER SUGAR ADDED _____
PREPARATION _____
_____

DATE FERMENTATION STARTED _____
ATMOSPHERIC TEMPERATURE _____
DATE FERMENTATION FINISHED _____
DATE OF FIRST RACKING _____
S.G. OF FINISHED WINE/MEAD/CIDER _____
TOPPED UP WITH _____
SULPHITE _____
SORBATE _____
FINING _____
DATE OF SECOND RACKING _____
APPEARANCE _____
STORAGE NOTES _____
_____

STORAGE TEMPERATURE _____
DATE BOTTLED _____
ARTIFICIAL SWEETENING ADDED _____
FINAL COMMENTS _____
_____
_____

A sample record card

Tannin – did you use grape tannin powder, liquid tannin, or cold tea, and if so how much?
Pectic enzyme – did you use it in powder or liquid form, how much and when?
Sulphite – did you use Campden tablets or 10% solution, how much and when?
Water – was this cold or hot, or boiled and left to cool?
Yeast – what variety did you use and was it granulated, liquid or culture? Was it activated? If so, how and when was it added?
Nutrient – did you use ammonium phosphate or sulphate, or a mixture of the two? Did you use vitamin B_1 Tronozymol, Gervin or another proprietary brand of mixed nutrients?

Method

Preparation of ingredients – liquidized, crushed or pressed, or fermented-on-the-pulp?
Sugar – were these crystals or syrup, how much and when added? Did you record the specific gravity of the must before any sugar was added and again after it had been thoroughly mixed in?

Fermentation

It is helpful to note the date fermentation started, the atmospheric temperature during fermentation, the date fermentation finished and the specific gravity of the wine. Details of a stuck ferment or other problems and the action taken should be recorded.

Racking

Note the date of the first racking, whether sulphite or any other substance was added and what was used for topping up. Record the appearance of the beverage: whether fining or filtering were necessary and if so what was used, when and with what result.

For other drinks

For beers record the kind of priming used and the quantity and date added. The same applies to sparkling wines, ciders and meads.

Evaluation

Finally, evaluate the beverage critically as regards:
Appearance: Bright, veiled or hazy.
Aroma: Strong, good or poor.
Bouquet: Vinous, fruity, slight or off-taint.

Taste: Balanced, sharp, bitter, astringent, dry, sweet, pleasant or off-taint.
General comment: Very good, good, fair or poor.
A sample record card is given on page 239.

You can, of course, make good wine, mead or cider by following the recipes in this book and without keeping records. When you are very experienced you may decide that you know everything there is to know and need not keep records. However, all the best winemakers I know keep records. These serve as a constant check and are an invaluable talking point when the wines, meads and ciders are being drunk with family and friends.

BREWING BEER

The History of Beer

Cereals have been used for making an alcoholic drink since before the Pharaohs built the pyramids; and according to archaeologists and historians, the slaves who built the pyramids were given beer to drink to quench their thirst.

IN BRITAIN

The Celts made a drink called curmi that they sometimes flavoured with nettles, burdock, yarrow or other herbs. The Danes were great beer drinkers and conferred the word 'ale' on to our native beverage. Other invaders from the north were also great drinkers and used giant horns from their cattle as drinking vessels.

All the ale was brewed by women, possibly because they also made bread and used the same yeast for each. This yeast was likely to be a lump of dough saved from one batch of bread to another, or the skimming from a fermenting ale. These women became known as ale-wives.

Types of ales

Two ales were brewed: a weak or 'small ale' drunk at breakfast and during the day, and a stronger and better-flavoured ale to drink with the evening meal.

Ale as a part of life
- The ale wives sold their ale to passers-by. Ales were also brewed to raise money for repairing bridges and building churches.
- The word 'ale' then had a meaning something akin to the word 'fête' that we use today. Drunkenness was rife and abbots imposed penances on monks found drunk; kings imposed fines on their drunken subjects, including a day in the stocks. King Edgar (959–975) closed countless ale houses, permitting each village to retain only one. The price of ale was controlled and even taxed – a blight that has never been lifted.
- For all their lack of scientific knowledge, at least some of the ale was of high quality. In 1158 two wagonloads were sent to the king of France, where his courtiers described it as 'most wholesome, clear of all dregs, equalling wine in colour and surpassing it in flavour'.

The introduction of hops
Hops were occasionally imported from the Low Countries during the thirteenth and fourteenth centuries, but the bitter flavour they imparted to the drink was not widely appreciated. When hops were boiled with the wort, the beverage was called beer, an adaptation of a German word for such a drink. A controversy developed between those who brewed ale with hops and those who did not; in London each had their own separate Guild! The beer brewers were charged a higher tax than the ale brewers, but the popularity of beer was increasing, especially when it was found that hops helped to preserve the beer as well as to give it flavour.

By 1492 the immigrant Huguenots were planting hops in Kent, where the best hops are still grown. By the end of the sixteenth century, hop-growing was supervized, the malting of the barley regulated and the size of the casks controlled; the brewing of beer was truly under way.

The growth of the breweries
By 1591, 25,400 barrels of beer were exported annually from London. It was made in small breweries. By the early eighteenth century breweries had become larger and more efficient. Saccharometers were used to control the sugar content and thermometers to check the mashing temperature. These breweries included the great names of today: Bass, Charrington, Coombe, Courage, Simmonds, Watney, Whitbread and Worthington.

Types of beer
The breweries offered three beers to the public: brown, old and pale ale. These were soon blended and became known as 'porter'. This was made for the next 150 years but production has now ceased.

Pasteur
In the nineteenth century, the famous scientist Pasteur contributed his own ideas on sterilization and the quality of beer improved still more.

HOME BREWING
With so much good beer on sale there was little need to brew beer at home. In any case few homes had adequate facilities. In 1880 home brewing was virtually stopped altogether by an Act of Parliament. This imposed a licence on the home brewer, the cost of which was based on the rateable value of his house. All beer was subject to excise duty. This situation continued until 1963 when the law on home brewing was rescinded.

In the 1950s and 1960s
Brewing at home had already started in a small way in the early 1950s and home brewers used malt extract and hops bought from local chemists. In the 1960s manufacturers started to produce beer kits that needed only dilution with water, sweetening with sugar and fermenting with the dried yeast provided. One firm even included a plastic bag in which to ferment the brew!

In the 1980s
Today, the majority of the beer brewed at home is made from kits, the contents of which continue to improve. Many people still like to experiment, however. Beer brewed from malt extract and hops with a few adjuncts added is quite widely made. There are also a good number of specialists who believe that the best beer is brewed at home from selected grains, adjuncts, hops, adjusted water and yeast. The following chapters cover all these aspects.

Styles of Beer

- Although the general styles of beer are common to all commercial brewers, the actual beers within the style vary considerably in colour, aroma, body, sweetness, bitterness, condition and overall quality.
- The same can be said about home brewers and their beers. Indeed, one of the great joys of home brewing is that you brew the beer that pleases you most. The relationship of the hop to the malt, the alcohol content, body and sweetness are all a matter of personal choice.
- The beer styles may be classified in the following way:

BITTER BEERS
Export ale
- This is sometimes described as Best Bitter, Burton Bitter or India Pale Ale (IPA for short). It is the most widely made and consumed beer and is traditionally made in the draught form and served by the pint from a keg. The best versions of this beer are, however, often bottled.
- The beer should be copper coloured with a noticeable taste of malt and hops. The original gravity can vary from 1.038 to 1.046 and finish at around 1.006 to 1.008. The taste should be dry, clean and refreshing. Mashing temperature should be maintained at 67°C (152°F) to enhance the maltose dextrin extraction.

Light ale
- This is the bottom end of the bitter scale. Although mashed from similar pale malt, less crystal malt is used and so the beer is light in colour, body and alcohol. The same hop is used for flavouring, although in a smaller quantity.
- The beer should be straw coloured and brilliantly clear. The original gravity may vary from 1.030 to 1.034. The beer is dry and often bottled rather than made into draught form.

Pale ale
- This beer comes between Export Ale and Light Ale in colour, flavour, texture and strength.
- The original gravity can vary from 1.036 to 1.040. It is more often bottled than casked and is often served as a luncheon ale.

STOUT

At one time only three beers were brewed. Malted barley was mashed to a high concentration of maltose and some wort was drawn off to make a strong beer. Hot water was then sprayed over the grains and, when drawn off, made a standard beer. The grains were then sprayed a second time with hot water and this wort was used to make 'small' beer. The word strong was gradually changed to stout and the dark colour was darkened still further.

Dry or Irish stout
- This is a full-bodied, somewhat bitter beer without any sweetness. It is often regarded as the most therapeutic of beers and is sometimes prescribed for convalescents in hospital.
- It is jet black in colour and has a substantial dark oatmeal-coloured, closely-grained head that remains longer than the head of all other beers. The original gravity should lie between 1.044 and 1.046.
- Dry stout is something of an acquired taste but one that is much appreciated by its devotees.

Sweet or milk stout
- The name is derived from the lactose (the sugar in milk) that is used for sweetening this beer. Also full-bodied, this stout is exceptionally smooth and has a flavour that is derived more from the malt than the hop.
- Its black colour may contain a hint of brown and its head may be a shade lighter than dry stout. It is also less strong since the original gravity should be in the region of 1.034–1.036.

BROWN ALE
- This is a somewhat broad grouping that covers numerous variations from brewer to brewer and from one part of the UK to another.
- In general the colour ranges from amber to dark brown. The flavour is smooth and sweet, less strong in alcohol and without the bitterness of the black malt used in stout. The sweetness is due more to the high dextrin content than to lactose, since the malts are mashed at 64.5°C (148°F). The original gravity should be around 1.030 and because of its high finishing gravity of 1.008 the alcohol content is low.

- In the UK, northerners tend to prefer their brown ales to have a slightly more noticeable hop content than southerners. Commercially, there is a distinct difference between a Newcastle Brown Ale and a London Brown Ale.

MILD ALE

- Once very popular, this beer is now rarely brewed. It is between a brown ale and a light ale in colour and style. Having a high dextrin and low alcohol content and being lightly hopped, it was the cheapest of the beers available. It is both easy and inexpensive to make at home.
- Mild ale used to be blended half and half with bitter beer but has now been superseded by keg beers carbonated at the pump.

LAGER

- This beer continues to grow in popularity commercially, although few British-made lagers seem to be comparable in quality with their continental equivalents.
- As with bitter beers there are a number of variations within the general style. They range from the golden, light, crisp and tangy, to the amber, strong, full-bodied and smooth. The original gravity can vary from 1.040 to 1.060.
- The best lagers are made by the decoction method from selected continental-grown grains, seedless hops and bottom-fermenting yeast. They are not easy to make at home and results are often nearer to a good pale ale than to a lager.

BARLEY WINE

- Having an alcohol content of around 10%, this beer is as strong as many light table wines and needs a long period of maturation.
- The colour can vary from a rich golden amber to a deep copper brown. It has little head retention but maintains a lively bead of condition. It should be full bodied, malty flavoured, very smooth and sweet from its high dextrin content. The original gravity can vary from 1.070 to 1.100 and the finishing gravity from 1.014 to 1.018.
- Commercially, this splendid beer is often sold in 142 ml (5 fl oz) bottles called 'nips'. At home it is best stored in $\frac{1}{2}$-pint bottles – enough for two glasses. Splendid barley wines can be made at home.

Equipment and Hygiene

Fermentation bin
- Buy one that can hold more beer than you ever intend to make in one go. Some space should always be left in the bin so that you can move it about without spilling the contents and there is room for the head of froth to lie on the top of the beer. Sometimes this can be as high as 10 cm (4 in).
- Natural polythene bins are best because they are inert to acids and alkalis and light and easy to clean. Most of them have volume graduations indented or printed on one side. This is a great help when making up the wort to a prescribed quantity. These bins also have fitting lids that keep out dust and air whilst allowing the fermentation gas to escape.
- Sterilize the bin with Chempro before use and rinse off with plenty of clean cold water. Failure to do so could cause a flavour reminscent of disinfectant. In the absence of Chempro, use a sulphite solution.

A long-handled stirring paddle
The paddle that has a flat surface pierced with holes is more suitable than a spoon shape for rousing up the wort.

Large saucepan
You need a large saucepan, fish kettle or preserving pan for boiling the wort and hops.

Beer bottles
Make sure that you have plenty for the quantity of beer you propose brewing. Before filling the bottles, thoroughly wash and sterilize them. Instead of bottles, you can also use a plastic cask.

Types of beer bottles
- Use returnable brown beer bottles and crown caps to seal them.
- Screw-stoppered beer bottles are no longer made but may be used if you have some.
- Do not use non-returnable beer bottles which are too thin for the varying pressures likely to be produced by home brewers.

Thermometer

Have one which has a scale from freezing to boiling. Medical thermometers are quite unsuitable as the glass can break and spill mercury into the wort.

Capping tool

For crimping crown caps onto beer bottles to seal them.

All the basic brewing equipment you will need: (**1**) boiling pan; (**2**) fermentation bin; (**3**) insulated mashing bin; (**4**) immersion heater; (**5**) thermometer; (**6**) hydrometer and trial jar; (**7**) plastic paddle; (**8**) J tube siphon; (**9**) plastic funnel; (**10**) brown beer bottles; (**11**) crown caps; (**12**) simple capping tool.

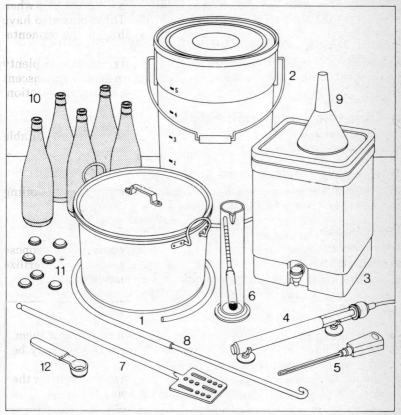

Crown caps or screw stops
Make sure that these have unperished rubber washers where applicable. Corks are quite unsuitable for sealing beer bottles since they are not gastight under pressure.

Siphon
This is used for transferring the beer from the fermentation bin to the bottles. Alternatively, a small jug and plastic funnel may be used, but this method disturbs the sediment and carries too much of it over into the bottles.

Hydrometer and trial jar
This is of great help in checking the original and final gravity of a beer, especially if you vary a recipe or make up your own.

Thermostatic immersion heater, heating belt/pad
This is used for fermenting in a cold place and for mashing at a precise temperature.

Mashing bin
Make sure you have one with a raised grid and a draw-off tap beneath. This is indeed for mashing grains. They lie on the grid and the wort is drawn off under them.

Calico sparging bag and stand
This is useful if you do not have a grid and draw-off tap in your mashing bin. After mashing the grains and wort are poured into the bag and the grains are then sparged to remove the maltose sticking to the surface of the grains.

Crushing mill
A mill is needed for crushing the grains. Use a food mincer with a coarse fitting. A coffee grinder is too small for the quantity of grains to be crushed.

HYGIENE
Cleanliness is important in home brewing (see pages 10–12).
- Sterilize all equipment before use.
- Keep wort and beer closely covered at all times.
- Wash and dry equipment after use and store it in a cool, dry place.

Ingredients

MALT

- Before being used for beer, barley grains must first be steeped in water for a period and then gently warmed until they begin to sprout. Growth is then stopped by raising the temperature to 50°C (122°F) and above. This process releases the starch and forms enzymes that can later convert the starch into sugar called maltose which gives beer its characteristic taste.
- Some malted grains are roasted until they are amber, or still more until they are chocolate coloured, or still more until they are black. **Chocolate and black malts** are used for brown ales and stouts.
Pale malts are the predominant malt used in all beers.
Crystal malts are mainly used as an adjunct in bitter beers.

MALT EXTRACT

- This is a toffee-like substance sometimes called **malt syrup** made by mashing a mixture of malted grains until all the starch has been converted into maltose. The wort is then concentrated until it contains only 20% water. Sometimes it is concentrated still more until only a powder is left; this is **malt flour**.
- Malt flour is available in a cream colour for bitter beers and in a brown version for darker beers. It is very hydrophilic (i.e. it attracts water), so keep it completely dry in an airtight container. Both colours are excellent for use in home brewing.

HOPS

- Only the flower, shaped like a pine cone, of the plant *Humulus lupulus*, is used. These are dried in a warm and mildly sulphurous atmosphere to preserve them from one year to the next. They are then packed very tightly into large sacks and stored in a cool, dry place until required.
- Today, with the aid of modern technology, the flowers can be finely shredded, the dross discarded and the essential parts compressed into pellets. These are then stored in airtight, foil-lined containers until required.

Hop varieties

There are several varieties of hops, the two best known being **Goldings**, mainly used for bitter-style beers, and **Fuggles**, mainly used for brown ales and stouts. Improved strains of these varieties are now also available – **Challenger** replacing Goldings and **Northdown** replacing Fuggles. A variety called **Northern Brewer**, sometimes used as a supplementary hop, has now been replaced with **Target**. The new strains have a higher alpha acid content than the old ones and so 20% fewer hops are required.

- Continental hops, such as **Hallertau** or **Saaz**, should be used when you brew lager, Saaz for the golden, lighter styles and Hallertau for the fuller and darker lagers.
- Most beers require between 14 and 28 g ($\frac{1}{2}$ and 1 oz) hops per gallon, depending on how bitter you like your beer.

WATER

The kind of water used in brewing beer is far more important than that used in making wine.

Hard water containing calcium sulphate and magnesium sulphate in particular, but with some sodium chloride, calcium chloride and calcium carbonate in addition, produces the best bitters and barley wines.

Soft water with an absence of calcium sulphate and a preponderance of sodium chloride, calcium chloride and a little calcium carbonate makes the best stouts and lagers.

To harden water: Add hardening salts (available in packets) to soft water when brewing bitter beers and barley wine.

To soften water: Add 2.5 ml ($\frac{1}{2}$ tsp) salt to soften 9 litres (2 gallons) of most hard water.

Tap water that is known to contain chlorine should always be boiled and cooled before it is used. Failure to do so will enable a disinfectant flavour to develop when the chlorine combines with the phenolics in the hops.

> **Quick tip**
> Off-flavours in beers are quite often caused by the water used. Do boil all the water you use for brewing, adjust it and leave it to cool.

YEAST

Beer yeast

Saccharomyces cerevisiae, the yeast used for brewing beer in Britain, is top fermenting. That is to say that it throws up a thick cloud of froth containing many dead cells as well as living cells. It ferments very quickly and usually finishes within five to seven days when the froth completely disappears.

- Beer or brewer's yeast is normally supplied in granulated form and should be activated before use to ensure a quick start to the fermentation. Make up a weak solution of malt extract by dissolving a rounded teaspoonful in 280 ml ($\frac{1}{2}$ pint) tepid water (40°C/104°F). Add the yeast and leave in a warm place until activity can be seen, usually within 15 minutes.
- The sediment from a bottle of some commercial stouts can be used to make a starter for stouts and brown ales. Similarly, the sediment from a bottle of some commercial bitter beers can be used to make a starter for bitter beer styles.
- Brewer's yeast ferments from the top and forms a very thick froth on the second and third days. This must be skimmed off each day and the beer thoroughly roused up to continue the fermentation.
- A liquid brewer's yeast is also available with kits. It ferments well and quickly without creating enormous heads which need to be skimmed. It settles out very firmly and all the beer can be removed from the sediment without disturbance or loss. It settles equally well in bottle after the priming fermentation. The beer can be poured to the last drop without disturbing it.

Champagne yeast

In addition, a Champagne yeast is sometimes added to a fermenting barley wine to ensure the maximum conversion of sugar to alcohol and to contribute to the development of a good flavour.

Saccharomyces carlsbergensis

- This yeast variety should be used for making lagers and can also be used for light and pale ales. It ferments from the bottom of the wort rather than from the top and so creates less froth on the surface.
- It can also function at low temperatures. Although this means that the fermentation may take six or eight weeks to complete, the bouquet and flavour is enhanced by the retention of volatile esters and aldehydes.

ADJUNCTS

These are used to provide additional alcohol and to enhance the flavour. The cereals also mop up some of the excess nitrogen in the malted grains.

Sugar

This is always used. Household granulated sugar (sucrose) is the least expensive and perfectly suitable. Try never to use more than will provide from one quarter to one third of the alcohol. Too much sugar makes the beer taste thin as it only produces alcohol which dilutes the water.

Barley

This is available as raw unmalted grain, raw grain roasted to the colour of a coffee bean, and as torrified barley – blown up like a popcorn.
Raw barley can be used in the brewing of bitter beers to sharpen their flavour.
Roasted barley imparts colour to a beer and adds its special flavour that makes a beer taste dryer than it really is.
Torrified barley imparts body to a beer as well as a little colour and flavour.

Wheat flakes

These make a useful addition to draught beers, imparting some body.

Flaked maize and flaked rice

These are widely used to add crispness to a beer, especially to pale ales, lagers and best bitters.

How much to use

All adjuncts should be used in moderation and should not amount to more than 25% of the weight of the pale malt or malt extract used. Of this 25%, 15% can be sugar and the remaining 10% grain adjuncts.

BEER INGREDIENTS SUMMARY

Malt
Barley grains that have been germinated and roasted } pale, crystal, chocolate, black } crush before use

Malt extract – toffee like; easy to use
Malt flour – pale or medium

Hops
Dried flower cones
Pellets
Golding/Challenger variety for bitter beers
Fuggle/Northdown variety for brown ales and stouts
Northern Brewer/Target variety for supplementary bitterness

Water
Hard water for bitters and barley wines
Soft water for brown ales, stouts and lagers
Boil chlorinated water before use.

Yeast
Brewer's years – top fermenting and fast, needs skimming and rousing
Lager yeast – slow fermenting from bottom in low temperatures
Liquid yeast – very clean fall out

Adjuncts
Sugar – the less used the better but always include some
Cereals – use some to mop up excess nitrogen
Unmalted barley – use in bitters for flavour
Roasted barley – enhances dry taste, colour and flavour; use in dry stouts
Torrified barley – adds colour and body; use in export ale
Wheat flakes – use 28 g (1 oz) to 1 gallon in draught beers
Flaked maize – adds crispness to best bitters
Flaked rice – adds crispness to pale ales and lagers

Principles of Brewing

ORIGINAL GRAVITY

A definition
- 'Original gravity' is short for 'original specific gravity', i.e. the specific gravity prior to fermentation. This is the factor that controls the alcohol content of the beer and determines the excise duty payable on commercially brewed beers.
- Home brewers do not have to pay excise duty and tend to make stronger beers than the commercial ones, usually because they make no attempt to control the original gravity.

How to calculate it
- The recommended original gravities of the different beer styles are given on pages 245–7. They may be calculated, at least approximately, by remembering that:

1 100 g **sugar** dissolved in **water** and made up to 1 litre produces a specific gravity of 1.037. Similarly, 1 lb **sugar** dissolved in **water** and made up to 1 gallon also produces a specific gravity of 1.037.

2 Malt extract consists of approximately 80% solids, most of which is fermentable sugar. We can therefore assume that 100 g malt extract in 1 litre of water, or 1 lb malt extract in 1 gallon of water, will produce a specific gravity of around 1.028 (approx 80% of 1.037).

3 Malt flour should be calculated in the same way as sugar.

- It follows that 1 lb malt extract (specific gravity of 28) and 8 oz sugar (specific gravity of 18, i.e. half of 1.037) dissolved in water and made up to 1 gallon would have a specific gravity of approximately 1.046 (28 + 18). Although this may only ferment down to around 1.006 because of the non-fermentable dextrins that are present in the malt, the alcohol content will be nearly 5%. This means that 1 pint of beer contains as much alcohol as $\frac{1}{2}$ pint of German wine!
- Other additives may increase the alcohol content even more, so the importance of sugar control, in particular, cannot be over-emphasized.

PRINCIPLES OF BREWING · 257

FERMENTATION

The correct temperature
● Brewer's yeast is a vigorous, fast-fermenting yeast that produces thick foam. It works fastest at a temperature of 24°C (75°F) but loses some esters and aldehydes in the tumultuous activity of the first few days. Better aroma and flavour can be produced by fermenting at 20°C (68°F).
● Once started, the fermentation rarely stops until all the fermentable sugar has been converted into alcohol and carbon dioxide.

Where to ferment
It is best to ferment the brew in a well-ventilated room because so much carbon dioxide is released into the atmosphere so quickly.

Method
1 Fermentation usually starts within a few hours, when the dried yeast granules are sprinkled on the surface of the wort, especially if they are fresh. As a wise precaution, however, it is best to activate the granules in a dilute malt solution, both to ensure that the yeast is alive and working and to achieve a faster start.

Skim off the froth during fermentation and rouse up the wort with a long-handled wooden spoon.

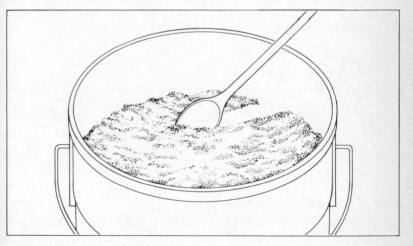

2 Once fermentation has started and a layer of carbon dioxide is resting on the wort, the brew will be protected from infection. Until then, however, the wort is at risk, even though it is covered, because spoilage organisms could be in the air beneath the cover.
3 On the second day the froth develops in uneven shapes and often contains dark green and brown particles. Skim off and discard it. At the same time wipe away the ring of pasty debris that collects on the bin just above the surface of the wort.
4 Then, thoroughly rouse up the wort to release entrained carbon dioxide and to admit some air to revitalize the yeast.
5 Repeat this process on the third day when the frothy head sometimes looks like a cauliflower.
6 Now leave the wort to finish fermenting. The whole period normally lasts from five to eight days.

RACKING

1 When fermentation has finished, move the beer to as cold a place as you can find, preferably on a concrete or tiled floor. This reduces the thermal currents and encourages the yeast cells and other debris to settle into a thick, creamy paste on the bottom of the container.
2 You can now siphon the clearing beer into bottles or a plastic cask, or into another container for priming. Better still, rack the beer into demijohns, fit airlocks and leave them in a cold place until the beer is bright – usually only a few more days. When the beer is bottled the deposit that forms from the priming fermentation will be much less and it will be much easier to pour the beer cleanly.

PRIMING

- This is the re-fermentation of the beer in bottles or cask. It imparts liveliness to a beer that would otherwise taste flat and dull.
- Use household sugar and take care to use sufficient to condition the beer adequately. Too much sugar creates a pressure that causes the beer to erupt in foam when the bottle is opened. Too little leaves the beer almost lifeless. 20 ml (4 tsp) per gallon produces a lively beer that is not too gassy.

How to add the sugar
The sugar may be added dry to the beer when it is in the bottle or cask or it may be dissolved in a little beer first and distributed evenly

between the bottles. More effectively, however, the sugar should be dissolved in a little beer and mixed into the bulk to ensure an even distribution in each bottle.

Beer in the cask
If the beer is casked, prime at the rate of 14 g ($\frac{1}{2}$ oz) per gallon. Never use more than a total of 56 g (2 oz) sugar per 22.5 litres (5 gallons).

Other methods
- Another method, which also aids head retention, is to withdraw about 5% of the wort before the yeast is added and to use this for priming. Leave the reserved wort well sealed in the refrigerator to keep it free from infection until it is required.
- Beer can also be primed with carbon dioxide at the moment of drawing off from a cask, but the result is never as satisfactory as from a secondary fermentation.

BOTTLING AND CASKING
Wash and sterilize beer bottles before use and fill them to within 3 cm ($1\frac{1}{4}$ in) of the top to allow space for the gas to collect.

Capping
1 Crimp crown caps on tightly with a capping tool.
2 After capping a bottle, shake gently and hold it close to your ear. If there is a hissing sound the seal is not perfect and should be renewed.

Casking
1 Casks, too, must be washed clean, sterilized and drained as dry as possible. Remember to rinse the cask well after using Chempro.
2 Fill the cask to within 5 cm (2 in) of the top and screw the cap down over the rubber washer as tightly as you possibly can to effect a gastight fit.

MATURATION
After priming, leave the beer in a warm place for four to five days while the sugar is fermented. Then store it in a cool place until it is ready for drinking. One week is the absolute minimum. A longer period is essential for better beers.

260 BREWING BEER

All the equipment needed for bottling and casking beer: a plastic beer keg and beer bottles, crown caps, crimping tool and labels.

Keys to success
- Use best-quality ingredients.
- Control the sugar content to the style of beer.
- Skim off and discard the froth and ring of pasty debris.
- Rouse up the wort thoroughly.
- Prime as recommended for best results.
- Always use proper beer bottles and gastight seals.

Brewing Problems: Causes and Cures

POOR FLAVOUR

This is almost certainly due to poor ingredients.

Water
This is the prime suspect.

Remedy: Boil all the water you require for the brew and leave it in a covered vessel to cool for topping up. Alternatively, change your water supply. Take an empty 22.5-litre (5-gallon) container to someone who makes good beer and fill it with water from his supply. Adjust the water as necessary with mineral salts.

Other ingredients
Malt extract deteriorates in a half-empty container; **malt flour** rapidly solidifies if not kept absolutely airtight, **malt grains** go slack if not equally well protected; **hops** become stale if not kept cool and away from light. **Yeast**, too, does not keep for ever and deteriorates with age.
- Poor-quality ingredients make poor beer. Use only fresh ingredients of the best quality available.

FLAT BEER

This can be due to inadequate priming or to inadequate sealing.

Remedy: Reprime and reseal and leave time for the beer to mature.

BEER GUSHES WHEN OPENED

This is due to bottling too soon and/or using too much sugar in the priming.

Remedy: Chill the beer hard, open the bottles, pour the beer into a sterilized bin, cover and leave to settle. When the beer is still and flat after stirring, re-bottle, prime and store for three weeks.

YEAST BITE

This is a bitterness that lingers in the mouth long after the beer has been swallowed. It can be caused by:
- using too much yeast and thereby creating a fermentation that is too vigorous.
- fermenting at too high a temperature.
- insufficient skimming and removal of the yeast ring.
- insufficient rousing.
- leaving the beer on its yeast too long after fermentation.

Remedy: There is no cure and if the bitterness is too severe then the beer should be discarded. Prevention is achieved by careful attention to brewing procedures.

LACK OF HEAD RETENTION

This is often caused by poor-quality malt or by inadequate maturation. Pouring the beer into a glass washed in a detergent and not subsequently rinsed in running cold water is another common cause. A wet glass, too, can have a similar effect. Oil or grease kills the head, and drinking beer with buttery or greasy lips can have a dramatic effect and cause the head to disappear.

Remedy: Heading agents are sometimes helpful but good ingredients and methods are the most effective prevention.

HAZY BEER

This is a rare ocurrence but one that can be caused by protein or yeast cells in suspension or by over-chilling.

Remedy: After boiling the wort and hops let it stand while the protein is being precipitated. You can add finings towards the end of fermentation if necessary.

WHITE SKIN ON THE SURFACE OF THE BEER

This is a wild spoilage yeast called *Candida mycoderma* that forms a powdery skin on the surface of the beer. It lives in the presence of air and will develop if a container has been inadequately sealed.

Remedy:
1 Gently slide some beer into the container so as to cause the minimum disturbance to the fungus. This should rise up with the level of the beer and be floated off.
2 Sulphite the beer at the rate of 100 parts per million (2 Campden tablets per gallon), seal and leave for two days.
3 Stir the beer well to release the sulphur dioxide, then prime and re-ferment with a little freshly activated yeast.

VINEGARY SMELL AND TASTE

This is due to infection by vinegar bacteria when the wort or beer was left uncovered.

Remedy: Convert to vinegar – see page 357 – or discard the beer and sterilize the container.

Kit Beers

Kits are an excellent way to begin brewing at home. Do begin with a 9-litre (16-pint) kit in the style of your choice. You may like the result so well that you decide to stay with kits and not progress onto specific recipes. They are undeniably easy and quick to make up. They require the minimum of equipment and take little time to prepare and mature. On the other hand, if you take a little more trouble you can make beers to suit your own palate more precisely.

DRY AND WET

- The first kit beers were produced in 'dry' form in the early 1950s. The ingredients, packed in a carton, consisted of: a plastic bag containing malt flour, a muslin bag containing hops and grains, and two small plastic bags containing yeast and finings.
- The home brewer had to provide sugar and water. Only two beer styles were then offered: bitter and stout.
- The 'dry' packs were very successful and still continue to sell well in an improved form, but they have now been largely superceded by the 'wet' kits which were developed in the late 1960s. These consist of a container of malt extract to which essential hop oils and essences have been added. They are marketed in a wider range of styles and have proved very successful. Again, all that has to be added is sugar and water.

Neither is perfect

- A common criticism of both kinds of kit is that too much sugar is required and the resultant brew tends to be on the thin side. Many manufacturers now suggest that you use rather less water than the amount recommended if you want a more full-bodied beer.
- There are a number of different brands from which to choose and, naturally, you will find the taste of some more appealing than others. It is worth making up small quantities of the same style from several brands so that you can compare one with another and choose the one you prefer. The kits come in varying sizes to brew from 4.5 to 22.5 litres (8 to 40 pints) at a time.

Kits for brewing beer. The dry kit contains a bag of hops and grains, a bag of malt flour, a sachet of beer yeast and a sachet of finings. The wet kit contains hopped malt extract and a sachet of yeast attached to the can. Full instructions are given on the labels. All that needs to be added is sugar and water.

MAKING UP THE DRY KIT

1 Put the bag of hops and grains into a large stewpan with about 2 litres (3½ pints) water and boil steadily for up to 1 hour.
The advantage of boiling the hops and grains in the muslin bag is that they can easily be lifted out when no longer required. There is also no problem with straining and getting rid of the individual hops and grains.
The disadvantage is that there is little opportunity for the hops to move about in the boiling water and the extraction of the essential oils and flavours is thereby diminished.

2 During the boiling process dissolve the malt flour and sugar in 1 litre (about 2 pints) warm water.

> **Quick tip**
> It is easier to dissolve the malt flour if it is first mixed with the granulated sugar. Otherwise it can form hard lumps that are quite difficult to dissolve.

3 When the boiling is finished, mix the hop and grain liquor into the malt and sugar syrup. Top up with cold water to the required quantity.
4 As soon as the wort is cool, sprinkle on the yeast. Fermentation soon starts and lasts from five to seven days.
5 Mix in the finings and, a day or two later, the beer will be ready for priming and bottling or casking.

MAKING UP A WET KIT

Directions for making up a wet kit vary slightly from one manufacturer to another but, in general, they are as follows:
1 Pour some hot water into a sterilized bin and stir in the malt extract.

> **Quick tip**
> The malt extract dissolves more easily if it is poured in slowly and the water is stirred briskly.

2 Wash out the container with some more warm water to ensure that no malt is wasted. Next, stir in the recommended quantity of sugar.
3 Some manufacturers recommend that the wort is now simmered for 5 minutes, others only that the wort is topped up with the required amount of water, covered and left to cool to 24°C (75°F).
4 Most manufacturers recommend that the yeast granules should now be sprinkled on the wort and the bin covered and left for five to seven days in the same even temperature. Liquid yeast cultures should first be activated in a dilute solution of malt syrup for 48 hours.
5 When fermentation is finished, rack the beer into bottles or a cask and prime, seal and store it for a week or two before drinking.

KIT BEERS · 267

Making beer from kits. Dry kit: **(1)** Boil the hops and grains. **(2)** Strain into a bin containing the dissolved malt flour and sugar.

Wet kit: **(3)** Empty the malt syrup into hot water, stirring all the time. **(4)** Add the sugar and stir until it is dissolved.

268 · BREWING BEER

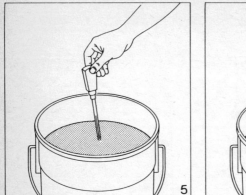
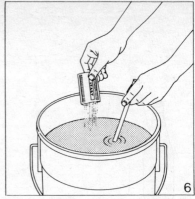

All beers: (5) Top up with cold water and check the temperature. (6) When the wort is 20–24°C (68–75°F) add the yeast.

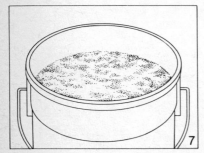
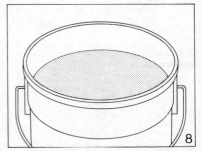

(7) Skim off the frothy yeast head and rouse up the wort. (8) When fermentation is completed, all the surface of the wort will be clear.

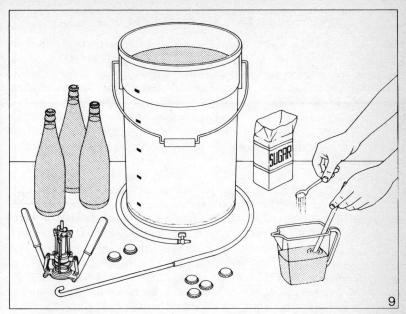

(9) Prime the beer by dissolving a little sugar in some beer and distributing it evenly between the bottles.

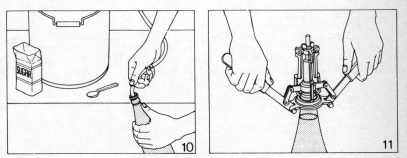

(10) Siphon the beer into bottles leaving some headroom. (11) Seal the bottles with crown caps.

ADDITIONAL HINTS AND TIPS

1 British beer yeast ferments on the surface, throwing up froth that contains solid particles of malt and hops. This should be skimmed off and the ring of dead yeast around the bin wiped off with a paper tissue. By getting rid of the dead yeast you will ensure that the beer is not contaminated by its decomposition.

2 The beer should also be roused up to admit some air to the wort so that the yeast cells can reproduce themselves and continue fermenting. Manufacturers rarely mention this so as to simplify the procedures.

3 Kit instructions also recommend fermenting at 24–25°C (75–77°F), a fairly high temperature, to avoid stuck ferments and ensure a speedy finish. Do be careful though, because too high a temperature can cause a bitterness that is unpleasant in the finished beer.

4 It is also worth increasing the recommended length of time the beer is allowed to mature. Whilst the beer is drinkable at the end of the seven-day period usually recommended by the manufacturer, it improves considerably if kept for much longer – four to six weeks for draught and three months or so for bottled beer. A good kit, properly made up, will produce a bottled beer that will keep for up to a year! This is particularly helpful if you like to keep a wide range of beer styles for drinking in different circumstances – especially if you enjoy an occasional glass of beer rather than a daily pint or two.

Malt Syrup Beers

Before kits were marketed, beer was brewed illegally at home. Small quantities were brewed from a jar of malt extract produced for medicinal purposes and sold by chemists along with other patent medicines. Hops could also be bought from chemists, for they were sometimes stuffed into pillows to induce sleep.

AN EARLY RECIPE

This is one of the earliest and best recipes for home-brewed beer.

>454 g (1 lb) malt extract
>28 g (1 oz) hops
>225 g (8 oz) sugar
>4.5 litres (8 pints) water
>Dried yeast

Dissolve the malt extract and sugar in 560 ml (1 pint) of warm water in a suitable container. Boil the hops in 1.1 litres (2 pints) of water for 15 minutes. Then strain the liquor onto the malt and sugar syrup.

Add a further 1.1 litres (2 pints) to the hops and boil again for 15 minutes. Strain the liquor onto the wort. Repeat this process once more. Then discard the hops.

Cover the wort and leave it until it has cooled to room temperature. Then measure the wort and make it up to about 4.8 litres (about $8\frac{1}{2}$ pints) with cold water. Sprinkle the yeast onto the wort.

The day after the fermentation starts, skim off the froth and rouse up the beer. Repeat this procedure the following day and then leave the beer for one week to finish fermenting and to begin clearing.

Siphon the beer into eight 1-pint beer bottles, prime with sugar at the rate of 2.5 ml ($\frac{1}{2}$ tsp) per pint, seal and store for three weeks.

This recipe gives a fairly strong bitter beer of good clarity, condition and flavour.

Variations

The same recipe can be followed today with variations to suit your palate.

- Malt extract can now be bought, the grain content of which has been adjusted to make it suitable for different beer styles. You can vary the basic recipe by changing the type of malt extract.
- The availability of better hops has improved and you can now choose between the different varieties. They are likely to be much fresher than those used when this recipe was formulated and a smaller quantity of hops – say three-quarters to two-thirds – may be sufficient. Choose the amount to suit your palate.
- The sugar quantity can be reduced or increased slightly or replaced with golden syrup. Alternatively, brown sugar may be used instead of white to darken the beer or black treacle (not more than 15 ml/1 tbsp).
- The malt and sugar mix can be boiled with all of the hops for 45 minutes and then strained or boiled with all but a handful of hops for 30 minutes and the remainder added for the last 15 minutes to enhance the hop flavour. Alternatively, the handful of dry hops can be added to the fermenting wort after the final skimming and left in until fermentation is finished.
- 15 ml (1 tbsp) flaked rice or maize, or a wheat biscuit can be boiled with the hops to vary the flavour.
- 15 ml (1 tbsp) raw, roasted or torrified barley can be boiled with the hops to impart colour and flavour.
- Crystal and chocolate malt can be boiled with the hops to make a brown ale and some black malt to make a stout.
- Lactose can be added to produce a slightly sweet ale or stout.

MILD ALE

900 g (2 lb) malt extract
11.25 litres (2½ gallons) medium water
25 g (1 oz) Fuggle hops
225 g (½ lb) brown sugar
Beer yeast
56 g (2 oz) priming sugar

Dissolve the malt extract in at least 2 litres (3½ pints) hot water and add the hops, pressing them down with a paddle until they are wet. Use up to twice the quantity of water if your pan permits.

Bring to the boil and simmer, covered, for 45 minutes. Leave to stand for 15 minutes, then strain out the hops. Stir the sugar into the liquor.

Make up to 11.25 litres (2½ gallons) with cold water, cover and leave to cool. Mix in the yeast, skim and stir on the second and third days, then leave to finish fermenting. Rack and prime as already directed.

This is a mild-flavoured malty beer that can be drunk by the pint if so desired.

DRAUGHT BITTER

1.8 kg (4 lb) malt extract
22.5 litres (5 gallons) medium water
56 g (2 oz) Golding hops
250 g (9 oz) crystal malt
125 g (4½ oz) flaked rice
25 g (1 oz) Fuggle hops
500 g (18 oz) brown sugar
Beer yeast
56 g (2 oz) priming sugar

Dissolve the malt extract in 4 litres (7 pints) hot water; mix in the Golding hops, crystal malt and flaked rice. Bring to the boil, and simmer gently, covered, for 40 minutes.

Add the Fuggle hops, wetting them thoroughly and continue to boil for a further 20 minutes. Leave to stand for 30 minutes and then strain out the solids. Rinse the solids with 2 litres (3½ pints) hot water and add this water to the container.

Stir in the sugar, top up with cold water, cover and leave to cool.

Mix in an activated yeast, skim and rouse. When fermentation has finished move the beer to a cold place for two days while the yeast settles.

Rack into a pressure keg, prime with 56 g (2 oz) sugar and mature for three weeks before drinking.

BEST BITTER

1.8 kg (4 lb) malt extract
18 litres (4 gallons) hard water
340 g (12 oz) crystal malt
125 g (4½ oz) flaked maize
125 g (4½ oz) roasted barley
85 g (3 oz) Challenger hops
14 g (½ oz) Target hops
500 g (18 oz) white sugar
Beer yeast

Dissolve the malt extract in 4 litres (7 pints) hot water; mix in the crystal malt, flaked maize, roasted barley and Challenger hops, wetting them thoroughly. Bring to the boil and maintain a good simmer, covered, for 45 minutes.

Add the Target hops, wetting them thoroughly. Continue to boil for a further 15 minutes and then remove from the heat and leave for 30 minutes while the solids and proteins settle.

Strain the liquor into a fermentation bin and stir in the sugar. Rinse the solids with hot water to release any maltose sticking to them and add this liquid to the bin. Top up with cold water and leave to cool, covered.

Remove 1 litre (1¾ pints) of wort and store it in a well-sealed bottle in the refrigerator.

Mix an activated yeast into the bin and ferment at around 19–20°C/66–8°F. Skim and rouse on the second and third days and then leave to finish.

Move the container to a cold place for two days, rack the beer into a fresh container and mix in the bottle of unfermented wort.

Siphon into bottles, seal and store for at least four weeks. This beer will continue to improve and will keep for many months.

LAGER

125 g (4½ oz) crystal malt
250 g (9 oz) flaked maize
42 g (1½ oz) Hallertau hops
9 litres (2 gallons) soft water
1 kg (2¼ lb) lager malt extract
250 g (9 oz) sugar
Carlsberg yeast
40 g (8 tsp) sugar for priming

Boil the crystal malt, flaked maize and Hallertau hops in 4 litres (7 pints) water for 30 minutes in a covered pan and then strain the liquor into a bin.

Stir in the malt extract and sugar and when it is dissolved top up with cold water. Cover and leave to cool.

Mix in an activated Carlsberg yeast and, as soon as fermentation starts, pour an equal quantity of the wort into two demijohns. Fit airlocks and move the jars to a cool place, about 10–12°C/50–54°F, until fermentation has finished and the lager is nearly clear. This takes between six and eight weeks.

Rack into bottles, prime with the sugar dissolved in some of the lager and distributed evenly between the bottles. Seal and store for three months.

BROWN ALE

908 g (2 lb) malt extract
9 litres (2 gallons) soft water
250 g (9 oz) crystal malt
70 g (2½ oz) chocolate malt
28 g (1 oz) Fuggle hops
100 g (3½ oz) dark brown sugar
Beer yeast
100 g (3½ oz) lactose
40 g (8 tsp) sugar for priming

Dissolve the malt extract in 2.8 litres (5 pints) hot water, add the crystal malt, chocolate malt and Fuggle hops, bring to the boil and simmer, covered, for 40 minutes. Leave for 20 minutes and then strain out the solids. Rinse them in 1 litre (1¾ pints) hot water and add this to the wort. Discard the solids. Then stir in the sugar.

Top up with cold water and when cool mix in an activated yeast.

Ferment, covered, at 20°C (68°F), skimming and rousing on the second and third days. Finish the fermentation, move the container to a cold place for two days, and then rack into a clean vessel.

Stir in the lactose and the priming sugar. When it is dissolved, bottle, seal and store for three weeks or more.

DRY STOUT

908 g (2 lb) malt extract
9 litres (2 gallons) soft water
250 g (9 oz) crystal malt
125 g (4½ oz) black malt
125 g (4½ oz) roasted barley
450 g (1½ oz) Northdown hops
500 g (18 oz) brown sugar
Stout yeast
40 g (8 tsp) sugar for priming

Dissolve the malt extract in 4 litres (7 pints) hot water, mix in the crystal malt, black malt, roasted barley and all but a handful of Northdown hops. Bring to the boil, cover the pan, and continue a steady rolling boil for 45 minutes. Remove from the heat and leave for 30 minutes.

Strain the liquor into a fermentation bin. Rinse the solids with hot water to remove any maltose and add the liquor to the bin. Stir in the sugar, top up with cold water and, when cool, mix in an activated yeast.

On the second and third days skim and rouse up the stout, then add the remaining hops, wetting them thoroughly.

Finish the fermentation and move the stout to a cold place to clear. Then bottle and prime with sugar at the rate of 5 ml (1 tsp) per 1.1 litres (2 pints).

Seal and store the stout for six weeks.

STRONG ALE

1.36 kg (3 lb) malt extract
9 litres (2 gallons) hard water
250 g (9 oz) brown sugar
28 g (1 oz) Challenger hops
250 g (9 oz) crystal malt
50 g (1¾ oz) roasted barley
Beer yeast
40 g (8 tsp) sugar for priming

Dissolve the malt extract in 2.27 litres (4 pints) hot water, bring to the boil, cover, and simmer for 5 minutes. Empty into a fermentation bin, stir in the sugar and cover.

Boil the hops, crystal malt and roasted barley in another 2.27 litres (4 pints) water in a covered pan for 1 hour, then strain the liquor into the bin.

Top up with cold water and when cool pitch an active yeast.

Ferment, skim, rouse and clear as usual, then rack into bottles and prime with sugar at the rate of 5 ml (1 tsp) per 1.1 litres (2 pints). Seal and store for three months.

This is a malty, mildly bitter strong beer that makes a splendid base for morello cherry ale.

Grain-mashed Beers

BLENDING THE GRAINS

- Good-quality grains, adjuncts and hops are now available from most home-brew shops. They can be bought in small and large quantities, crushed or otherwise. Unless you have suitable facilities for crushing them it is better to buy them ready to use.
- Every style of beer depends on a plentiful supply of maltose from pale malt to provide most of the alcohol. Crystal malt is added to supplement the pale malt, to enhance the malty flavour and to impart a little colour; chocolate and black malts add only colour and flavour to a brew.
- As a general guide, use 75% pale malt in all brews, varying the remaining 25% with other malts, adjuncts and sugar.
- The quality of the barley varies with the season, its variety and where it is grown. It is impossible, therefore, to be precise about the yield of maltose from a given quantity of pale malt.
- When formulating a recipe, however, you can assume that 454 g (1 lb) pale malt when properly mashed and sparged will yield a specific gravity of around 1.024 in 1 gallon of water.

MASHING THE GRIST

Mashing is steeping the mixture of grains and adjuncts in water at a specific and constant temperature for 2 or 3 hours so that the enzymes can convert the starch into maltose. To get the best maltose/dextrin extraction you must watch several points:

Temperature

- Mashing at a temperature of 65–68°C/150–154°F produces a wort containing more dextrins than one mashed at 60–63°C/140–145°F. At the lower temperature slightly more maltose is produced. The dextrins give body and a hint of sweetness to a beer.
- It is not easy to maintain an even temperature throughout the 2 or more hours of mashing. Wrapping the container in a blanket or similar material is often the best that can be done and most home brewers have to mash at a temperature that fluctuates between 64 and 67°C/147–153°F.

Liquidity
- The quantity of grains being mashed in the quantity of water is also significant. For example, a mash containing 2.25 kg (5 lb) grains per gallon produces less maltose than one containing 1.8 kg (4 lb) or less per gallon. But be careful not to go to the other extreme. If you use more than 1 gallon of water in the mashing and sparging of 680 g (1½ lb) grains, you will also extract unconverted starch and albuminous material.
- A good rule of thumb is to mash the grains in roughly three-quarters of the liquor and to sparge with the other quarter. For example, mash from 680 g to 1.36 kg (1½–3 lb) grains in 3.4 litres (6 pints) water and sparge with the other 1.1 litres (2 pints).

Time
- The length of the mashing is important too. After 1 hour, 4 parts maltose to 1 part dextrin are extracted. After 6 hours, 16 parts maltose to 1 part dextrin are extracted.
- The ratio affects the style of beer being brewed. Low temperature, high liquidity and long mashing produces the highest ratio of maltose to dextrin. In turn, this produces high alcohol and a thin beer.
- The art of brewing from grains is to balance the liquidity of the mash with the temperature and the length of the mashing to obtain the best maltose/dextrin ratio for the beer that pleases you most. In general, a mashing period of about 2 hours is sufficient.

End point
This is the moment when all the starch has been converted to maltose and dextrin. To check that it has been reached, remove 15–30 ml (1–2 tbsp) of the wort, place it in a white saucer and mix in 1 or 2 drops of household iodine. If the wort turns blue or darkens, then some starch remains and the mash should be left for a further 30 minutes before testing again.
- When no colour change is observed in a sample after the addition of iodine, mashing is completed.

Sparging
- The wort must now be run off and the grains sparged, i.e. rinsed in hot water (74–76°C/165–169°F) to remove the particles of sticky maltose and dextrin clinging to them. It is best to spray the water on to the grains but this is easier said than done in a confined space. In

practice it is sufficient to trickle a thin column of water over them, directing it from one area to another.

- If your mashing bin is not fitted with a fine-meshed drainer above a draw-off tap, suspend a calico sparging bag on a stand over a boiling pan and empty the mash into the bag. Start sparging immediately and continue until the allocated quantity of water has been used up. Use at least 1.1 litres per 1.8 kg grains (2 pints per 4 lb) but again, do not overdo it or you will wash out undesirable substances.

Boiling

1 Hops must now be added to the wort and thoroughly wetted. Their lightness and slightly oily nature enables them to float on the surface. Press them down and thoroughly wet them before boiling begins.

2 Cover the pan to increase the pressure and thus reduce the heat required, as well as minimize the odour – alas, not to everyone's liking! Close the kitchen door and open the window. A rolling boil is required so that the hops are constantly moved about in the wort to facilitate the extraction of the essential oils and flavours.

3 Some brewers include a little Irish moss with the hops to assist in the clarification of the wort prior to fermentation. This is not essential to produce a bright beer, however.

4 The boil should last from 45 to 60 minutes, other hops being added if you wish for the last 10 or 15 minutes. Then remove the pan from the heat and allow to stand for about 30 minutes. During this time the proteins will be precipitated and the hops will settle down on the bottom of the pan.

5 Pour off the wort through a fine-meshed strainer that will collect the hops, seeds and debris of the boil. Press the hops gently with the back of a wooden spoon to release any trapped wort.

6 Top up with cold water to the required amount, cover and leave to cool. Then pitch the yeast and continue as for any other beer.

GRAIN-MASHED BEERS · 283

Making grain-mashed beers: (1) Hops on the **vine**. (2) Sparging or rinsing the grains with hot water. (3) Boiling the hops which have been added to the wort.

PALE ALE

1 kg (2¼ lb) pale malt grains
100 g (3½ oz) torrified barley
100 g (3½ oz) flaked maize
9 litres (2 gallons) hard water
28 g (1 oz) Challenger hops
250 g (9 oz) glucose chips
Beer yeast

Mash the malt, barley and maize at 66.5°C (152°F) to end point in 3.4 litres (6 pints) hard water, then strain and sparge with a further 1.1 litres (2 pints).

Boil the wort with all but a handful of hops in a covered pan for 1 hour and then leave it to stand for 30 minutes.

Strain off the liquor into a fermentation bin, stir in the glucose chips, and top up with cold water. When cool, remove 420 ml (16 fl oz) of the wort for later priming. Store this wort in a corked bottle in the refrigerator.

Mix the yeast into the rest of the wort, skim, rouse and on the third day add the remaining hops, wetting them well.

Leave the fermentation to finish and then move the beer to a cold place to clear. Rack into sixteen 1-pint bottles, each containing 28 ml (1 fl oz) unfermented wort.

Seal and store for four weeks. Serve cool.

BEST BITTER

9 litres (2 gallons) hard water
1.36 kg (3 lb) pale malt
200 g (7 oz) crystal malt
100 g (3½ oz) flaked maize
28 g (1 oz) Challenger hops
7 g (¼ oz) Target hops
125 g (4½ oz) glucose chips
100 g (3½ oz) brown sugar
Beer yeast

Heat 3.4 litres (6 pints) hard water to 75°C (167°F) and stir in the crushed pale malt, crystal malt and flaked maize. Cover and maintain a temperature of 66.5°C (152°F) until end point.

Strain off the liquor into a large pan and slowly sparge the solids with 1.1 litres (2 pints) hot water at 75°C (167°F). Add this liquor to the pan.

Wet the Challenger hops into the wort and boil for 45 minutes with the pan covered, then wet in the Target hops for a further 15 minutes' boil.

Remove from the heat and leave for 30 minutes. Strain out into a fermentation bin and lightly press the hops. Stir the glucose chips and brown sugar into the wort, top up with cold water and, when cool, withdraw 420 ml (16 fl oz) of the wort for subsequent priming. Store in a corked bottle in the refrigerator.

Mix an activated yeast into the rest of the wort and ferment, skim and rouse in the usual way.

Move the beer to a cool place to clear, then rack into sixteen 1-pint bottles each containing 28 ml (1 fl oz) unfermented wort.

Seal and store for six weeks.

DRAUGHT BITTER

22.5 litres (5 gallons) hard water
2.7 kg (6 lb) pale malt
454 g (1 lb) crystal malt
85 g (3 oz) Golding hops
14 g ($\frac{1}{2}$ oz) Fuggle hops
454 g (1 lb) brown sugar
Beer yeast
56 g (2 oz) granulated sugar for priming

Heat 6.8 litres (1$\frac{1}{2}$ gallons) hard water to 75°C (167°F) and stir in the crushed pale malt and crystal malt. Cover and maintain a temperature of 65.5°C (150°F) to end point.

Strain out the liquor into a large pan and sparge the grains in 7 litres (4 pints) hot water (75°C/167°F). Add this liquor to the pan.

Cover the pan and boil the wort and Golding hops for 45 minutes, add the Fuggle hops and continue to boil for a further 15 minutes.

Stand for 30 minutes and then strain out the hops into a fermentation bin. Stir in the sugar, top up with cold water and, when cool, add the yeast.

Ferment, skim and rouse in the usual way, then clear and rack into a pressure cask.

Prime with the sugar, seal and leave for three weeks.

BROWN ALE

9 litres (2 gallons) soft water
908 g (2 lb) pale malt
250 g (9 oz) crystal malt
85 g (3 oz) chocolate malt
28 g (1 oz) Northdown hops
250 g (9 oz) brown sugar
Beer yeast
85 g (3 oz) lactose
40 g (8 tsp) granulated sugar

Heat 3.4 litres (6 pints) soft water to 75°C (167°F) in a large pan, stir in the crushed pale malt, crystal malt and chocolate malt; cover and maintain a temperature of 64.5°C (148°F) until end point.

Strain out the grains into a fermentation bin and sparge them with 1.1 litres (2 pints) soft hot water at 75°C (167°F).

Wet in the hops, cover the pan and boil for 45 minutes. Leave to stand for 30 minutes and then strain out the hops. Stir the sugar into the wort, top up with cold water and when cool add an activated yeast.

Ferment, skim, rouse and clear as usual. Then dissolve the lactose and granulated sugar in some of the brown ale and distribute this between the bottles. Siphon in the rest of the ale, seal and store for three to four weeks.

DRY STOUT

9 litres (2 gallons) soft water
1 kg (2¼ lb) pale malt
250 g (9 oz) crystal malt
125 g (4½ oz) black malt
100 g (3½ oz) roasted barley
100 g (3½ oz) flaked rice
42 g (1½ oz) Northdown hops
250 g (9 oz) brown sugar
Stout yeast

Heat 3.4 litres (6 pints) water to 70°C (158°F) in a large pan and stir in the crushed pale malt, crystal malt, black malt, roasted barley and flaked rice. Cover and maintain a temperature of 65°C (149°F) to end point.

Strain out the solids into another large pan and sparge with 1.1 litres (2 pints) soft water at 70°C (158°F). Add this liquor to the pan.

Add all but a handful of the hops and boil for 1 hour, covered, then leave for 30 minutes.

Strain into a fermentation bin, stir in the sugar, top up with cold water and withdraw 420 ml (16 fl oz) wort for subsequent priming. Store this in a corked bottle in the refrigerator.

Mix an activated stout yeast into the rest of the wort, then ferment, skim, rouse and clear as usual.

Pour the unfermented wort equally into sixteen 1-pint bottles, siphon in the rest of the stout, seal and store for six to eight weeks.

LAGER

9 litres (2 gallons) soft water
1.5 kg (3 lb 5 oz) lager malt grain or the palest you can find
28 g (1 oz) Hallertau hops
Carlsberg yeast

Only very soft water, preferably with a low salt content, is suitable for this beer.

Pour 3.4 litres (6 pints) cold water into a large pan and stir in the crushed lager malt grains. Heat the mash to 55°C (131°F), stirring steadily, and then maintain this temperature for 15 minutes by adjusting the heat as necessary.

Remove one third of the mash, place it in a second pan, bring it to the boil and simmer for 15 minutes, stirring from time to time.

Return the boiling mash to the main brew, stir it well and check the temperature. The combined mash should now stand for 1 hour at a constant temperature that does not exceed 65°C (149°F).

Repeat the removal of one third of the mash, bring it to the boil, simmer for 15 minutes and then return it to the main mash, stirring it well. Let it stand for 30 minutes and then check for end point. If it is not reached then let it stand for a further 30 minutes and check again.

When end point is reached, strain off the wort into another large pan and sparge the grains with 1.1 litre (2 pints) soft water heated to 82°C (180°F). Add this water to the pan.

Boil the wort and hops for 45 minutes and then strain out and discard the hops. Top up with cold water and when cool pitch in an activated Carlsberg yeast. Pour into demijohns, fit airlocks and ferment in the coolest place you can find that will maintain fermentation.

Rack, prime, seal and store for three months.

BARLEY WINE

9 litres (2 gallons) hard water
2.2 kg (5 lb) pale malt
500 g (18 oz) crystal malt
100 g (3½ oz) roasted barley
28 g (1½ oz) Challenger hops
400 g (14 oz) brown sugar
Ale yeast
1 lemon
Pinch of salt
40 g (8 tsp) sugar for priming

Heat 6.8 litres (1½ gallons) of water to 75°C (167°F) in a large pan and stir in the crushed pale malt, crystal malt and roasted barley. Cover and maintain 65.5°C (150°F) to end point.

Strain out the grains into a large pan and slowly sparge with 1.7 litres (3 pints) hot water (75°C/167°F). Add this liquor to the pan.

Wet in the hops, and boil for 1 hour, covered. Leave it to stand for 30 minutes and then strain out the hops. Stir the sugar into the wort, top up with cold water and cover. When cool, mix in the yeast, the expressed and strained juice of the lemon and salt. Ferment, skim, rouse well and clear.

Rack into ½-pint bottles and prime with 40 g (8 tsp) sugar dissolved in a little of the beer and distributed evenly between the bottles.

Seal and store for nine months.

BREWING SUMMARY

Grain-mashed beers

1. Mash between 63–68°C/145–154°F in 3.4 litres (6 pints) water per 1.36 kg (3 lb) grain for 2 hours plus.
2. Sparge with 1.1 litres (2 pints) hot water per 1.8 kg (4 lb) grain.
3. Boil the wort with hops for about 1 hour, then leave to stand for about 30 minutes.
4. Strain, top up, cover and cool to 20°C (68°F).
5. Yeast and ferment for five to eight days.
6. Skim and rouse on second and third days (dry hop if desired).
7. Clear and prime at the rate of 20 ml (4 tsp) sugar per gallon of beer.
8. Bottle or cask, seal and store.
9. Mature for three to four weeks or longer.
10. Serve cool at about 15°C (59°F).

Malt extract beers
Follow numbers 3–10.

Kit beers – dry
Follow numbers 3–10.

Kit beers – wet
Dissolve the syrup in hot water and boil if so required, then follow numbers 4–10.

Fruit and Other Beers

Before the hop finally became the definitive flavouring for beer, wild herbs, fruits and even vegetables were used. When commercial breweries took over the production of beer they used only the hop and these other beers were made occasionally by countryfolk.

With all the experimentation going on in home brewing these old beers are now being revived. I have described a few in the following pages.

ALE-BERRY

560 ml (1 pint) strong old ale
2.5 ml (½ tsp) ground ginger
6 crushed cloves
1 small piece of cinnamon
30 ml (2 tbsp) sugar
1–2 thick slices of wholemeal bread

The word 'berry' is derived from 'bre', an old word for broth.

Slowly warm the ale with the ground ginger, cloves, cinnamon and sugar. Stir gently to dissolve the sugar, then add the wholemeal bread cut into cubes.

When the temperature of the ale reaches 60°C (140°F), serve it in soup plates and consume at once. This is enough for two or three people.

BEETROOT STOUT

900 g (2 lb) freshly dug beetroot
454 g (1 lb) sugar
2.7 litres (4 pints) stout
20 g (4 tsp) sugar for priming

This beer derives from Bedfordshire and Lincolnshire. Gather the freshly dug beetroots in the autumn, top and tail them and scrub them clean from every trace of soil.

Cut them into thin rings and place them with the sugar in layers in a suitable bin. Cover and leave overnight. The next day pour on the stout.

Leave the brew to ferment to a finish under a close cover, giving it an occasional stir.

Strain the beer into bottles, prime in the usual way, seal and store for three months.

BRAGGET

560 ml (1 pint) strong ale or sweet stout
15 ml (1 tbsp) runny brown honey
4 crushed cloves
2.5 ml ($\frac{1}{2}$ tsp) ground ginger
2.5 ml ($\frac{1}{2}$ tsp) ground cinnamon

Made and drunk when Chaucer was writing his *Canterbury Tales*, this is a strong ale, flavoured with spices and sweetened with honey.

Mix together the ale or sweet stout, honey, cloves, ginger and ground cinnamon. Warm to 60°C (140°F) and serve at once.

Variation
You can vary the quantities of spices and honey to suit your taste.

COCK ALE

1 gallon basic malt extract beer (see pages 271–272)
Trimmings from 1 chicken
1 bottle white wine (see method)
20 g (4 tsp) sugar for priming

This very fine beer was once brewed in hostelries called the Cock Inn, the name being derived from the ale. The following version has been adapted and scaled down.

Make 1 gallon of the basic malt extract and hops beer as described on page 271.

After the second skimming, take the wingtips, parson's nose, carcase and scraps from the serving of a plainly roasted chicken, chop up and place them in a bowl. Cover them with white wine, such as apple or gooseberry, and leave overnight in the refrigerator.

Next day strain the wine into the fermenting wort and suspend the chicken bones and pieces in it, loosely tied in a muslin cloth.

Leave for three days, then remove and discard the chicken, finish the fermentation, rack, prime and seal in the usual way.

Mature this splendid beer for six weeks and serve in modest quantities.

ELDERBERRY ALE

454 g (1 lb) fat ripe black elderberries
2.27 litres (4 pints) water
454 g (1 lb) malt extract
Beer yeast
20 g (4 tsp) sugar for priming

Clean and wash the elderberries. Place them in a pan, pour on the water, bring to the boil and simmer, covered, for 20 minutes.

Strain the liquor into a fermentation bin and gently press the berries. Stir in the malt extract, top up to 4.8 litres/$8\frac{1}{2}$ pints with cold water, cover and leave to cool.

Mix in an activated yeast and ferment in the usual way. Rack, prime, bottle and store for three months or longer.

GINGER BEER

28 g (1 oz) root ginger
1 lemon
4 litres (7 pints) water
14 g (½ oz) cream of tartar
225 g (8 oz) white sugar
Beer yeast
Saccharin pellets

Crush the ginger with a mallet or steak hammer; thinly pare the lemon and cut up the parings. Pour on boiling water, mix in the cream of tartar and stir in the sugar until it has dissolved. Cover and leave to cool.

Mix in the expressed and strained juice of the lemon and an activated yeast, cover and leave in a warm place.

Next day remove the frothy scum and two days later strain into strong, screw-stoppered mineral water or beer bottles. Sweeten with saccharin – 2 pellets per 560 ml (1 pint). Seal and store for one week.

Chill well before serving.

Wise tip
Do not use more sugar than recommended, nor bottle any sooner. (This beer should contain little alcohol.)

MORELLO CHERRY ALE

454 g (1 lb) ripe morello cherries
454 g (1 lb) sugar
2.27 litres (4 pints) strong old ale

This is an old recipe from Kent, the Garden of England, where morello cherries are still grown in abundance.

Stalk, wash and pierce each cherry with the two sharp prongs of a pastry fork. Place them in a large sweet jar or similar container, sprinkle on the sugar, shake the jar so that each cherry is well covered, and then leave for 24 hours.

Pour the beer down the inside of the jar to make the minimum froth, then cover and leave to ferment out.

When the beer is clear, siphon into half-size wine bottles, cork and store for six months or more.

Serve in wine glasses at room temperature.

Variations
- The cherries can be served afterwards in a pastry case with cream.
- Ripe damsons may be used instead of morello cherries.

NETTLE BEER

908 g (2 lb) young nettle tops
4 litres (7 pints) hot water
454 g (1 lb) malt extract
Beer yeast
Sugar for priming

This is a modern version of a beer that was once widely made in the south of England.

Gather the tops of the nettle stalks only, place them in a preserving pan, pour on hot water and boil, covered, for 15 minutes or so.

Strain out the liquor into a fermentation bin and press the nettles. Stir the malt extract into the wort and when cool add an activated yeast. Leave to ferment, rack, bottle, prime and seal in the usual way. Then store for three weeks.

SPRUCE BEER

454 g (1 lb) malt extract
2 litres (3½ pints) hot water
5–10 (1–2 tsp) spruce essence
Beer yeast
20 g (4 tsp) sugar for priming

This beer was widely made in the north of England and Scotland from the tips of the spruce tree. Nowadays you can buy a spruce essence or extract from home-brew shops.

Dissolve the malt extract in the hot water, top up with cold to the 4.5-litres (1-gallon) mark, add the spruce essence and the activated yeast. Leave to ferment.

Rack, bottle, prime, seal and store for three weeks.

TREACLE ALE

454 g (1 lb) golden syrup
115 g (4 oz) black treacle
4 litres (7 pints) water
Beer yeast
2.5 ml (½ tsp) citric acid
2.5 ml (½ tsp) nutrient
20 g (4 tsp) sugar for priming

Dissolve the syrup and treacle in hot water, top up with cold water to 4.5 litres (1 gallon), and when cool add the yeast, acid, and nutrient.

Ferment, then rack, bottle, prime and seal in the usual way. Store for three weeks.

The black treacle imparts a bitter flavour and dark colour to the ale.

Serving Beer

TEMPERATURE

- People often disagree about the best temperature for serving beer. Americans, Australians and Continentals prefer their beer to be well chilled. British people on the whole prefer to drink their beers less cold. In many pubs beers are served at room temperature, but whether this is due to poor management or customer preference is open to question.
- At home you can serve your beer at the temperature you prefer. **Light beers** and **lagers** are generally better when lightly chilled, especially in warm weather. **Heavier beers** and **barley wines** may be served a little warmer but they are best at below room temperature, about 15°C (59°F).
- If the beer is too warm it will pour with a large amount of froth that quickly fills the glass. If it is cooled, it pours more evenly and the head will collect more slowly.

POURING

- Many beer yeasts do not settle as firmly as could be wished and it is better first to pour the beer from the bottle into a large jug, returning the bottle to the upright as the sediment reaches the neck of the bottle.
- Liquid yeasts settle much more firmly and every drop of beer can be poured from the bottle without disturbing the sediment when the beer is fully matured. With other yeasts, some beer is lost with the lees.
- When pouring beer from a bottle or drawing it off from a cask, always tilt the glass and run the beer down the side of the glass rather than directly into the bottom. This also reduces frothing and enables you to fill the glass with beer.

THE CORRECT GLASS

- A plain glass, incurved at the top, shows off beer well. The colour, clarity and condition can be seen easily and enjoyed. The pleasant aroma of the beer is also retained by the incurved bowl. Glass tankards have a handle and so save handling the bowl.
- Glazed earthenware, pewter and silver tankards are thought to

SERVING BEER · **299**

Assorted beer glasses and food, which makes a good accompaniment to beer.

keep the beer cool for longer but all the visual attraction is lost.
● Containers should be rinsed in clear cold water after washing, drained dry and then polished with a lint-free cloth. Store them mouth up to avoid stale air collecting in them.

COOKING WITH BEER

● Half a glass of stout enriches a beef casserole, steak pie or meat pudding. Sausages can be poached in beer. Stout or barley wine is an important ingredient in Christmas pudding or rich cake.

🍎 CIDERMAKING 🍎

The History of Cider

THE FIRST CIDER
- Cider was well known in Biblical days. The word cider comes from the Hebrew word *shekar* and there are several references to it in the Bible. The Romans made cider and called it *sicera*.
- It is unlikely that cider was made in England before the Roman invasion. However, apples had long been associated with the Druids who then moved westwards from the subsequent invaders of the east coast of England.
- Our first piece of recorded evidence of cidermaking is dated 1205 and comes from Norfolk, still famous as a cidermaking county.

A POPULAR DRINK
- During the Middle Ages cider became increasingly popular. Wine was, of course, imported, mainly from France, and increasingly so after the marriage of Henry II to Eleanor of Aquitaine in 1152.
- Cider, mead and ale were the alcoholic drinks of the countryman and his family and, of the three, cider was the most prestigious. The wild apple trees from which cider was originally made had been cultivated and the strain improved by stock selection, especially in the western counties of England.
- Cider was made by farmers in small quantities for their farm workers and surplus quantities from the larger farms would be taken for sale in the markets of nearby large towns.

THE GOLDEN AGE

- In a delightful book, *Vinetum Britannicum*, published in 1676, John Worlidge describes how:

    The cider made in Herefordshire, Gloucestershire and Worcestershire, being in great quantities carried to London and several other places of this Kingdom and sold at a very high rate, is valued over the wines of France, partly from its own excellency and partly from the deterioration of the French wines which suffer in exportation and adulteration that they receive from those who trade in them.

IN DECLINE

- Cider's very success, however, was partly the cause of its demise – it was taxed by the government to increase the state revenue.
- The other and perhaps major cause of its decline was the drift of population from the countryside to the towns at the time of the Industrial Revolution. No benevolent factory employers gave their workers free cider! Tea was the new drink with cheap gin drunk to help forget the exhaustion of a hard life and miserable living conditions.
- Consequently, the orchards growing the special mixture of sweet, sharp and bitter apples used to make cider were neglected. The trees grew old and were not replaced. Many were grubbed out and the land planted with other crops to feed the increasing population. For about 100 years cider was little made and little loved except by its devotees in the West Country.

A NEW START

- In about 1890 interest in cider reawakened. Companies built small cider-making factories, planted orchards and also encouraged farmers to do so. They bought in apples from a wide area, even from Normandy, and the businesses prospered.
- The years of the First and Second World Wars and the Great Depression between 1929 and 1933 caused momentary lulls. But the popularity of cider continued to increase, especially in the past 25 years. New varieties of cider-apple trees have been developed and present-day cider is better than it has ever been.

Using a Kit

THE KIT

- As soon as home winemakers and brewers started to take an interest in cider, the suppliers of concentrated grape juice and hopped malt extracts quickly produced concentrated cider apple juice and a true cider can now be made as easily as wine. There are now a number of brands from which to choose.
- As with wine and beer kits there are also several sizes, the two most popular making 9 and 18 litres (16 and 32 pints) respectively.
- Additional sugar is required to provide sufficient alcohol but dried yeast is usually supplied in a sachet with the kit.

Method

Follow the detailed instructions on how to make up the concentrate which are printed on the label. The main points are:

1 Sterilize all the equipment.
2 Dissolve the concentrate in cold water.
3 Wash out the container with hot water to ensure that no concentrate is wasted.
4 Dissolve sugar at the rate of 170 g (6 oz) per gallon in hot water and then mix it in before you make up the total must to the prescribed quantity with more cold water.
5 Mix in the yeast.
6 A fast fermentation is best and should be finished in seven or eight days, by which time the specific gravity should be down to 1.005.
7 Leave the cider for a day or two in a cool place to clear, siphon it into beer bottles and prime it at the rate of 2.5 ml ($\frac{1}{2}$ tsp) sugar per 560 ml (1 pint). Seal the bottles.

- The manufacturers do say that only a week or two is necessary for the priming sugar to ferment before the cider is ready for drinking. But they admit that it will improve if kept longer!

The result

Made according to the instructions the cider is lively but somewhat veiled with a slight haze. It is light in flavour and thin in body but clean and pleasant to drink, being not quite dry and with a hint of sweetness.

Variations

If you are interested in experimenting you can:
- Reduce the quantity of water recommended by at least 10% and up to 25%. This will strengthen the flavour and body of the cider.
- Adjust the sugar to make a must of specific gravity 1.050 and conduct the fermentation more slowly at a lower temperature.
- Mature the cider slightly longer. This is really essential to produce a cider worthy of the name.

Equipment and Hygiene

ESSENTIAL EQUIPMENT

The equipment available for crushing and pressing apples determines the quantity of cider that you can make. Depending on the juiciness of your apples, and your ability to crush and press them, you need some 10 kg (22½ lb) of fruit to make 5 litres (8¾ pints) of cider.

> ### A general tip
> With adequate equipment it is no more trouble to make 10 gallons of cider than it is to make 1. Furthermore, cider is a beverage that is consumed by the half pint, not by the wineglass. A single gallon of cider soon disappears.

Cider press
It is very difficult to make real cider without a press. There are several different sizes to choose from but the smallest is better than none at all.

Crusher
For more than 50 kg (1 hundredweight) of apples, a crusher is also necessary.
- Alternatives to the apple-cum-grape crusher are the slicer/shredder attachment to food processors. A stainless steel blade on a stainless steel shaft can be fitted into a powerful electric drill.

Fermentation bin
In addition you will need a fermentation vessel of suitable size. The 25-litre (5½-gallon) natural polythene bins with graduated quantity markings on one side and a fitting for a fermentation lock in the top or lid are best. A carrying handle makes this bin easy to move when full.

OTHER EQUIPMENT

Other pieces of equipment required are:
- a straining bag for the press
- a funnel
- a thermometer, hydrometer and trial jar
- storage jars. These will be required, together with bungs and labels, while the cider matures
- When the cider is ready for drinking, beer or mineral water bottles may be used, or a plastic beer keg or, for a still cider, a bag-in-the-box.

HYGIENE

As with winemaking and brewing, hygiene is of the utmost importance (see pages 10–12 for fuller instructions).
- Do clean and sterilize all vessels and pieces of equipment before use. Afterwards wash and dry them and put them away in a dry and airy place.
- Chempro SDP is ideal for cleaning and sterilizing. But wash it off with plenty of cold water afterwards.
- Sulphite is a safe sterilizer. Do not wash it off. Merely drain off or shake off the surplus moisture.
- Before crushing the apples wash them thoroughly in plenty of water containing sulphite at the rate of 50 parts per million. This reduces the number of micro-organisms on them and stuns the rest.
- Always wipe up any apple juice or cider spills at once with a cloth that has been dipped in a sulphite solution. The fewer opportunities for moulds, fungi and bacteria to grow, the safer it is to make cider.

Ingredients

THE MIXTURE

- The base ingredient of cider is, of course, apples. To make a well-balanced cider, however, you must have a mixture of apples – some sufficiently sweet to produce enough alcohol, some sufficiently acid to impart a sharp freshness and others sufficiently bitter to give firmness and character.
- A blend in the ratio of 4 sweet to 2 sharp and 1 bitter produces the best results. The sweet apples have some acid, of course, and the sour apples some bitterness, while the bitter apples have some sugar and some acid.
- It is equally important to use strongly flavoured apples; otherwise the cider will be lacking in appeal.

Cider apples

- True cider apples are not easy to come by in the relatively small quantities required by the home cidermaker. A visit to the West Country in October/November could be worth while. A drive around country lanes may lead you to a farmer who would let you pick up a few bags of mixed apples at a price just above what he could expect from one of the cidermaking companies.
- It is unlikely that you will be able to buy them at a country market and you are never likely to see them in a shop.

Other apples

Failing proper cider apples, seek out some of the following varieties which are available from farm shops and pick-your-own farms:

Sweet: Cox's Orange Pippin, Discovery, Egremont Russet, Ellison's Orange, Golden Delicious, James Grieve, Laxton's Fortune, Lord Lambourne, St Edmond's Russet, Spartan, Sunset and Worcester Pearmain.
Sharp: Bramley's Seedling, Golden Noble, Howgate Wonder, Lane's Prince Albert.
Bitter: Crab apples – Dartmouth, John Downie, Red Sentinel, Veitch's Scarlet.

CIDER CONCENTRATE

In winemaking some concentrated grape juice improves the wine made from country fruits. Similarly some concentrated cider apple juice improves the cider that can be made from other varieties of apples. Do remember to add some.

SULPHITE

- Sulphite is essential at the crushing stage to prevent oxidation. Some apples begin to turn brown the moment you cut them. Ideally, apples should be pressed immediately after crushing but since this is rarely possible do the best you can in the circumstances.
- Although some apples are notorious for oxidizing quickly, others are much slower to do so. It is worth testing each variety you have so that you can do all the 'safe' ones together and then all the 'difficult' ones.

PECTOLYTIC ENZYME

- Apples are fairly pectinous, so include a good measure of a pectic enzyme when the apples are crushed. This helps to extract the juice as well as to prevent haze.

SUGAR

- In a good season and with the right blend of apples you may well have sufficient sugar in the juice to produce a natural cider. In a poor season you may need some additional sugar.
- White granulated sugar is best. Use only sufficient to make the strength of cider you require (see page 310).

YEAST

- Professional cidermakers use *Saccharomyces uvarum* but a Champagne wine yeast also makes good cider. Make sure that it is well activated before adding it to the must.
- Include 3 mg of vitamin B_1 per gallon to help prevent the formation of hydrogen sulphide. It also enables the yeast to ferment out all the sugar in the must.

Making the Cider

PREPARING THE APPLES

1 First check that your apples are mellow enough. Real cider apples are usually left for two or three weeks in the long grass under the trees. During this period ripening finishes and the fruit begins to soften. The crushing and pressing are then easier and more effective.
2 Lay out your apples in trays, inspecting each one for bruising or maggot markings. Remove the imperfect apples and deal with them separately.
3 Cut away and discard bruised and maggoty parts.
4 Dip the remaining apple in a sulphite solution before crushing.

CRUSHING AND PRESSING

1 Whether you crush, thinly slice or mince the apples, prepare only as many as you can handle quickly at a time. Pressing 50 kg (110 lb) apples is quite an arduous task.
2 Wash them free from any grass, mud, bird droppings etc., then crush them in whatever way is most convenient. Crush just sufficient to fill a sterilized nylon or hessian straining bag that fits your press.
3 Arrange your equipment so that as you press, the juice runs into a narrow-necked container like a demijohn that can be filled fairly quickly.
4 Put a crushed Campden tablet or its equivalent and an adequate measure of pectic enzyme in the jar. As the juice runs into the jar it will be protected immediately from oxidation and infection.
5 A soon as the jar is full, bung it tight and leave it for 24 hours.

The second pressing

1 After the first pressing, release the pressure, remove the bag and

Opposite
Cidermaking: (**1**) Place the crushed, minced or thinly sliced apples in a nylon bag (**2**) and press dry (**3**). A larger press may also be used (**4**). It is essential to add 1 Campden tablet per gallon and pectic enzyme. Check the specific gravity with a hydrometer (**5**) and stir in sugar if required. This is best done in a polythene bin (**6**) with a plastic paddle or spoon.

MAKING THE CIDER

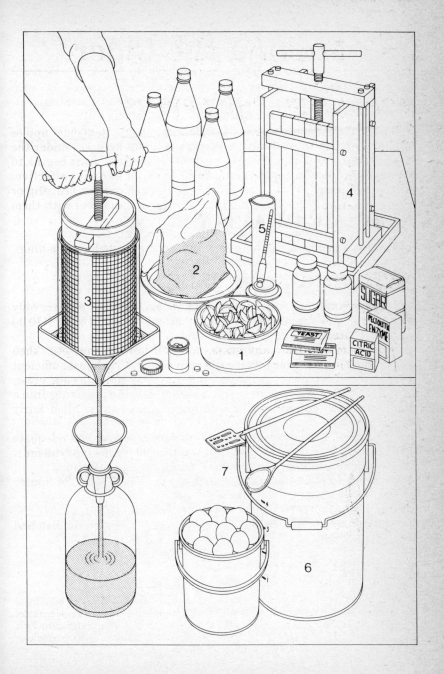

turn it upside down, replace the plate and resume pressure. More juice will flow.

2 When it stops, open the press again and turn the bag on its side for a further pressing, then on its other side for a fourth pressing. By this time the apple cake should be quite dry and easy to handle without breaking up. You can now discard it on the compost heap.

3 If you need a break, have one now before you crush the next batch of apples. When they are all finished, wash, dry and put away the crusher, press and bag.

4 Leave the juice in a warm place, 24°C (75°F), for 24 hours while the pectic enzyme acts.

SPECIFIC GRAVITY

- Siphon a sample of the juice into a trial jar containing a hydrometer. When the stability of the hydrometer is obtained, check the reading. A minimum of 1.046 is required but it can be up to 1.060.
- If the reading is lower than 1.046 stir in enough sugar to raise the next reading to about 1.050. This can be fermented out to a dry cider.
- You can safely stop fermentation at about 1.010 with potassium sorbate and sulphite, or with stabilizing tablets containing the same substances. At this point, however, get the original gravity right for the cider you wish to make.

ACIDITY

- It is also wise to check the acidity of the juice with an acid-testing paper. A pH of 4 is the ideal if you have graded papers. If you are using one coloured for low, normal and high, you need to be on the low side of normal.
- If the colour shows a clear 'low' add 2.5 ml ($\frac{1}{2}$ tsp) malic acid to each gallon of the must.
- If the colour shows 'high' add a similar quantity of potassium carbonate instead. This will cause some frothing but will reduce the acidity sufficiently.

FERMENTATION

- Now mix the activated yeast and vitamin B_1 into the juice. If possible combine the entire collection in one container and fit an airlock.

- The lower the temperature at which fermentation proceeds, the better the cider.

Commercially cider is either fermented in giant vats holding 315,000 litres (70,000 gallons) in the open air during the winter or in refrigerated containers under cover. The larger the container, the more heat is produced by the fermentation.

At home it might be possible to leave the fermentation in a garage or outhouse where it would be protected from frost but still have a low atmospheric temperature of around 10°C (50°F).

- Fermentation may take as long as ten weeks, the units of specific gravity decreasing by only 4 or 5 each week. When all movement stops, either naturally or artificially, the cider is ready for racking.

Key to success
- Make sure that your apples are really mellow.
- Only prepare as many apples as you can handle at a time.
- Check the specific gravity and acidity carefully.
- Ferment the cider at as low a temperature as possible.

Cellarcraft

RACKING
- The clearing cider must now be removed from the deposit of dead yeast cells, particles of apple pulp and other debris that have collected at the bottom of the vessel.
- Use a siphon and rack the cider in exactly the same way as for wine (see page 91). Don't forget to include sulphite at the rate of 50 parts per million to prevent oxidation and infection.

CLEARING
- Normally cider clears by itself. But if a haze persists you can fine or filter the cider. The problem is often suspended protein and a fining agent has been specially developed to precipitate these particles. But the haze could also be pectin. Check first for this by mixing 10 ml (2 tsp) cider into 30 ml (2 tbsp) methylated spirits. Shake them together vigorously and then leave for up to an hour.
- If dots or threads appear the cause is pectin. Stir in additional pectic enzyme and leave for a few days before racking a second time.

SWEETEN TO TASTE
Should all the sugar have been converted, leaving the cider with a taste that is too dry for your palate, you can add 4 or 5 saccharin pellets per gallon to remedy the situation.

MATURATION
After racking leave the cider in bulk for a few months to mature. It is usually ready for drinking in about six months.

BOTTLING
Depending on the quantity you have made, cider can be bottled in beer or mineral water bottles. Use crown caps or screw stoppers rather than corks; in this respect cider is more akin to beer than to wine.

- If the cider has only been lightly sulphited, it is possible that a partial malo-lactic fermentation will occur, creating a little gas as a by-product. The cider will then pour with a few bubbles that impart a pleasing freshness and tang.

DRAUGHT CIDER

- Alternatively, you can siphon the cider into a beer keg and carbonate it slightly so that it pours with rather more of a sparkle.
- A completely still cider may be siphoned into a bag-in-the-box for serving by the glassful. Only ever use still ciders – which are safe from further fermentation – in a bag-in-the-box. Any pressure from fermentation will cause the bag to blow up with disastrous results.

SPARKLING CIDER

- Sparkling cider can be made by the *méthode champenoise* as described for sparkling wine (see page 184). Few people think that it is worthwhile, however, and a carbonated cider is more commonly produced as described on page 188.
- Alternatively you can prime the cider in the same way as beer with granulated sugar (see page 258). The rate is 5 ml (1 tsp) per 1.1 litres (2 pints).

THE PLEASURES OF CIDER

The great interest in making wines and beers in the home includes cidermaking. At its best, cider is a most appealing and satisfying drink. Its pale golden hue, fragrant aroma, slightly sparkling freshness, cleanliness and cider flavour masks an alcohol content that is stronger than beer. It is best enjoyed in moderation and should be served cool.

Cidermaking Problems: Causes and Cures

Several problems can occur in cidermaking. The four most common are described below.

VINEGAR

- A faint vinegary smell and taste will develop if the fruit was not whole and sound and if sulphite was not used at the outset.
- Ripe and possibly bruised or damaged fruit lying uncovered attracts the fruit fly. This often carries the spoilage organism *Mycoderma aceti* on its feet. The wild yeast, *Hansenula*, or some member of the lacto-bacillus family may settle on the fruit. All produce acetic acid from the apple juice.
- Use only sound apples and wash them in a sulphite solution before crushing them to avoid the problem.
- Keep crushed fruit closely covered so that infection cannot occur before pressing.
- Finally, sulphite the juice and leave it sealed for 24 hours before adding an activated yeast.

Remedy: If the odour and flavour is too pronounced, the cider can be used in cooking or converted into vinegar (see page 357).

OXIDATION

- When apples are cut or crushed and allowed to turn brown they develop a particular and recognizable flat, dull taste. This taste can be carried through to the finished cider. It can also develop after the fermentation has finished, if the cider is left uncovered and exposed to the air.
- Oxidation is easier to prevent than cure. Use sulphite and protect the fruit from the air.
- Be careful not to use bruised fruit with brown patches, nor to leave crushed fruit uncovered. A sulphited cloth pressed close to the fruit is helpful here.

- Keep the finished cider well covered in containers that are full to the bung.

Remedy: It is sometimes possible to reduce this taint by a re-fermentation but not always. You can drink the cider as it is if the taint is not too bad, otherwise use it in cooking.

POOR FLAVOUR

- Even if the cider is clean and free from vinegarish or oxidized taints it may lack flavour. This is almost certainly due to the blend of apples used. Sufficient acid is essential to develop good bouquet and flavour. Strong-flavoured apples are also necessary.
- If you cannot get crab apples, use hard pears in their place. You could also add 5 ml (1 tsp) grape tannin per gallon.

Remedy: Commercial ciders are usually a blend of different ciders made from different batches of apples as they ripen between September and December. You could improve your cider by blending different batches together or by making up a cider kit and blending it with that.

FOUL ODOUR AND TASTE

- There is no excuse for this and no remedy. It is caused by leaving the finished cider on its lees. The dead yeasts decompose along with the particles of pulp and other debris. This problem can occur with all fermented beverages if they are not racked from the deposit of sediment at the end of fermentation.

OTHER FAULTS

- Cider can become infected like wine musts and develop mousiness and ropiness. Poor yeast can cause the bad-egg smell of hydrogen sulphide. These are rare occurrences, however, and you may never meet them.

A general hint
Cleanliness and care should avoid all cidermaking problems.

Serving Cider

- Cider looks best in a colourless glass with a fat, tulip-shaped bowl, incurved at the top and standing on a short leg. Guinness is often served in this shape glass to help retain its magnificent head. The shape also enables cider to hold its fragrant aroma and keep the occasional bubble of gas that imparts freshness to the taste.

TEMPERATURE

- The temperature at which to serve cider is a matter of personal taste. Since a good cider lies somewhere between a light ale and a white wine, it usually tastes best when served at about 10°C (50°F).
- Some people prefer their cider at room temperature, claiming that this emphasizes the flavour. If you appreciate cool beer you will probably prefer cool cider.

WITH FOOD

- Cider is not only a clean, flavoursome and refreshing drink on a warm day but also a splendid companion to meals which include ham or pork, such as ham salads and sandwiches and roast pork.
- Cider also drinks well with both cold and hot plainly roasted chicken and with grilled fish.

COOKING WITH CIDER

- Cider is good in marinades and in cooking. Joints of ham that are to be boiled or baked usually have to be soaked beforehand so you can add a cup of cider to the mixture. When boiling or baking, the liquid could be half cider and half water.
- Fish, such as whiting or haddock, can be marinated with cider and then baked in the liquor.
- Apples, prunes and plums can all be stewed in cider to enhance their flavour.
- Mild cheese, crusty bread and cider make a splendid snack at any time, but avoid strongly-flavoured cheese.

CIDER (1)

4.5 litres (1 gallon) water
Pectic enzyme and 4 Campden tablets
16.32 kg (36 lb) eating apples
8.16 kg (18 lb) cooking apples
4 kg (9 lb) crab apples or pears
1 kg (2¼ lb) cider concentrate
1 sachet Champagne wine yeast
6 mg (2 tablets) vitamin B_1

These ingredients produce about 18 litres (32 pints) of cider. No additional sugar should be necessary, but check the specific gravity before you mix in the yeast.

Dissolve the pectic enzyme and Campden tablets in the water in a plastic bin, and drop in about 9 kg (20 lb) apples as soon as they are crushed or sliced. Stir occasionally to make sure that the latest additions are mixed into the water.

Strain out the apples and press them dry. Collect the juice in a demijohn and seal it when full. Repeat the process twice more to deal with all the apples. Dissolve the cider concentrate in the water previously used for the apples and when dissolved, mix it with all the pressed juice. Seal and leave for 24 hours.

Next day check the specific gravity and acidity, although adjustments are unlikely to be necessary. Gently stir in the activated yeast and vitamin B_1 and ferment under an airlock in a cool place.

CIDER (2)

5.44 kg (12 lb) eating apples
2.75 kg (6 lb) cooking apples
1.36 kg (3 lb) crab apples or pears
Pectic enzyme and 1 Campden tablet
sugar if necessary
1 sachet Champagne wine yeast
3 mg (1 tablet) vitamin B_1

These ingredients produce about 4.5 litres (8 pints) of cider if made up as described on pages 308–12.

MEAD

The History of Mead

Mead is the product of the fermentation of honey after dilution in water.

THE FIRST MEAD

There is little doubt that early man would have found colonies of wild bees and tasted the thick honey oozing in their hives. A dry and empty gourd would have served as a container to take some back to his family. Some honey left in a gourd, rain, a day or two's delay and then a bubbling liquid was there to be tasted and enjoyed. Archaeologists believe that this could have happened as long as 12,000 years ago.
- As man's standard of living improved, corn and vines were planted and ways were found of colonizing bees. This honey was used for sweetening cakes as well as for making into a pleasing drink.
- The bee was domesticated several thousand years ago. Over the centuries new varieties have been bred that are more resistant to disease and, therefore, more reliable.

THE ANGLO-SAXONS

- The making and drinking of mead has always been popular. The Anglo-Saxons were especially fond of it and in the country mead was the superior drink for special occasions.

- It has been suggested that it was drunk every day by a new bride and bridegroom for the 28 days after their wedding – the four phases of the moon. The intention was, no doubt, to increase their fertility. The custom is thought to have been the origin of our modern word 'honeymoon'.

THE MONASTERIES

Mead was widely made and drunk in the pre-Reformation monasteries. Indeed, the monks did much to improve the standards of beekeeping. They used the wax for candles as well as for polish.

FLAVOURINGS

Mead was frequently flavoured with fruit juice, flowers or leaves and sometimes with herbs or spices. Many meadmakers had their own favourite recipe and in the seventeenth century recipe books were published and widely bought.

THE MAZER

- Mead was often served in a wooden beaker called a mazer. Sometimes a patterned wood like bird-eye maple would be used or the mazer would be embellished with silver. Large mazers with three handles were used as 'loving-cups' and were filled with mead and passed from one person to another to take a drink as a symbol of love and unity.
- In some monasteries and private homes people had their own mazers with their individual mark or initials engraved on them. Mead was a very precious part of the lifestyle of many people up to the end of the eighteenth century.

TODAY

- The break-up of monastic life and the coming of The Industrial Revolution ended the Golden Age of mead. But making mead never completely died out and enthusiasts still make it today.
- Most winemaking enthusiasts make mead, at least occasionally. It is also possible to buy mead that has been made commercially. Making mead is not really expensive because no sugar is required. Indeed, a bottle of home-made mead costs no more than a bottle of wine made from concentrated grape juice.

Honey

THE DIFFERENT FLAVOURS

The nectars that bees extract from different flowers make honeys with specific flavours that carry over to the mead. Honey can be bought from countries all round the world – Australia, Mexico, the USA, Canada, and Spain to name a few and, of course, from the UK. Honey from particular flowers, such as acacia, orange blossom, clover and leatherwood, can also be bought.

WHAT HONEY CONSISTS OF

The chemicals that actually make the flavour are present in trace quantities only. An analysis of honey reads something like this:
- water – about $17\frac{1}{2}\%$
- fructose – between 40 and 50%
- glucose – between 32 and 37%
- sucrose – about 2%.

The remaining $5\frac{1}{2}\%$ consists of salts of calcium, iron, maganese, phosphorus, potassium, sodium and sulphur; together with traces of citric, formic, malic and succinic acids; albumen, dextrin, enzymes, fats, gums, oils, pollen, protein, vitamins and waxes.

Specific gravity
The specific gravity of honey at 20°C (68°F) varies between 1.452 and 1.486, depending on the quantity of water present. It follows that 1 measure of honey should be diluted with at least 4 measures of water to reduce the specific gravity to around 1.090.

Sugar
One measure of honey is the equivalent of only three-quarters of the same measure of sugar, i.e. 1 kg honey is the equivalent of 750 g sugar, and 1 lb honey is the equivalent of 12 oz sugar.

Different types of honey
- Honey is usually available in two forms, brown and runny, or cream-coloured and set firm. Generally the brown honey has a

stronger flavour and is used for sweeter and stronger meads, while the cream-set honey is usually lighter in flavour and used for table meads.
● A strongly-flavoured dry mead is not acceptable to every palate and these are best finished with a sweet taste.

MEAD STYLES

Every mead style can be made from the different honeys – dry table, sweet table, dessert, sparkling and social.
● Orange blossom makes excellent dry table mead. It also can be used as an aperitif, as the subtle fragrance of the orange comes through into the mead.
● Clover makes splendid sweet and dessert meads.
● Any light, cream-set honey may be used to make a sparkling mead.
● The great range of melomels, cysers and pyments make fascinating social meads, while the metheglins make superb mulls for a cold night.

The melomels
These can be made from a mixture of mead and fruit juices – canned and cartoned fruit juices are particularly suitable. Flower melomels are also delightful, since all melomels should be served medium sweet, either as table or social meads.

Cyser
This is a mixture of mead and apple juice. It was a great favourite in days gone by when the range of available fruit was much more limited.

Pyment
This is a mixture of mead and grape juice. It was often made in the wine-producing countries. Before sugar was available to add to grape juice in poor seasons, honey was used instead. Pyment is only made as an interesting speciality today. Sometimes spices or herbs would be mixed with it, often for medicinal purposes. This was called hypocras after Hypocrates who is regarded as the founder of medicine.

Metheglin
This is a strong and well-flavoured mead in which a mixture of herbs or spices has been steeped during fermentation. A dry metheglin is an acquired taste but a sweet one can be a delight, especially if it is warmed to 60°C (140°F) and drunk when hot.

Other Ingredients

Honey contains very little acid or nitrogen, certainly not enough to produce a good fermentation to a level of alcohol that will keep the mead safe for any length of time. This is no doubt why, long ago fruits – with their acid and nitrogen – were so often added to the honey.

ACID

- Modern meadmakers, with their knowledge of the ingredients in honey and of wine technology, always add at least 14 g (½ oz) acid per gallon to their straight meads. Ideally, 20 g (¾ oz) should be added for the best results.
- Citric acid is most commonly used because it is the cheapest but tartaric acid probably confers a better flavour.

YEAST NUTRIENT

Include 5 ml (1 tsp) yeast nutrient if you wish to ferment sufficient sugar to produce 10–15% alcohol.

TANNIN

Mead benefits from some tannin so include 3 ml (between ½ and ¾ tsp) of grape tannin powder.

YEAST

Maury yeast: Honey can be fermented by any wine yeast, although the best results are produced by this yeast, named after a French village where especially good mead is produced.
Sauternes yeast: This is very suitable for making all the different meads.
Champagne wine yeast: This can also be used to make dry table mead from orange blossom honey.
Baker's yeast and brewer's yeast: These are not recommended. The baker's yeast causes foaming during fermentation with a consequent loss of bouquet and flavour, as well as alcohol. It is also

slow to settle and difficult to rack. Brewer's yeast often causes a bitterness to develop in the mead, possibly from its former association with hops. It also produces foaming.

PECTIC ENZYME

When making melomels, cysers and pyments, it is as necessary to include pectic enzyme as in the making of a fruit wine.

Equipment

The equipment used for winemaking can also be used for making mead (see pages 21–30 for further details).

You will need:
- a pan in which to dissolve the honey.
- a plastic or wooden spoon to help disperse the honey by gentle stirring.
- a fermentation jar.
- a funnel.
- a bored bung.
- an airlock.
- a siphon.
- a storage jar and bung.
- bottles, corks and labels.
- a thermometer and hydrometer with trial jar.
- a nylon strainer or straining bag – this will be necessary when melomels are made from fruits other than cartoned fruit juices.
- a small, wide-meshed nylon bag to hold the herbs and spices in suspension while the metheglins ferment.
- champagne bottles, hollow-domed plastic stoppers and wire cages if you are making sparkling mead.

Making Mead

PREPARING THE MUST

Bought honey

- Honey is usually sold in 454 g (1 lb) jars, although occasionally you can buy catering packs. Select your honey, bearing in mind the kind of mead that you would like to make. Normally three jars of honey are required for a dry mead and four for a sweet one.
- It was once common practice to boil the diluted honey for about 15 minutes. This not only sterilized the honey but also caused the coagulation of the waxes, gums and general debris into a scum that could be skimmed off. Some flavour and other volatile elements are, however, lost in the boiling, even if the pan is kept covered.
- Nowadays the honey is normally dissolved in hot water (60°C/140°F). This kills most of the micro-organisms present and dissolves the waxes and gums which precipitate with other particles after fermentation.

1 To make a gallon of mead you will need about 4 litres (7 pints) water. Pour about two-thirds of this quantity, approx 2.8 litres (5 pints) hot water into a polythene bin, remove the lids from the jars and empty the honey into the hot water, stirring gently to prevent the honey collecting in one place and sticking tight to the bottom. Rinse out the jars with hot water once or twice so that none is wasted.
2 Stir in the acid and tannin, cover the bin and leave the must to cool to about 24°C (75°F).
3 If you are making the melomel with a canned or cartoned fruit juice, use less water equivalent to the quantity of juice. Add the juice and pectic enzyme when the must is cool. Fresh white fruits should also not be added until the must is cool. The same applies to cyser and pyment.
4 Mix in black fruits, jams and flowers, however, while the honey solution is still hot. This helps to extract the colour from the black fruit, the fragrance from the flowers and to dissolve the jam.

From the comb

- Only beekeepers are likely to have access to honeycombs. After the

326 · MEAD

The ingredients for making different meads: (1) honeycomb; (2) honey; (3) grapes to make pyment; (4) apples to make cyser; (5) oranges, blackberries or other fruits to make melomel; (6) nylon bag of herbs or spices to make metheglin.

honey has been strained out, a fair amount still remains stuck to the frame. You can wash this off in hot water and then strain it clear from particles of bees and other debris. It will contain more wax and gum than the free-run honey, so simmer it gently and skim it.
• After cooling to 60°C (140°F) check the specific gravity and make it up to 1.090 with honey. Don't forget to make the temperature allowance indicated on the table on page 76.
• The must can now be used as described for bought honey.

FERMENTATION

1 When the prepared honey solution is cool enough, remove the cover and pour it into a demijohn. Mix in the yeast, top up with cold boiled water and fit an airlock.
2 Remember to activate the wine yeast before adding it to the must. You must include a full measure of nutrient, especially if you are making a straight mead or metheglin, rather than a melomel, cyser or pyment. The yeast would also benefit from the addition of one 3 mg Benerva tablet (vitamin B_1) if you are making a high-alcohol mead.
3 Even with the inclusion of sufficient nutrient, wine yeasts ferment honey more slowly than other musts. It is likely to take three months rather than three weeks, especially if you ferment in an atmospheric temperature around 15–17°C (59–63°F). This produces a better flavoured mead than one fermented at 24 or 25°C (75–77°F). As soon as fermentation is vigorous, move the jar to a cooler place if you can.
4 If you are making a melomel, cyser or pyment, you will need to ferment the fresh fruits on the pulp for four or five days. Keep the vessel covered and press down the fruit cap twice each day.
5 Strain out the fruit, press it dry, pour the must into a demijohn, top up and fit an airlock.

Stuck fermentation

A steady, even temperature is more important when fermenting a mead must than any other. Stuck fermentations are fairly common and are often difficult, although never impossible, to re-start. Fortunately most mead musts ferment out with no difficulty.

RACKING AND STORAGE

When fermentation is finished the mead will clear quickly, especially if it is left in a cold place for a few days. It should now be racked into a storage jar, topped up, sulphited at the rate of 50 parts per million (1 Campden tablet per gallon) to protect it from oxidation and infection, and then put away in a cool place.

Light meads: These mature more quickly than strong and heavy meads. I have drunk excellent mead that was only six weeks old, yet others have taken almost as many years to mature.

Sherry-style meads: Matured in jars not quite full and closed with a cotton wool plug, these take five years to develop a good sherry flavour and lose their honey aroma and flavour.

Bottling
It would be reasonable to mature every mead for at least a year before bottling and then to use a mixture of different-sized bottles. Drink the smallest at six-monthly intervals until you judge the mead to be fully mature. Even so, it may be that the last bottle is the best.

Keys to success
- Select your honey according to the type of mead you would like.
- Always add acid and nutrient to straight meads and pectic enzyme as well to melomels, cysers and pyments.
- Add white fruits to a cool must, black fruits to a hot one.
- Ferment at a steady, even temperature.

DRY MEAD

1.36 kg (3 lb) orange blossom honey
15 ml (3 tsp) tartaric acid
2.5 ml ($\frac{1}{2}$ tsp) tannin
5 ml (1 tsp) nutrient
4 litres (7 pints) hot water
Sauternes wine yeast
1 Campden tablet

Dissolve the honey, acid, tannin and nutrient in the hot water, 65°C (149°F), pour it into a demijohn and when cool add the activated yeast. Fit an airlock and ferment out in a temperature of 18°C (64°F).

Rack into a storage jar, add 1 Campden tablet, top up and store until bright, then rack again.

Keep for one year. Serve as a light table wine.

SWEET MEAD

1.8 kg (4 lb) acacia honey
20 ml (4 tsp) tartaric acid
4 ml ($\frac{3}{4}$ tsp) tannin
5 ml (1 tsp) nutrient
3.6 litres (6$\frac{1}{2}$ pints) hot water
Sauternes wine yeast
1 Campden tablet

Make as described for dry mead but finish this mead sweet.

Variation
Other honeys may be used as available. The different honeys bestow different flavours on the meads made from them.

SPARKLING MEAD

1.25 kg (2¾ lb) cream-set honey
20 ml (4 tsp) tartaric acid
2.5 ml (½ tsp) tannin
5 ml (1 tsp) nutrient
4 litres (7 pints) hot water
Champagne wine yeast
1 Campden tablet
70 g (2½ oz) priming sugar
Champagne wine yeast

Make the mead as already described on page 329 and mature for at least six months.

Dissolve the priming sugar in some of the mead and empty this into a clean demijohn. Siphon in the maturing mead and mix in an activated Champagne yeast. Fit an airlock, leave the mead in a warm place for a few hours where you can keep an eye on it.

Prepare six champagne bottles, hollow-domed, plastic stoppers and wire cages. As soon as the mead is fermenting, pour it into the bottles. Fit the stoppers, wire them on and lay the bottles on their sides in a warm place for one week.

Label the bottles with the date the mead was made and the date it was sparkled. Then store the bottles on their sides for at least another six months. Disgorge the sediment as described on page 186.

OTHER MEADS

CYSER

1.36 kg (3 lb) cream-set honey
3 litres (5¼ pints) hot water
15 ml (3 tsp) tartaric acid
2.5 ml (½ tsp) tannin
5 ml (1 tsp) nutrient
1 litre (1¾ pints) apple juice
Sauternes wine yeast
1 Campden tablet

Dissolve the honey, acid, tannin and nutrient in the hot water, 65°C (149°F) and when cool, mix in the apple juice and activated yeast. Pour into a demijohn, fit an airlock and ferment out. Rack into a storage jar, add the Campden tablet, top up, seal and store for one year.
  Sweeten to taste before serving if so required.

Variation
Other cysers can be made by replacing part or all of the sugar in an apple wine recipe with honey. Remember that 1 kg honey is the equivalent of only 750 g sugar (1 lb honey is the equivalent of 12 oz sugar).

MELOMEL (1)

1.8 kg (4 lb) liquid honey
10 ml (2 tsp) tartaric acid
2.5 ml ($\frac{1}{2}$ tsp) tannin
5 ml (1 tsp) nutrient
3 litres (5$\frac{1}{4}$ pints) hot water
1 litre (1$\frac{3}{4}$ pints) orange juice
Sauternes wine yeast
1 Campden tablet

Make as described for cyser but finish this stronger mead fairly sweet.

MELOMEL (2)

1.3 kg (3 lb) liquid honey
454 g (1 lb) redcurrant jelly
3.6 litres (6$\frac{1}{2}$ pints) hot water
5 ml (1 tsp) pectic enzyme
10 ml (2 tsp) tartaric acid
5 ml (1 tsp) nutrient
2.5 ml ($\frac{1}{2}$ tsp) tannin
Sauternes wine yeast

Dissolve the honey and redcurrant jelly in the hot water, 65°C (149°F). When cool enough, 24°C (75°F), mix in a measure of pectic enzyme, the acid, nutrient, tannin and yeast. Pour the must into a demijohn and fit an airlock.

When fermentation is active, move the melomel to a cooler position (18°C/64°F). Finish this quite strong melomel medium-sweet.

Variation
Other jams may be used in the same way but don't forget the pectic enzyme.

PYMENT (1)

1 kg (2¼ lb) concentrated grape juice, red, white or rosé
454 g (1 lb) liquid honey
approx 3.4 litres (6 pints) water
Maury mead yeast and 1 Campden tablet

Make up the concentrated grape juice following the instructions but instead of adding sugar, mix in the honey. To be on the safe side, sterilize the honey by loosening the lid, without removing it, and standing the jar in a saucepan of water. Bring to the boil and simmer for 20 minutes. Fasten the lid until the honey is required.

PYMENT (2)

9 kg (20 lb) home-grown grapes, red or white
Pectic enzyme and 2 Campden tablets
approx 454 g (1 lb) liquid honey
Sauternes wine yeast

Stalk, wash and crush the grapes, add the pectic enzyme and 1 crushed Campden tablet, cover and leave for 24 hours in a warm place.

Remove a sample of pulp and juice and press out sufficient to take a hydrometer reading. Calculate how much honey you will need to raise the reading to 1.090 (454 g/1 lb honey will raise it by about 30 units).

For white wine strain out the skins and pips and press them dry. Mix in the honey and the activated yeast, pour the must into a demijohn, fit an airlock and ferment out.

For red wine mix in the honey and activated yeast and ferment-on-the-pulp for ten days. Keep the bin covered and press down the floating skins twice each day. Strain out and press the pulp, pour the pyment into a demijohn and finish the fermentation.

Quick tips
- Wine made from home-grown grapes sometimes lacks flavour, especially if the end of September and first half of October have not been warm and dry. The addition of the honey not only adds essential sugar but also improves the flavour.
- Serve these pyments dry or medium sweet to suit your taste.

HYPOCRAS

This is a spiced pyment. Make up either of the pyment recipes as far as fermentation and suspend a muslin bag of spices in the fermentation. A suitable mixture can sometimes be bought from specialist homebrew shops but it can be made up as follows or to suit your own taste:

1 large piece of crushed root ginger
1 lemon or orange, thinly pared, rind only
12 cloves
1 small stick of cinnamon

(Rosemary leaves, coriander, aniseed, mace and juniper berries are alternatives.)

Suspend the bag in the fermentation for about four days. Alternatively, suspend the bag in the hot honey solution while it cools.

Another way is to suspend the spices in the finished pyment (tasting it every few days) until the flavour is to your liking.

> **Quick tips**
> Hypocras often tastes better sweet rather than dry. It also makes a fine mull.

METHEGLIN

This is a spiced mead and any of the spices and herbs mentioned for hypocras may be used. Although you may enjoy a dry metheglin, it is probable that you will enjoy a very sweet metheglin even better.

Make up a sweet mead with any honey and add the sachet of spices or herbs. Washings of the honeycomb are excellent for metheglins since the subtle flavourings of the prepared honeys are overwhelmed by the spices or herbs.

Metheglin also makes a superb mull. You can often buy spices for a mull that can be added to a sweet and strong mead during the heating to 60°C (140°F).

HONEY BEER

14 g (½ oz) Golding-type hops
4.5 litres (1 gallon) water
454 g (1 lb) liquid honey
5 ml (1 tsp) nutrient
Carlsberg lager yeast

Boil the hops and water in a covered pan for 15 minutes, leave for a further 15 minutes to cool, then strain into a bin and mix in the honey and nutrient.

When cool, add the activated yeast and stir well to admit some air. Pour the wort into a demijohn, fit an airlock and ferment out.

Stand the jar in a cold place for a few days to clear, then siphon into eight 1-pint beer bottles, leaving an air space of 5 cm (2 in). Add 5 ml (1 tsp) liquid honey to each, seal and store for three weeks. Serve this old and once very popular beer cold but not chilled.

Quick tips
It is important to use the bottom-fermenting Carlsberg yeast. Ordinary beer yeast is not recommended because it makes too much froth during the fermentation. If a Carlsberg yeast cannot be obtained, use a Champagne wine yeast.

Serving Mead

TEMPERATURE

Like white wines, meads need to be served cold, 9–10°C (48–50°F). Red melomels and red pyments, because of the tannin in the fruit, are best served at 18–20°C (64–68°F). Hypocras and metheglins should be served at this temperature too, but taste even better hot, 60°C (140°F).

WITH FOOD

Table meads, cysers, pyments and **melomels**, make excellent companions to roast chicken, chicken in cream sauce, pork and ham.
Dry red pyments may be served with casseroles, goulash and similar well-flavoured dishes but are less attractive with plain roast beef or lamb.
Sweet meads may be served with the dessert course of a meal.
Dessert meads that are strong and sweet are best served after meals.
Hypocras and **metheglins** are also best served on their own or with spiced ginger cake or rich fruit cake.
- The strong honey flavour of all meads tends to overwhelm the more delicate flavour of most fish dishes. Grilled mackerel and herring are, perhaps, the exceptions.
- As with wine, serving mead is partly a matter of taste and there are some very interesting experiments to be made with different dishes. You may eventually decide, however, that you prefer all your meads between dry and medium sweet and served on their own so that you can enjoy their flavour to the full.

LIQUEURS

Commercial or home-made?

LIQUEURS – PAST AND PRESENT

- A liqueur is defined as a strong alcoholic liquor sweetened and flavoured with aromatic substances. It is usually drunk in small quantities after a meal.
- Liqueurs have been made and drunk for several centuries. The somewhat rough spirit at first produced by heating wine and collecting the vapour that came off was often ameliorated with sugar, fruits, herbs and spices to make it more palatable.
- The ever-increasing price of liqueurs is causing more people to make their own. It must be appreciated, even so, that making liqueurs at home is more expensive than making wine.

COMMERCIAL PRODUCTION

Three methods of production are employed commercially:

Distillation: Fruit wine, such as apple, is distilled to make Calvados. Similarly, plum wine is distilled to make Slivovitz.

Infusion: Fruits, herbs and spices are infused, i.e. steeped, in a spirit for seven–fourteen days to extract the aromatic substances. An example is Apricot Brandy. Some of the herb and spice liqueurs made in this way are then distilled to concentrate the flavours.

Essence: Sweetened spirit is flavoured with the essential aromatic oils of various fruits, herbs and spices.

AT HOME

- Since it is *totally illegal to distil spirits in any way in the home*, home liqueur-makers are left with the second and third methods – infusion and essence.
- Many commercial liqueurs are both less strong and sweeter than might at first be imagined and the following short list of the more popular liqueurs is interesting to consider:

	Alcohol	Approx Specific Gravity
Anisette	25%	1.150
Apricot Brandy	28%	1.070
Cherry Brandy	24%	1.090
Chocolate Mint	27%	1.140
Crême de Menthe	28%	1.110
Framboise	29%	1.080
Peach Brandy	24%	1.070

The strong liqueurs are the most expensive to make. They include:

	Alcohol	Approx Specific Gravity
Benedictine	40%	1.060
Cointreau	40%	1.040
Curaçao	40%	1.070
Drambuie	40%	1.080
Grand Marnier	38%	1.040
Green Chartreuse	54%	1.000
Mandarin	40%	1.050
Yellow Chartreuse	40%	1.090

PERSONAL TASTE

- How closely you want to match your liqueurs with the commercial equivalents depends on your knowledge and enjoyment of commercial liqueurs and how much money and effort you are willing to spend on them.
- The more dedicated can produce 'make alike' liqueurs at home, and more specialized books than this one will explain how to do so.

Equipment and Hygiene

EQUIPMENT

Very little equipment is needed to make liqueurs at home. You will need:
- a large jug for mixing ingredients.
- a plastic spoon for stirring.
- a plastic funnel to guide the liquid into bottles.
- some 1.1-litre (quart-size) storage or Kilner jars for infusing fruit.
- a fine-meshed straining bag for removing the fruit.
- a measuring jug to ensure the correct quantity of spirit and/or wine is used.
- a pair of kitchen scales for weighing sugar and fruit.
- some bottles, corks and labels.

HYGIENE

Hygiene is of course essential and everything coming into contact with the liqueur should be clean and sterile (see pages 10–12 for fuller instructions).

Ingredients

THE SPIRITS

- Most spirits are labelled as so many degrees proof or as percentage alcohol by volume. To convert the proof figure into a percentage, divide by 7 and multiply by 4: thus 70° proof becomes 40° alcohol.
- The spirit is the most expensive ingredient. It is therefore important to use the most suitable and least expensive spirit in the smallest quantities.

Vodka/Polish spirit: The most widely used is vodka at 65.5° proof or Polish spirit at 140° proof, because they are tasteless and colourless, and can be used for every liqueur.

Gin: At 70° proof gin may be used with a number of fruits, especially damsons, oranges and sloes.

White rum: At 70° proof, this is sometimes used with blackcurrants.

'Eau de vie pour les fruits': This French spirit, 40° alcohol, is particularly good for making fruit brandies – notably apricot, cherry and peach.

SUGAR

Most liqueurs are very sweet and have a high specific gravity.

Granulated white sugar is the least expensive of the sugars and the most suitable to use but is a bit slow to dissolve.

Caster sugar, at almost twice the price, may be used instead, or the granulated sugar could be ground more finely if you are impatient to get on.

Sugar syrup is not recommended because it contains water that dilutes the spirit.

Specific gravity

- **Alcohol dilutes water**, consequently additional sugar is required in the liqueur to allow for this. The stronger the spirit used, the more sugar is required. Indeed for every percentage point of alcohol in the finished liqueur, you need approximately an extra 4 g (just under 1 tsp) sugar.

The ingredients for liqueur making.

- **Sugar occupies volume** and is therefore also a dilutant in the dry form: 80 g sugar occupies 50 ml (8 oz sugar occupies 5 fl oz of volume) and *pro rata* each does so in the ratio of 8 to 5.
- In 1 litre (1¾ pints) water the sugar equivalent of specific gravity is as follows:

50 g	=	1.020	200 g	=	1.080
100 g	=	1.040	250 g	=	1.100
150 g	=	1.060			

WINE

- When making the weaker liqueurs with essences, a strong, bland wine is sometimes used to minimize the quantity of spirit required. A white wine is best for all but the red liqueurs.
- You can make this from a plain white concentrated grape juice fermented to a maximum alcohol content with repeated small doses of

sugar. If you use a Tokay yeast and some additional nutrient and vitamin B_1, as much as 15 or even 16% alcohol can be produced.

GLYCERINE

- All liqueurs taste rich and silky as well as sweet, strong and highly flavoured. This richness can be obtained by the addition of from 10 to 25 ml (2–5 tsp) glycerine per litre bottle.
- Use only glycerine of BP quality (*never* use industrial glycerine) and add the smaller quantity at first. Taste and then mix in a further dose until you are satisfied with the result.

THE FRUITS TO USE

- The most suitable fruits to use for making liqueurs at home are: apricots, blackberries, blackcurrants, damsons, morello cherries, oranges, peaches, pineapples, raspberries, sloes and strawberries.
- It is also worth experimenting with kumquats, mandarins, tangerines, passion fruit and prunes, but use only the best-quality examples.
- Most fruits contain around 80% of their weight in the form of juice and you must allow for this when making the liqueur. The juice contains no alcohol and therefore also dilutes the spirit used.

OTHER FLAVOURINGS

- Herbs, spices, cocoa powder and coffee are used commercially but are not easy to use at home because of the great variety required in minute quantities – often as little as 1 g.
- Commercially prepared essences are best to use for these liqueurs. I recommend the T. Noirot brand. They are not cheap but have a truer flavour than many of the less expensive brands.

CAPSICUM TINCTURE

- When making liqueurs from essences and from wine and spirit mixtures, a few drops of capsicum tincture can be added to impart a sense of warmth. This is especially worth while when you are keeping the spirit to the minimum possible.
- The tincture is stocked in bulk by most pharmacists. Explain that you only want about 25 ml for adding in drops to your home-made liqueurs. Make sure that a dropper is supplied with the bottle.

Methods and Recipes

WITH ESSENCES OR INFUSION

- As explained, liqueurs can only be made in the home with essences or by infusion.
- The easiest and quickest way is to mix the essence of your choice into a sweetened spirit or into a sweetened mixture of strong wine and spirit. This liqueur is immediately ready for drinking.
- The second way, not much more difficult although it does take longer, is to steep the fruit of your choice in a sweetened spirit for a few days or weeks.

ESSENCE METHOD

Read the information on pages 340–2 very carefully to calculate how much sugar you need to make the liqueur of your choice and decide on the spirit that you will use to obtain the alcohol content required.

Please note that in the calculations and recipes in this chapter metric rather than imperial measurements have been used, principally to make them easier to follow.

Example one (Peach Brandy using vodka)

Assume that you wish to make 1 litre of Peach Brandy with an alcohol content of around 24% and a specific gravity of about 1.070 (see page 338). You need:

$$285 \text{ ml strong wine } 16\% \text{ alcohol}$$
$$520 \text{ ml vodka } 65.5° \text{ proof}$$
$$270 \text{ g sugar}$$
$$25 \text{ ml peach essence}$$

The calculations are made as follows:
- Convert the vodka into % alcohol, i.e. $65.5 \div 7 \times 4 = 37.4\%$
- Sugar to provide specific gravity 1.070   = 175 g
- Sugar to compensate for dilution by alcohol   = 96 g
  (i.e. $4 \text{ g} \times 24$)
- Total sugar   = 270 g
- Total sugar (270 g) occupies 170 ml of volume (because 8 g of sugar = 5 ml of volume).

Therefore:

520 ml vodka at 37.4%	= 194.5 (5.2 × 37.4%) units of alcohol per 100 ml
285 ml wine at 16%	= 45.6 (2.85 × 16%) units of alcohol per 100 ml
170 ml sugar	= 0 units of alcohol per 100 ml
25 ml essence	= 0 units of alcohol per 100 ml
1000 ml liqueur	= 240 units of alcohol per 100 ml
	= 24% alcohol per litre

Method: Mix together the wine and vodka, stir in the sugar and, when it is dissolved, add the essence (about three-quarters of the quantity at first). Taste the liqueur and add the rest as required until you are satisfied with the result. It improves a little if left to homogenize for a week.

Example 2 (Peach Brandy using Polish spirit)

Assume that you wish to make the same liqueur again but this time using Polish spirit at 80% alcohol instead of vodka. The calculations are made as follows:

Sugar and essence – no change in quantity or volume

175 ml Polish spirit at 80% alcohol = 140 (1.75 × 80) units per 100 ml
630 ml wine at 16% alcohol = 100.8 (6.3 × 16) units per 100 ml
Total = 240.8 units per 100 ml
= 24% alcohol per litre.

Although Polish spirit is twice as expensive as vodka, only a third as much is required.

Example 3

By the addition of some glycerine and capsicum tincture, however, the richness and warmth of the liqueur can be enhanced and the alcohol content reduced by several percentage points.

330 ml vodka
500 ml strong wine
200 g sugar
25 ml essence
20 ml glycerine
15 drops capsicum tincture

The alcohol content of the liqueur will be approximately 20%.

- The difference in alcohol content between the three examples is not likely to be noticed by anyone other than those very familiar with liqueurs. The glycerine and capsicum tincture takes care of that.
- If Polish spirit is used instead of vodka, you can use 750 ml strong wine and only 100 ml Polish spirit.
- The flavours will be further enhanced if you use a wine made from the same ingredient, i.e. a peach wine with a peach brandy liqueur essence.

Stronger liqueurs

The higher alcohol liqueurs are made in the same way and by the same calculations. Naturally more spirit should be used, even in the 'cut the cost' example (No 3), but you may find that you are satisfied with 25% alcohol in the finished liqueur, even for those that commercially contain 40% or more.

INFUSION METHOD

- Fresh ripe fruit may be used instead of essences. The precise quantity to use depends on the strength of flavour of the fruit and how noticeable you want this to be: 340–454 g (12 oz–1 lb) fruit to make 1 litre (1¾ pints) of liqueur is recommended.
- Because the juice from the fruit will occupy some volume, additional spirit will be required to make up for this further dilution. Ensure that the fruit is of the highest quality, remove the stalks and stones and crush the fruit. 340 g (12 oz) ripe fruit will yield up to 272 ml of juice and an allowance of at least 250 ml should be made for it.
- You will also have to allow for the sugar content of the fruit. Refer to the tables on page 45.
- Polish spirit is usually necessary when making liqueurs with fresh fruits. The extra liquid, together with the sugar, dilutes ordinary vodka too much.

For example: Fruit 340 g   = 250 ml juice
               Sugar 250 g   = 150 ml
               Vodka (65.5° proof)   = 600 ml
               Alcohol content 22.4% approx
               Specific gravity 1.070 approx

- The alcohol impression could be enhanced with, say, 15 ml of glycerine and 10 drops of capsicum tincture, since many of the fruit brandies are relatively low in alcohol.

If Polish spirit were used instead of vodka, the recipe could be as follows:

        Fruit 340 g (12 oz)   = 250 ml
        Sugar 250 g (9 oz)   = 150 ml
        Polish spirit   200 ml
        Strong wine   400 ml
        Alcohol content 22.4%

or:

        Fruit 340 g (12 oz)   = 250 ml
        Sugar 250 g (9 oz)   = 150 ml
        Polish spirit   300 ml
        Strong wine   300 ml
        Alcohol content 28.8%

These figures are very close to the commercial fruit brandies.

Method

1 Select the fruit carefully, using only the largest, ripest and best pieces. Clean and wash the fruit, remove the stones and crush or liquidize it. It is helpful to add some pectic enzyme and bentonite at this stage. A tablet is marketed which contains these two ingredients combined. The tablet aids juice extraction and clarification.

2 Dissolve the sugar in the spirit, or spirit and wine, and then mix in the fruit pulp and juice.

3 Seal the vessel, leave it somewhere accessible and give it a shake every day for a week or so. Precise timing is not critical – a good colour is more important. Leave the pulp to settle down and when the liqueur is fairly clear strain it through a fine-meshed nylon bag or filter paper and funnel into a 1-litre bottle.

4 If some very fine pulp carries over, it should settle out if the bottle is left in a cold place for a few days. The liqueur can then be racked again. If it doesn't clear fairly quickly, filter the liqueur in the manner specified with your filter set. Fortunately this is rarely necessary and is not necessary at all if pectic enzyme and bentonite are used at the outset.

5 The liqueur should now be given some time to mature. The minimum period is three months but a year is better. You may, if you wish, store your liqueur in smaller quantities and in bottles with attractive shapes. Make sure that they are thoroughly clean and sterilized before filling them and never use a bottle that has ever contained any obnoxious substance. Label the bottles with full details for further reference.

EXCEPTIONS

SLOE GIN

1 bottle gin 70° proof (700–750 ml)
454 g (1 lb) ripe sloes
250 g (9 oz) sugar

This delicious liqueur is made from blue-black, soft and fully ripe sloes. The stone is so large in proportion to the fruit, however, that it cannot easily be extracted. Stalk and wash the sloes, then pierce each one in several places with a bodkin or a sharp-pronged pastry fork.

Place the sloes in a container, add the sugar and gin, seal and shake. A dessertspoonful of glycerine may be added if you wish, but do not add capsicum tincture.

Regular shaking for a month or two will extract a rich, dark red colour from the sloes.

After three months strain out and lightly press the sloes. The liqueur should then be bottled and left to mature for a further nine months.

DAMSON GIN

Damsons may be used instead of sloes and in exactly the same way. When the damsons are strained out, however, do not discard them but serve with cream and ratafia biscuits as a very special dessert.

ORANGE GIN

Instead of sloes or damsons in the above recipes, use the thinly pared rind of a sweet orange, a mandarin and a lemon; avoid all white pith.

Cut the parings into small pieces and add them to the sweetened gin.

Leave them in for just one week, shaking the container daily, then strain out the parings. Add 15 ml (3 tsp) glycerine and mature the liqueur for three months or so. (The glycerine is an important addition to this liqueur.)

DRIED FRUIT CORDIALS

Some liqueurs that are not commercially comparable can be prepared from certain dried fruits, notably apricots, figs, muscatels and prunes. Again use only the best-quality fruit. To use poor-quality, undersized or stale fruit is just a waste of spirit and effort, for the result will be disappointing.

Make up a strong, bland wine and fortify it to about 20% alcohol with vodka or *eau de vie pour les fruits*.

Wash and pierce the fruit in several places with a pastry fork. Place the fruit in a container, add the sweetened wine and spirit mixture, seal and store for three months, shaking the container once a week.

Strain off and drain the fruit. Bottle the cordial and set it aside for another month or two.

Serve the fruit with or without ice cream or fresh cream, together with wafer biscuits, as a very special dessert. If all the fruit is not required at once it should be sealed in an airtight container and refrigerated. It will keep safely for a week or two.

APRICOT CORDIAL

250 g (9 oz) dried apricots
500 ml strong wine
330 ml vodka
200 g (7 oz) sugar
15 ml glycerine

FIG CORDIAL

125 g ($4\frac{1}{2}$ oz) dried figs

Other ingredients and method as for Apricot Cordial

MUSCATEL CORDIAL

220 g (7 oz) muscatels

Other ingredients and method as for Apricot Cordial

PRUNE CORDIAL

250 g (9 oz) prunes

Other ingredients and method as for Apricot Cordial

FRESH FRUIT CORDIALS

Whole fresh fruits may be used instead of dried. Larger fruits, such as apricots, nectarines, peaches and plums should be halved and stoned. Smaller fruits, such as blackberries, cherries, loganberries, mulberries, raspberries and strawberries should be left whole.

Pierce them with a large needle but try not to damage them.

When shaking the container, do so gently and use a swirling action – again so as not to damage the fruit. It then looks more attractive when drained and served as a dessert.

You can make as much as you wish, but follow the general proportion of 454 g (1 lb) fruit, 200 g (7 oz) sugar, 500 ml strong wine, 330 ml vodka.

Polish spirit may, of course, be used, it is more economical than vodka. Use 100 ml Polish spirit with 750 ml strong wine (16% alcohol).

Leave the fruit in the mixture for six weeks.

Although a great deal of flavour is extracted by the wine and spirit mixture, much less juice is extracted. Care should be taken in the straining and draining not to squash the fruit.

Leave the cordial for two to three months to mature.

> **Quick tip**
> Frozen fruit is not suitable because it collapses when thawed.

Serving Liqueurs

WHEN TO DRINK THEM

● Because of their high alcohol content and sweetness, liqueurs are normally served at the end of a meal when the stomach is full. The alcohol can then be absorbed into the bloodstream more slowly.
● Again because of their high alcohol content and sweetness, liqueurs are normally served in the smallest glasses containing no more than 25 ml (approx 1 fl oz).
● The cordials and less strong liqueurs are also very pleasant around four o'clock in the afternoon when their sweetness particularly appeals.

TEMPERATURE

Liqueurs and cordials are usually served at room temperature and are slowly sniffed and sipped. They have a delicious aroma and flavour which deserve to be enjoyed to the full.

WITH FOOD

Liqueurs and cordials can be mixed into or poured over ice cream, poured over sponge cake to make delicious trifles, mixed into fruit salads, poured over quartered pineapples and melons, or mixed into summer 'cups' – but not winter mulls.
● A serving of liqueur or cordial poured into a champagne glass and then topped up with sparkling wine is also excellent.

COOKING WITH LIQUEURS

Sweets made in the home can also be flavoured with liqueurs. Crême de menthe in peppermint creams is an obvious example but fudges, too, can be flavoured with liqueur.
● Chocolates and marzipan fruits with different liqueurs are other great delights.
● The ready availability of a wide range of liqueurs gives the imaginative cook countless opportunities for enhancing dessert dishes and sweetmeats.

VINEGARS

What is Vinegar?

SOUR WINE

- The word vinegar comes from the French word *vinaigre* which means a sour wine.
- Left open to the air a weak wine or mead, or a beer or cider for that matter, is soon likely to be infected by a micro-organisim called *Mycoderma aceti* – a member of the acetobacter family. These organisms live in the presence of air and convert the alcohol in the wine into acetic acid. It is this acid that imparts the sharp, sour odour and taste of vinegar.
- The word acetic comes from the Latin. In Roman times any vessel in which vinegar was kept or from which it was served, was called an *acetabulum*.

IN BIBLICAL TIMES

One of the earliest recorded references to vinegar comes from the Bible in that heart-touching verse from the Book of Ruth: 'And Boaz said unto her, "At mealtime come thou hither and eat of the bread, and dip thy morsel in the vinegar."' In the New Testament, too, there is a reference to vinegar at the crucifixion.

Clearly, vinegar was widely known and used thousands of years ago. It is probable that it preceded wine, for the berries of the wild grapes would have been less sweet than the cultivated grapes of today, thus producing a weaker wine which probably acetified as it fermented.

VINEGAR VARIETIES

- Wherever wine was used, it is likely that vinegar was close at hand. Cooks no doubt used it in the preparation of tasty foods.
- Once fully appreciated it was a small step to making a great variety of different vinegars for culinary use. These include wine vinegar (both red and white), malt vinegar from beer, cider vinegar from apple juice and honegar from honey. There are also a great many vinegars flavoured with fruits or flowers such as raspberry or rose petal, or with herbs such as basil, garlic and tarragon.

NOT TOO MUCH ALCOHOL

- A base with an alcohol content of between 4 and 6% is the most suitable for conversion into vinegar.
- Beverages containing 10% alcohol or more keep better and are less prone to infection than weaker ones. They can be converted into a suitable base from which to make vinegar by diluting them with an equal quantity of water, thus reducing the alcoholic strength by half.

PURPOSE MADE

- As with so many other drinks vinegar is best purpose made. Prepare an all-liquid must or wort with a specific gravity of 1.036, ferment out to dryness, rack and clear and then convert to vinegar.
- Wines that have an acetic taint can be converted into vinegar but the result is that of making the best of a bad job, rather than a good vinegar.

THE ORLEANS' METHOD

- Making vinegar in the home is based on the Orleans' method. A cask large enough to hold 200 litres (45 gallons) of wine was rested on a cradle set up in an orchard. Holes were bored in the upper half of the end plates to admit air.
- A diluted wine was poured into the cask until it was half full, leaving as large a surface as possible in contact with the air.
- After 24 hours the holes were lightly plugged with cotton wool to keep out flies and insects.
- Within a few days a film of acetobacter covered the surface and became known as the 'mother of vinegar'.

- The vinegar was made in the summer when the weather was often dry and warm, thus encouraging the conversion of the alcohol to vinegar. Even so, it took three months to complete.
- The vinegar was then drawn off through the tap into jars or bottles.

PASTEURIZATION

- New vinegar must be pasteurized or heavily sulphited (150 parts per million) to prevent spoilage by other members of the acetobacter family.
- The most dangerous are *Acetobacter rancens*, which can convert the acetic acid to carbon dioxide and water, and *Acetobacter xylinum* which forms capsules of cellulose that clog the tap and build up inside the cask. *Anguillula aceti* are tiny worms that feed on acetobacter. They flourish in acetic acid and their presence ruins the vinegar.

Equipment and Hygiene

EQUIPMENT

The container
You can use one of the following containers for making your home-made vinegar but No 1 is the most successful.
1 You can buy vinegar from large supermarkets and grocers in a 5-litre (1-gallon) plastic container. Other beverages such as concentrated grape juice or fruit squash are also sometimes sold in these large containers.
• When the container is empty, wash it out – even if it contained vinegar – and sterilize it with Chempro SDP or sulphite.
• Lay the container on its side – broadest part to the surface – and with a hot skewer bore holes in the top and the upper third of the sides. The container for your vinegar is then ready.
2 You can use some of the jumbo-sized plastic bottles used for beer.
• Devise a small rack to support the necks to prevent the bottles from rolling and again pierce holes in the upper part of the bottles to admit the air.

A container for making vinegar. When the wine, water and vinegar have been mixed, the container should be left in a warm, airy place for three months before the vinegar is bottled and pasteurized.

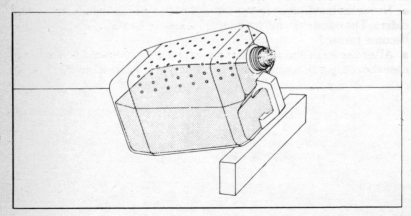

- Use a piece of nylon netting to cover the container when in use to keep out flies and insects and a plug of cotton wool for the mouth of the bottle.

3 You can also use an ordinary glass demijohn, half fill it and plug the neck with cotton wool. Since air can get to the vinegar solution only through the cotton wool the demijohn is not as effective as the plastic container (1) laid on its side with holes pierced in its upper portion. This exposes a larger surface of solution to the air and enables much more air to get in and out with draught and temperature changes.

Other equipment

You will also require the following:
- a glass or polythene funnel.
- a number of bottles – the 283 ml (10 fl oz) glass mineral water bottles with screw caps are admirable.
- a fish kettle or preserving pan in which to sterilize the bottles of vinegar.
- a few labels to tie on or stick on to the bottles, describing the contents and the dates the vinegar was started and bottled.

HYGIENE

- As with home-made wines and beers, hygiene is essential in the making of vinegars (see pages 10–12 for fuller instructions).
- Keep some equipment exclusively for the making of vinegar. Keep it clean and sterilize it before use.
- Never make vinegar in the same place as wines, meads, beers and ciders. The odour of vinegar can be picked up by these beverages and become tainted.
- After use wash and *sterilize* the equipment before putting it away in case there are any acetobacter on it that would spoil some other brew.

How to Make Vinegar

THE BASE INGREDIENTS

● First select a suitable bland and dry wine, either red or white or, preferably, make up a new one from some concentrated grape juice and a general-purpose wine yeast. Aim to produce about 5–6% alcohol from an original gravity of 1.036.
● If you decide to use an existing wine, look up your records, check the approximate alcohol content and dilute the wine with cold water to about 5 or 6% alcohol.
● Mead may be used instead of wine. Use as dry a mead as you can, although the presence of some sugar is not harmful. Dilute it in the same way as the wine.

THE FIRST STAGE

1 You will need 5 measures of wine or mead to 1 measure of a commercial vinegar.
2 Calculate the quantity of vinegar that you can make in your container. The gallon-sized plastic container should hold at least 2.5 litres (4½ pints) of vinegar.
3 Place a small block of some kind under the shoulder of the container. Pour in the vinegar and the diluted wine or mead. The vinegar level should be just below the mouth of the container.
4 Place the container in a warm, airy place, plug the mouth with cotton wool and cover the container with the nylon net. Leave for about three months.

THE VINEGAR MOTHER

● If you can see into the container you will notice that after a few days the solution becomes hazy. Subsequently a thick, crumpled, sticky-looking skin will develop on the surface. This is called the 'vinegar mother', or 'the mother of vinegar'.
● It will remain until the alcohol has been converted into acetic acid when it will break up, fall to the bottom of the container and the vinegar should clear.

BOTTLING

1 Prepare the bottles in which you propose to store your vinegar, or honegar if you have used a mead base. Wash and sterilize them and fill them with the new vinegar, leaving a small gap in each.
2 Fit screw caps and twist them just a turn to fasten them on, but not to seal the bottles. Cork stoppers may be used; just lay them loosely in place.

PASTEURIZING

1 Get out your preserving pan or fish kettle, lay some thin struts of wood or a cloth folded several times across the bottom and place it on a stove.
2 Stand the bottles of vinegar in the pan and fill it with cold water until the level of the vinegar in the bottles is reached.
3 Turn on the heat and when the water comes to the boil reduce the heat. Simmer for about 20 minutes.
4 Turn off the heat, screw down the metal caps until they are tight, or push in the stoppers to their maximum.
5 Lift out the hot bottles, taking care not to burn your fingers, and stand them on a folded cloth, both to absorb the water and some of the heat. A very cold surface might crack a bottle.

LABELLING AND MATURATION

When the bottles are cold check the seals again and tighten them if necessary. Attach the labels and put the bottles away in store for a few weeks for the flavour to develop.

VINEGAR VARIETIES

Beer and cider

- Use any cider or a strong but lightly hopped beer for vinegar.
- Use both as they are, without dilution, but again in the same proportion of 5 to 1 and make them exactly as described above.

Fruit vinegars

1 Strong-flavoured and rather sharp fruits seem to give the best results. Use 250 g (9 oz) blackcurrants, blackberries, loganberries,

mulberries, raspberries, redcurrants or strawberries for every 2.5 litres (4½ pints) of vinegar solution.
2 Wash, clean and crush the fruit, mix it into the solution and leave it there while the vinegar is made. The fruit pulp will settle on the bottom of the container and can be discarded when the vinegar is poured off into the bottles.
3 Having made up your base vinegar solution you can divide it into two or more portions and flavour each one with an appropriate proportion of a different fruit. You will need to use a separate container for each portion. Tie a label on to each one with a description of the contents. Otherwise it is very easy to get them muddled.

Herb vinegars
1 Almost any herb may be used and the following are known to be successful: basil, bay, borage, dill, garlic, mint, shallot and tarragon.
2 Prepare the herb as you would for any other purpose, wash and crush it, or cut it into small pieces, and mix it into the solution.
3 How much to use depends on how strongly flavoured you would like your vinegar to be: 25 ml (5 tsp) in 2.5 litres (4½ pints) is recommended for most herbs but you may prefer to make smaller quantities of each one at first.
4 Make up your basic solution, divide it into portions, and add an adjusted measure of a different herb to each. Next time round you can add more or less of a given herb to suit your taste.

VINEGAR USES
- You can use vinegars in so many ways, apart from sprinkling them on fish and chips! Home-produced vinegars are excellent for pickling little onions and shallots, and for making chutney of all kinds.
- They mix well with vegetable oils to make dressings for salads.
- They are splendid for marinating fish, ham or bacon in particular, but with wine also for marinating venison, hare, pigeon and mutton. A variety of vinegars greatly extends the range of your cuisine.

Quick tip
2.5 litres (4½ pints) of solution comfortably produces 8 mineral water bottles of vinegar, each containing 283 ml (10 fl oz). The remainder is lost with the lees and is not worth bothering about.

SOCIETIES AND SUPPLIERS

Clubs and Competitions

One of the most enjoyable things about making wine, beer and other drinks is forming friendships with other winemakers and brewers. It is much more pleasant to drink with friends than alone and home winemakers and brewers have the added benefit of being able to discuss the ingredients and methods they have used.

CLUBS
- Winemakers and brewers all over the UK and in a number of other countries too such as Australia have organized clubs with membership open to anyone who makes wine or beer. There are more than 1000 such clubs of all sizes in the UK and all have a common purpose: to provide a forum for talks and discussion on every aspect of homemade wine, beer, cider and liqueurs, for tastings and for fellowship.
- Social activities, such as outings to pick fruit or to visit a vineyard are often arranged. There are also social evenings and functions. The attraction here is that people with a shared interest, but from a wide range of occupations, can meet.

Organization
Most clubs meet in the evening once a month, although a few meet fortnightly. The secretary organizes the talks and social activities and quite often there is a supplies officer who buys certain ingredients in bulk and offers them to members at a small discount.

Meetings

After the speaker has given his talk there will be a discussion, sometimes with a tasting of a particular wine. During the evening members taste their own or their neighbours' wines and perhaps nibble a biscuit or a piece of cheese. The atmosphere is friendly and convivial.

COMPETITIONS

- In many regions clubs have formed federations that arrange an annual competition, often associated with lectures or seminars. The wines and beers are usually assessed by members of the National Guild of Wine and Beer Judges.
- There is also a National Association of Wine and Beermakers to which many federations and some circles are affiliated, as well as some hundreds of individual winemakers and brewers. Again, an annual competition is held in which there are often as many as 4000 bottles submitted for adjudication over a very wide range of classes.

Read the schedule

At whatever level wines or beers are submitted the same care is necessary in entering them. The competition secretary will issue a schedule stating the date and place of the competition, the names of the different classes (dry red, dry white, dessert, bitters, stouts, lagers and so on) and the rules to be followed regarding bottles, corks and labels. If you are interested in entering, first read the schedule carefully and make sure that you understand it.

Assess your wines

Next, assess your own stocks and decide in which classes you have suitable bottles to enter. Examine them one by one in a slow and methodical manner and consider the following points:

Colour: Pour a little wine into a glass and match the colour of your wine with that of the class in which you propose to enter it. Incredible though it may seem some people actually enter a red wine in a white class or a white wine in a red class!

Bouquet: Swirl the wine in the glass and smell it. The odour should be clean, fresh and attractive. If it isn't, don't enter it.

Taste: If everything is satisfactory, then take a good mouthful of wine, chew it and move it around with your tongue before swallowing it. The taste should be above all clean and attractive.

Bacterial infection: The judge sometimes finds a wine with a most unpleasant odour and taste, usually due to a bacterial infection. If your wine has this then please do not enter it. It will not be awarded a prize and can only spoil the judge's palate for other wines. If, by some chance, you have such a wine, take a sample to a senior member of your wine club and ask for advice.

Taste classification: If the class name includes the words 'dry' or 'table' then there should be no obvious sweetness in your wine. If it includes the words 'sweet' or 'dessert' then there should be a positive taste of sweetness, not just an absence of dryness. In almost every class at a competition a judge is likely to find at least one wine that is too sweet for a dry class or not sweet enough for a sweet class.

How to enter your wines and beers

Having found suitable entries for different classes, send off your form to the competition secretary who will send you the appropriate labels for your bottles. In the meantime prepare them.

Bottle preparation: The standard bottle in which home-made wines are exhibited in the UK is the 75 cl Sauternes bottle. This is virtually colourless, has rounded shoulders and a deep or shallow punt. Beer is exhibited in crown-capped or screw-stoppered 1-pint brown beer bottles.
• You will need a T-flange stopper and the schedule will prescribe whether it should be all cork or have a white plastic top. Wash the bottles clean, both inside and out, and ensure that every trace of previous labels, including the gum, has been removed. Sterilize and drain each bottle before it is filled. When the stopper is fully inserted there should be an airgap of 13–18 mm ($\frac{1}{2}$–$\frac{3}{4}$ in) between the bottom of the stopper and the surface of the wine.

Labelling: Stick the labels carefully on to the side of the bottle, equidistant between the two seams that run from top to bottom. They should also be at the height from the bottom of the bottle prescribed in the schedule. Ensure that there are no surplus gum marks around the label and that the bottle as a whole looks clean and neat. Give the bottle a final rub over with a clean cloth to wipe off your fingermarks and then wrap the bottle in tissue paper.

Learn from the results
After the adjudication try to speak to the judge and ask for comments on your entries. There is always something to learn and he or she may be able to give you some useful tips.

ADJUDICATION
With the rapid growth of home winemaking and brewing in the 1960s it became clear that adjudication had to be properly organized and controlled. Adjudication demands keen eyesight, a sensitive nose and a trained palate as well as a proper understanding of how wines and beers should be made and the ability to make an objective assessment.

THE GUILD OF JUDGES
- Relatively few people are gifted with the ability to evaluate the merits of home-made wine and beer. It is as important to choose the right people as to devise a system of adjudication which means that all judges apply the same standards. With this in mind a guild of judges was formed with an executive committee to devise adjudication regulations and to control the admission of new members.
- Since 1964 all home-made wines have been adjudicated in the same, precisely specified manner, and all new members have to pass a comprehensive entrance examination. In 1978 the judging of beer was included and the name of the guild was changed to The National Guild of Wine and Beer Judges.

THE HANDBOOK
The handbook is called *Judging Wine and Beer: A Handbook for the Guidance of Judges, Competitors and Show Organizers* and it is published by The National Guild. As well as advice on organizing competitions, both for stewards and judges as well as for exhibitors, it also includes definitions of the different wine, beer and mead styles and a glossary of technical terms. It can be obtained from Mr V.H. Goffen, Hon. Secretary, The National Guild of Wine and Beer Judges, 13 Monks Orchard, Petersfield, Hampshire, England.

Putting the judges through their paces
- In addition to having a thorough knowledge of winemaking technology or brewing and of judging procedures, judges must also prove their own winemaking or brewing abilities by winning prizes at major competitions; they must also have been a steward to a national judge. There is a practical palate examination in which they have to place in the same order of merit six or eight bottles of wine that have previously been assessed by three experienced judges.
- Training does not stop after a judge has passed this difficult examination and been admitted to the guild. They must continue to train their palates by attending seminars, regional meetings with other judges, commercial wine tastings tutored by a Master of Wine or by one of their own members with a specialized knowledge of a wine region or style. They also receive a quarterly newsletter and are encouraged to learn as much as possible about commercial as well as home-made wines.

JUDGING PROCEDURE

After entering on the marking sheet the name of the class (for example, Dry, Red Table Wine), and the exhibitor's number, the judge visually examines each exhibit and the steward writes down the number of points allocated for presentation, clarity and colour. The steward then pours some wine from the first bottle into a suitable glass and the judge examines the wine with his eyes, nose and tongue. The marking system of the adjudication is as follows:

For wine
Presentation (2 points): This covers the appearance of the bottle, cork and label. Marks are deducted for imperfections. These include using the wrong bottle or one that is chipped or dirty; wrong, dirty or proud corks; labels stuck in the incorrect position.
Clarity (4 points): Marks are deducted for hazes, imhogeneity (the non-mixture of a sugar syrup for example), and for particles of debris or sediment.
Colour (4 points): Marks are deducted for poor or wrong colour according to type, e.g. a pink wine in a red wine class.
Bouquet (10 points): The wine should smell clean and attractive,

vinous or fruity, mature, balanced and appropriate to the style. Marks are awarded according to the degree of perfection.

Flavour and Balance (30 points): The wines are not swallowed but moved around the mouth with the tongue and, after some consideration, ejected into a spitoon. Marks are deducted for a lack of balance in dry wines between the acids, tannins, alcohols and texture, and in sweet wines, the sugar content. Faults such as oxidation, immaturity, instability, over-sulphiting or microbial infection lose marks according to their degree. Sweet wines in dry classes and dry wines in sweet classes are obviously not according to schedule and are marked NAS.

When adjudicating sparkling wines 10 points are allocated from the final 30 for condition and effervescence.

For beer

Colour and clarity (4 points): These are combined with deductions similar in content but appropriate to the different beers.

Head and Condition (4 points): Marks are deducted for lack of head or head retention, and for lack of a continuing bead of bubbles.

Presentation (2 points) **and bouquet** (10 points): Similar points are awarded and marks are deducted as for wine, but appropriate to the different beers.

Flavour and Balance (30 points): Beers are also awarded up to 30 points with deductions for imperfections as appropriate to beers. The extremes of gushing and flatness lose points.

Finalizing

After adjudication the judge makes a note of the marks awarded and any comments against the exhibitor's number on the marking sheet. There is no indication on the bottle as to the identity of the exhibitor other than the number allocated by the entries' secretary.

When a judge has marked all the wines or beers in the class, those with the highest marks are tasted again and placed in an order of merit. The exhibitor's number is related to the placings and the information is given to the show secretary who announces the result.

General tip
- Consult the Judges' Handbook for fuller details.
- When you enter wines or beers in a competition that will be judged by a member of the National Guild of Wine and Beer Judges you can be sure that your exhibits will be assessed fairly.

Sources of Supply

SPECIALIST SHOPS

Most large villages and suburbs will have a shop that specializes in selling equipment and ingredients for the home winemaker and brewer. These shops are usually owned and staffed by winemakers who are always willing to give advice to their customers.

See what is available

An extremely wide range of stock is maintained in such shops and prices are reasonable. It is well worth spending a few minutes just looking at the different items on sale. You will be impressed, for example, by the number of manufacturers of concentrated grape juice. These concentrates are available in great variety in several qualities and also in different-sized containers from 240 g to 5 kg ($8\frac{1}{2}$ oz–$11\frac{1}{4}$ lb).

Read the small print: Make sure that you read the small print on the label, for some cans contain a quantity of liquid sugar and possibly a fruit juice other than, or in addition to, that of the grape.

Other stock items

Here you can also buy a variety of yeasts in the form of tablets or dried granules and all the different acids, nutrients and other additives, as well as a comprehensive assortment of equipment. Indeed, most of these shops are like an Aladdin's cave where you can buy virtually everything you may ever wish to use in making wine, mead, beer, cider and liqueurs in the home.

HIGH STREET SHOPS

Many leading chemists stock ingredients and equipment and some have a complete range with items for both the beginner and the more experienced winemaker.

Some DIY and gardening centres as well as supermarkets (especially in their larger stores and in the out-of-town shopping centres) stock a limited range of the more widely used items.

Service

Unfortunately in all of the High Street outlets it is often very difficult to find anyone who knows anything about the stock, let alone someone who could answer a question on the subject. If the item you want is on show there is no problem, but if you want anything else you may find that no one can help you. For this reason in particular, as well as because of the very extensive range of equipment and ingredients stocked, I would strongly recommend that you use the services of the specialist shops.

MAIL ORDER

For those who do not live within reach of a suitable outlet there are a number of mail order businesses. Write for a catalogue first and then place your order. You will have to pay postage on your purchase but you do save on bus or train fares to town. The following are three of the best-known mail order services in the UK:

- Loftus, 9 Oakleigh Way, Mitcham, Surrey CR4 1AU.
- Luton Winemakers, 50A Alton Road, Luton, Bedfordshire, LU1 3NS.
- Moorsales, 55 Bancroft, Hitchin, Hertfordshire.
- Gervin, 61 Church Road, Woodley, Reading, Berkshire.

A large s.a.e. should accompany your catalogue request.

CLUB STOCKS

If you join a winemaking club you will find that one of the members acts as the supplies officer and that a limited range of frequently required items will be available for purchase as well as some 'specials'. These sometimes include catering packs of canned fruits, jams and pie fillings that are ideal for making fast-maturing wines. The supplies officer is often able to purchase at a discount which is usually passed on to members.

Note to Australian readers

For further information write to the Secretary of the National Amateur Wine and Beer Show, Mr R.E. Head, PO Box 29, McLaren Vale, SA 5171, Australia.

Glossary

Acetic acid   The acid in vinegar. Alcohol in wine can be converted into acetic acid if left exposed to the air and infection by vinegar-forming bacteria. It is also present in sour beer.

Acid   The cornerstone of bouquet and flavour. The three main acids of wine are citric, malic and tartaric. A dry wine needs from 4 to 6 parts per thousand, a sweet wine 5 to 7.

Other acids, notably succinic, are formed during fermentation and give off a wine-like odour.

Acidity   The degree of sharpness or tartness of a wine is measured by its hydrogen ion concentration. A pH reading of between 3 and 3.4 is desirable.

Acid-testing kit   Test tube, conical flask and chemicals for measuring the quantity of acid in a must, i.e parts per thousand.

Acid-testing papers   Chemically treated paper for measuring the degree of acidity of a must, i.e. its pH.

Adjuncts   Beer is made from malt, hops, water and yeast. All other items included in a recipe are adjuncts. They include sugar, flakes, syrups and other cereals.

Aerobic/Anaerobic   Yeast cells have the ability to live and thrive not only in the presence of oxygen – aerobic – but also in its absence – anaerobic. During fermentation-on-the-pulp, air containing oxygen (aerobic) is readily available to the yeast in the must. During fermentation under an airlock when air is excluded (anaerobic), the yeast can still flourish. Most spoilage organisms are aerobic. By excluding air from the must spoilage organisms are both prevented from infecting it and, if present, prevented from developing.

Aftertaste   Poetically referred to as the 'farewell' of a wine. It is the taste that slowly develops on the uvula at the back of the throat after the wine has been swallowed.

Airlock   A device fitted to a container of a fermenting must to exclude air whilst permitting carbon dioxide to escape. The actual lock is usually a weak sulphite solution poured into a glass or a plastic cylindrical shape. During fermentation the pressure inside the container is greater than that outside and large globules of gas are forced through the sulphite solution. Because of the imbalance of pressure the external air cannot pass through the lock into the must.

Alcohol A common expression for ethanol, i.e. ethyl alcohol. This is the intoxicating spirit that is formed from a sugar solution during fermentation. Several other alcohols are also formed but in very small quantities. They include amyl, butyl and methyl alcohol.

Aldehydes Substances formed by the partial oxidation of alcohol and interaction with acids. In most wines they contribute to the pleasant odour and taste of the wine. Some are formed during fermentation, others during maturation.

Ale Originally ale was a beer brewed without hops. Now the word means exactly the same as beer.

Amateur winemaker A person who makes wine for personal use but not for sale. The phrase was first used as far back as 1835.

Ammonium phosphate/sulphate Although yeast cells can flourish without oxygen, they cannot exist without nitrogen. Most fruits contain some nitrogenous matter but it is always a wise precaution to add 5 ml (1 tsp) of either ammonium phosphate or ammonium sulphate to each gallon of must to ensure an adequate supply of readily available nitrogen to the yeast.

Anthocyanins These are the red, blue and purple pigments of fruits and other plants which are water soluble. The colour is usually in the skin, hence the need for steeping in hot water or for pulp fermentation to extract it.

Anti-oxidant A substance added to a must or wine to prevent oxidation (browning). The two most commonly used are sulphite and, to a lesser extent, ascorbic acid.

Aroma The odour of the main ingredient in the wine, e.g. apple, elderberry, orange. (See also **Bouquet**.)

Astringent The tingling feeling around the gums when tasting certain wines – mostly red wines containing an excess of tannin.

Attenuation The thinning of the wort during fermentation.

Autolysis The decomposition of dead yeast cells by enzymes previously secreted by them. This causes off-flavours and even complete spoilage.

Balm or **Barm** An old name for yeast that is sometimes used in the fermentation of lagers.

Barley The cereal that is most widely used for brewing beer.

Bead The bubbles in sparkling wine or a glass of beer.

Beer A hopped ale brewed from malted barley and other ingredients.

Bentonite A grey-powdered clay used for fining wines. It is also available more expensively as a gel and as soluble granules. The powder is difficult to dissipate unless mixed with a small pinch of salt in warm water.

Bleach Domestic bleach is an excellent cleaning agent for stained decanters, glass jars, bottles and glazed earthenware vessels. It should be well diluted, 10 ml (2 tsp) per gallon of water is adequate, and the vessel should be left full for 24 hours. Afterwards it should be emptied and the vessel thoroughly rinsed five or six times in running cold water. Bleach should not be used with plastic containers or wood.

Blending The mixing together of two or more wines to improve them. Each wine must be sound and free from infection or off-flavours, albeit deficient or excessive in some factor.

Bloom The waxy dust coating on grapes and plums in particular.

Body The 'thickness' or 'fullness' of a wine or beer. Wines are said to be 'thin' if they have little body, i.e. watery, or 'fat' if they are full bodied.

Bottle Throughout the wine and mead section of this book the word bottle refers to proper wine bottles as used commercially for wine. Brown or green bottles should be used for the storage of wine. Only Champagne bottles may be used for sparkling wines.

Thick brown glass is usually used for beer bottles although some plastic bottles are now available. Non-returnable wine, spirit or other thin bottles should never be used.

Bottle fermentation 1. The deliberate secondary fermentation of a sugared still wine in a sealed bottle to produce a sparkling wine. 2. The renewed fermentation after bottling of a wine thought to be stable. Sometimes caused by lactic acid bacteria. (See also **Priming**.)

Bottoms Usually refers to the small amount of beer and yeast left in a bottle after pouring out the clear beer.

Bouquet The pleasing odour that develops in a wine during fermentation and maturation due to esterification and oxidation. Not to be confused with aroma.

Brewer's grains Cereals that have been used for making beer and sold off for cattle food.

Brewer's yeast The *Saccharomyces cerevisiae* variety of yeast used for brewing in the UK. It is top fermenting and causes mounds of foam during fermentation which protects the beer from infection.

Bru-keg A pressurized plastic cask developed for use at home.

Cake The residue of fruit pulp after all the juice has been pressed out. It should be dry enough to handle without breaking up.

Campden tablet The proprietary name of a small white tablet of potassium or sodium metabisulphite that, when dissolved in 4.5 litres (1 gallon) of a liquid, releases some 50 parts per million of sulphur dioxide. Very useful for adding to small quantities of wine when a prescribed dosage is required, e.g. after the first racking.

Cap A solid layer of fruit pulp supported by carbon dioxide on the surface of a must. It should be broken up and mixed into the juice to ensure proper extraction and to prevent its infection.

Capping tool Used for crimping crown caps onto beer bottles.

Capsules Foil or plastic covers that fit neatly over the cork and neck of a bottle. They protect the cork and enhance the appearance of the bottle.

Caramel A colouring agent sometimes used to darken beers.

Caramelized A wine tasting of burned sugar or toffee. Dark brown sugar imparts this flavour to a wine as does prolonged storage in a warm place. Madeira wines are deliberately caramelized.

Carbohydrates The ingredients containing starch and sugar used in brewing to produce alcohol.

Carbon dioxide The gas given off during the fermentation of must or wort. It can be seen passing through the airlock as a large bubble of colourless gas. The thousands of small bubbles rise constantly to the surface of a must or wort and burst with a soft hissing sound. Almost half the weight of the sugar in the must or wort is converted into carbon dioxide and the other half into alcohol. It is also produced during the fermentation of the priming sugar in beermaking, whether in bottle or cask, and in the making of sparkling wine. It causes the lively bubbles when the wine or beer is poured.

Cellar Any place where wine is stored for maturation, not necessarily the basement of a house. For preference, however, it should be cool and dark.

Chempro A chlorine-based sterilizing agent widely used by brewers and winemakers.

Clarify Clearing a hazy wine by fining or filtering.

Cloying The feeling of excessive sweetness in the mouth, especially after swallowing a wine or liqueur.

CO_2 injector A device that injects carbon dioxide into a plastic pressurized cask.

Condition The liveliness or otherwise of a beer when poured.

Cream of tartar In very cold conditions tartaric acid combines with the potassium present in most fruit wines and precipitates as glass-like crystals or thin, slate-like flakes of potassium hydrogen tartrate. The crystals may be colourless but usually contain some anthocyanin or colouring if any is present. The wine is often smoother and mellower as a result of the precipitation.

Crown caps Discs of thin metal lined with plastic or cork used for sealing bottles of beer.

De-acidification The reduction of an excess of acid in a fruit must by the addition of calcium or potassium carbonate.

Decant To pour wine carefully from a bottle, in which a sediment has been deposited during maturation, into a carafe or decanter suitable for serving the wine. It is important not to allow the sediment to mix into the wine and make it cloudy.

Deposit Insoluble substances that fall out of a beer or wine during fermentation or maturation. It collects on the bottom of containers and should be removed.

Dextrins Substances produced during the mashing of grains which impart body and sweetness to a beer.

Dextrose Another name for glucose.

Diammonium phosphate The correct name for ammonium phosphate.

Diastase A combination of enzymes formed in the barley grain during malting. It converts starch into maltose during mashing.

Disgorge To remove the secondary sediment from a bottle of sparkling wine prior to serving. You decant a clear, still wine leaving the sediment behind, but disgorge the sediment from a sparkling wine leaving the clear wine behind.

D.M.S. Diastatic malt syrup. A malt extract containing some diastase required for converting the starch in adjuncts into fermentable sugar.

Draught The name given to beer conditioned and matured in a cask instead of in bottles.

Dry The term used to describe a wine or beer in which there is no taste of sweetness.

Dry hopping The addition of dried hops or hop pellets to a beer during fermentation to enhance the hop flavour.

End point The moment in the mashing of grains when all the starch has been converted into maltose and dextrins.

Enzymes Substances produced by living cells that cause changes in other substances without being changed themselves. They each effect only one change but a group of different enzymes can cause a sequence of changes.

Esters   Sweet-smelling substances formed by the interaction of fruit acids and alcohols during maturation.
Farewell   (See **Aftertaste**.)
Fermentation   The process by which yeast converts sugar in a must or wort into alcohol and carbon dioxide.
Fermentation bin   A natural-coloured polythene bin with a fitting lid used for fermenting must or wort into wine or beer.
Fermentation-on-the-pulp   Fermenting the sugar in the presence of crushed fruit to extract colour, acids, flavouring substances etc.
Ferment-on   To continue the fermentation after the addition of sugar.
Ferment-out   To continue the fermentation until all the sugar has been converted to alcohol and carbon dioxide.
Ferment-to-a-finish   To continue the fermentation until the yeast stops working due to the high concentration of alcohol.
Filtration   The removal of minute, solid particles suspended in a wine by passing it through a mixture of cellulose powders or a cellulose pad.
Fining   The precipitation of minute, solid particles in suspension by the admixture of fining agents such as bentonite, chitosan, gelatine, isinglass etc.
Flakes   The generic term given to flaked adjuncts, e.g. flaked rice.
Flat   A wine that tastes dull and insipid; often of low alcohol and acid content and slightly oxidized. A lifeless beer in which there are no gas bubbles.
Flowers of wine   *Candida mycoderma* A film of white dust-like organisms that can appear on the surface of a wine or beer exposed, however slightly, to air. A poorly fitting stopper would admit sufficient air and with it the spoilage yeast.
Fortification   The addition of spirit, usually vodka, to a wine to increase its alcoholic strength.
Fructose   A readily fermentable single sugar, also called levulose, that combines with glucose to form sucrose (household sugar).
Gelatine   A tawny, transparent and brittle substance used for fining. Sometimes sold in granule form. Must be completely dissolved in hot water before mixing into a cloudy wine.
Glucose   A readily fermentable single sugar, also called dextrose, that combines with fructose to form sucrose (household sugar). Sometimes added to a wort to increase its alcoholic strength.
Glucose chips   Solid pieces of glucose as opposed to powder.
Glycerine   A transparent syrup sometimes added to sweet and

dessert wines as well as liqueurs to enhance their richness. A little is formed during fermentation.

Goods   A generic name for all the solid ingredients from which beer is brewed.

Grist   The name given to all the grains from which beer is brewed.

Hardening salts   A mixture of mineral salts, especially sulphates and carbonates, used to make soft water hard. Hard water contains these salts naturally.

Haze   A lack of clarity in a wine due to tiny particles of matter that remain in suspension. Sometimes caused by pectin, starch or proteins or by contact with copper or iron.

Head   The froth on a glass of beer.

Heading liquid or **Powder**   Substances added to a wort to stimulate and maintain the head on a glass of beer.

Headroom   The space between the surface of a wine and the cork or bung. This should be kept to a minimum at all times except in the maturation of sherry-style wines. The space is sometimes referred to as ullage, especially in casks.

Hock   The generic name given to the golden wines produced along the banks of the Rhine, primarily from the Riesling grape. The word comes from Hochheim, a village from which Prince Albert imported wine for Queen Victoria and the court. This wine is still very popular and is often imitated by country winemakers using ripe gooseberries and similar ingredients.

Hop   The plant *Humulus lupulus*, the flower of which is used for flavouring and preserving beer.

Hot break   The precipitation of proteins during the boiling of wort.

Hydrogen sulphide   A colourless gas that has the odour of bad eggs and is sometimes found in wines.

Hydrometer   A simple instrument for measuring instantly the specific gravity (s.g.) of a must, wine, wort or beer in which it is floated. For home winemakers this shows the approximate quantity of sugar present.

Inhibitor   A substance that prevents the growth or development of organic cells. In the context of winemaking sulphite inhibits the growth of spoilage organisms. During fermentation the carbon dioxide that lies on top of the fermenting must also acts as an inhibitor. Sulphite additionally inhibits oxidation.

Invert sugar   A *mixture* of fructose and glucose in their readily fermentable, separate selves. Household sugar (sucrose), which is a *combination* of fructose and glucose, cannot be fermented until it is split into two parts by the enzyme sucrase, more commonly called invertase.

Irish moss A dried and powdered seaweed used during the boiling process for clarifying wort. Sometimes called carragheen moss.

Isinglass A substance produced from the swim bladder of certain fish and used for fining white wines.

Krausening The priming of beer by the addition of unfermented wort instead of sugar.

Lactic acid The mild acid found in milk and produced in small quantities during fermentation. Some spoilage organisms flourish in it. One variety can convert malic acid into lactic acid. (See also **malo-lactic fermentation**.)

Lactose Milk sugar that is not fermentable by wine or beer yeasts. It is only one third as sweet as household sugar. In white powder form it is used for sweetening brown ales or stouts.

Lees Insoluble substances that settle on the bottom of a jar or bin during fermentation and storage. It consists of minute particles of decomposing ingredients, dead yeast cells and similar debris and should be removed promptly to avoid spoilage of the wine or beer.

Levulose Another name for fructose.

Liquor The brewer's name for water after it has been adjusted for hardness or softness.

Lupulin The golden-coloured powder found in the base of the hop flower. It contains the essential oils and resins.

Macerate To extract flavour from flower petals by steeping them in hot water and rubbing them against the side of the container with the back of a wooden or plastic spoon.

Maderized A white or rosé wine that has become oxidized, developed a tawny tinge, a sharp, musty odour and a woody taste. Sometimes caused by storage in too warm a place.

Malo-lactic fermentation The conversion of some of the sharp-tasting malic acid into the milder lactic acid by lactic acid bacilli. It often occurs in fruit wines during maturation unless they have been sulphited. Carbon dioxide is also produced and can be sufficient to blow out the cork. It is not a fault, the wine may taste smoother and the slight effervescence can be attractive in white wines.

Malt Barley grains after they have been artificially germinated and then roasted to produce pale, crystal, chocolate or black malt.

Malt extract/syrup A toffee-like, concentrated solution of maltose and dextrin.

Malt flour Malt extract that has been dried and spun into a powder.

Maltose The fermentable sugar produced from the starch in the malted barley by the action of the diastase enzymes.
Marinate To steep meat, fish and fruit in wine, beer, cider or vinegar to enhance their tenderness and flavour.
Mash The mixture of crushed malt grains, adjuncts and hot liquor.
Mashing The process of converting the starch in the malted barley and the adjuncts into maltose by steeping it in hot water for several hours.
Mashing bin A container used for mashing.
Maturation The process of improving a wine, mead, cider or beer by storage in a cool, dark place until it reaches the point at which it tastes best.
Mead A solution of honey in water with added acid and nutrient that has been fermented by wine yeast, racked and matured.
Melomel A mead flavoured with fruit juice or flower essence.
Metabisulphite (See also **Campden tablet** and **Sulphite**.)
Metheglin A mead flavoured with herbs or spices.
Methyl alcohol A spirit formed in minute quantities during fermentation. Very poisonous in large quantities.
Micro-organisms Single-celled plants or animals too small to be seen by the naked eye but clearly visible under the lens of a powerful microscope. They include bacteria, viruses, fungi (including yeasts) and moulds. Most micro-organisms spoil wine but can be inhibited or killed by sulphite. Although invisible they are present everywhere floating in the air.
Mousy The name given to the odour of a wine infected by certain spoilage organisms. It is reminiscent of rats and mice.
Mull A wine that has been sweetened, spiced and heated.
Muselet A wire cage used to fasten the stopper to the projecting rim of the neck of a champagne bottle.
Must A solution of fruit or vegetable juices, honey etc. that has been adjusted with acid, sugar, nutrient etc. for fermentation into wine by yeast.
Musty The smell given off from a vessel that has been put away damp with the result that moulds have formed.
Mycoderma aceti Vinegar-forming fungi that form a film or skin on the surface of a low-alcohol wine that has not been sulphited. They convert the alcohol to acetic acid.
Mycoderma vini (See also **Flowers of wine**.)
Nutrient A substance containing nitrogen in a form easily accessible to yeast cells. But yeast cells also need some amino acids, many

trace elements of inorganic salts and some vitamin B_1. Grapes contain all these nutrients, which is one of the reasons why some fresh or dried grapes, or concentrated natural grape juice should be added to all musts.

Oenophile A person who loves wine for all the pleasure it gives: its appearance, bouquet and flavour, its history, social and therapeutic benefits and so on; *not* an alcoholic.

Original gravity The specific gravity of a wort prior to the mixing in of the yeast.

Oxidized An excess of aldehydes in low-alcohol wine due to the admission of too much oxygen. The wine develops a flat, 'brownish' taste, similar to that in over-ripe fruit. (The wine is in fact over-ripe.) Wine should be protected from contact with air at all times. The exception is sherry-style wine that has a high alcohol content where the oxidation is attractive.

Palate The roof of the mouth. Mostly used as a term referring to the sense and sensitivity of taste as experienced mainly by the tongue. A person who is said to have a 'good palate' is one who is very sensitive to the varying nuances of taste.

Pearson's square A method for calculating the quantity of spirit required to increase the alcohol content of a wine to a given degree.

Pectin A soluble, gum-like carbohydrate that surrounds the molecules of fruit juice. It gels and sets when heated. Sometimes causes a haze in fruit wines not treated with a pectin-degrading enzyme.

Pectolytic enzymes Compounds which break down pectin and enhance juice extraction from fruit. Proprietary brands include Pectozyme, Pectolin, Pectolase etc. A desirable additive to all fruit musts.

pH The measure of the hydrogen ion concentration in a liquid, the degree of acidity (or alkalinity). A very sharp-tasting wine would have a low pH, a bland wine would be somewhat higher. The scale is from 0 to 14, with a crossover from acidity to alkalinity at about 7.

Pith The white, spongy substance surrounding citrus fruits. It is very bitter and highly pectinous. All traces of it should be excluded from wine musts.

Potassium carbonate A white, chalk-like powder used to reduce the tartaric acid in the juice of unripe grapes or in wines containing an excess of tartaric acid.

Potassium metabisulphite (See also **Campden tablet**.)

Potassium sorbate A white powder used in conjunction with sulphite to terminate fermentation.

Pressure cask A strong plastic container developed for use by home brewers. Available in sizes from 10 to 25 litres (2.2–5½ gallons).

Priming The addition of a small and precise quantity of sugar together with some activated yeast cells to a mature, still wine so as to start a second fermentation in the bottle and thus create a sparkling wine. Also the addition of a small quantity of sugar or unfermented wort to a fully attenuated wort. It causes a secondary fermentation during maturation, producing a liveliness in the finished beer.

Prolonged fermentation The frequent addition of small quantities of sugar to a fermenting must to increase the alcohol content. High-alcohol wines are produced in this way.

Punt The indentation in the bottom of a wine bottle.

Pyment A mead flavoured with grape juice.

Racking The removal of a clear wine from its deposit of lees without disturbing them. Usually performed with a siphon. In beermaking the removal of the clear beer from its sediment of dead yeast cells, hop particles and fermentation dross.

Robe The colour of a wine – used especially of red wines of exceptional colour.

Rohament P The trade name for a preparation of pectin glycoside used to assist in juice extraction. Sometimes used instead of or in conjunction with a pectolytic enzyme.

Ropiness An oily appearance in a wine or beer caused by lactic acid bacteria hanging on to one another and so forming ropes. A fairly rare ailment.

Rousing The stirring up of a wort from the bottom of the bin during fermentation.

Saccharin A non-fermentable sweetening agent.

Saccharomyces Literally sugar fungi, the family name for yeast. Wine yeast is derived from the variety *S. cerevisiae* and is of the strain *S.C. elipsoideus*. There are further sub-strains with slightly different characteristics suitable for different styles of wine.

Sediment Another name for lees.

Siphon In its simplest form a plastic tube used to remove a clear or clearing wine from its sediment into a clean jar or into bottles.

Sorbitol Like lactose sorbitol is a sugar that cannot be fermented by wine yeasts and may therefore be used for sweetening dry wines.

Sparging The process of washing the maltose off the grains with hot water after mashing has been completed and the wort drawn off.

Specific gravity The weight of a given volume of a liquid compared with the same volume of water at a given temperature – usually 15°C (59°F). For the home winemaker the difference between the two weights is mainly sugar. The specific gravity (s.g.) of a liquid is measured with a hydrometer.

Stable/stabilizing A stable wine is one in which there is no activity associated with fermentation and the wine is still and inactive. A stabilizing tablet, usually made from a mixture of potassium sorbate and metabisulphite kills yeast, stops the fermentation and makes the wine still and stable.

Stainless steel The only metal that may be used in winemaking. All other metals react with the acids in the must and wine to form poisonous salts.

Starbright A brilliantly clear wine.

Starch A polysaccharide found in grains and vegetables. Yeast is unable to ferment it into alcohol until it has been converted into single sugars.

Starter bottle A sterilized bottle in which dormant yeast cells are reactivated. The contents of the bottle are subsequently added to a waiting must or wort to start the fermentation.

Sterilize To kill or inhibit all the micro-organisms on the surface of every piece of equipment likely to come into contact with the must or wine and also on all the ingredients from which wine is made.

Stuck ferment A fermentation that has stopped prematurely, i.e. before an appropriate quantity of alcohol has been formed.

Succinic acid The principal acid in the formation of esters that provide the winy odour. Usually formed during fermentation.

Sucrose The proper name for household sugar, whether produced from sugar beet or sugar cane. It consists of equal molecules of fructose and glucose in combination.

Sulphite The short and popular name for potassium or sodium metabisulphite from which sulphur dioxide is released in solution. (See also **Campden tablet**.)

Sulphur dioxide A pungent, colourless gas given off by metabisulphite in solution. It kills or inhibits most micro-organisms and retards oxidation. It also temporarily bleaches red wines. It irritates the eyes, nose and throat and inhalation should be avoided, especially by asthmatics and bronchitics.

Sweet The term used to describe a wine that contains residual sugar and therefore sweetness after fermentation has finished. Also used to describe a beer containing sweet-tasting dextrins or lactose.

Tannin Substances in the skin, pips and stalks of some fruits, notably black grapes, that impart a slight bitterness and astringency to a wine. An essential constituent of well-balanced red wines. Tannin is also a preservative.

Thin A wine or beer that lacks substance or body; watery.

Torrified barley Barley so heated that the grains swell and increase in size. Used as an adjunct.

Ullage (See also **Headroom**.)

Wheat Used in the form of flakes, flour or syrup as an adjunct.

Wine yeasts Microscopic, single-celled plants that secrete enzymes which convert sugar into alcohol and carbon dioxide. (See also **Saccharomyces**.)

Wort The mixture of malt and hop essences in solution prior to fermentation.

Zymase The popular name given to the apo-zymase complex of enzymes and co-enzymes secreted by wine yeast for the conversion of sugar into alcohol. Many by-products are produced in small quantities, notably a number of different acids, alcohols, glycerol etc. that enhance the bouquet and flavour of the wine.

Index

Page numbers in italics refer to illustrations

acids
  fruit 80, 122
  and honey 322
  importance 80
  quantity 49, 81
  right balance 80–81, 84, 140, 229
  testing 28, 81–3, *82*, *83*, 310
  type 49
  using 49
airlocks 15, *22*, 24, *27*, 122–3
alcohol content 74, 75, 138, 157, 219, 222, 352
alcohol tolerance 218–19
ale-berry 292
ammonium sulphate crystals 28
aperitifs 18–19, 172, 176
apple and blackberry wine 144
apple and elderberry wine 142
apple and plum wine 153
apple juice and grapefruit wine 224
apple wine 124
apricot cordial 348
apricot jam wine 175
apricot wine 143

bag-in-the-box 29–30, 103–5
barley wine 247, 290
beer, history of 242–4
  see also beer kits; brewing; individual types of beer
beer kits 264–70, *265*, *267*
beetroot 'madeira' 216
beetroot stout 293
beetroot wine 125
beggarman's wine 126
bentonite 28

best bitter 275, 285
bilberry and elderberry 'ruby port' 210
bilberry and elderberry 'tawny port' 211
bitter beers 245
  see also best bitter; draught bitter
blackberry and apple wine 144
blackberry and elderberry wine 145
blackberry 'port' 127
blackberry 'port' wine 212
blackberry table wine 127
blending 96–8, 156
bottles and bottling
  beer 248, *249*, 259, *260*, *269*
  cider 312–13
  mead 328
  vinegar 357
  wine *22*, 26, 99–102, 206–7, 230
bouquet
  in dessert wines 204–5
  lack of 108
  in table wines 138
bragget 293
bramble jelly wine 175
breweries, growth of 243
brewing
  equipment 248–50, *249*
  home 244
  ingredients 251–5
  principles 256–60
  see also beer kits; individual names of beers
brown ale 246–7, 277, 287

Campden tablets *22*, *309*
  care in use 7
  in country wines 122

first used 15
  sterilizing with 30, 52
  and stuck ferments 107
canned fruit wines 177–82
capping tool 249, *249*, 259
capsicum tincture 342
carafes 233
carbonating 188
carrot and orange wine 158
casks and casking 28–9, 50, 52, 259, *260*
Chempro 28, 30, 32, 33, 99–100
cherry wine 128, 146
cider press 304
cidermaking 9, 13, 300–317, *309*
citric acid 28, 49, 122, 322
citrus fruits 69
clubs 7, 16, 359–60, 366
cock ale 294
colouring 55
competitions 16, 360–4
cooking
  with beer 299
  with cider 316
  with liqueurs 350
  with wine 236–7
corks and corkers *22*, 26, 100–101, *100*, 249
country wines 121–37
crimping tool *260*
crown caps *249*, 250, *260*, *269*
crushers and crushing
  fruit 29, 64–5, *65*, 250, 304, 308
cyser *326*, 331

damson gin 347
damson jam wine 175
damson wine 129, 147
date wine 130
decanting 207, 233

382 · INDEX

demijohns 15, *22*, 24, 122–3, *194*
  padded covers 25, *25*
dessert wines 20, 204–17
diabetics, wines for 222–5
diammonium phosphate crystals 28
draught bitter 274, 286
draught cider 313
dry mead 329
dry sherry 198
dry stout 278, 288
dry wines 18–19

eau de vie pour les fruits 218
elderberry ale 294
elderberry and apple wine 142
elderberry and bilberry 'ruby port' 210
elderberry and bilberry 'tawny port' 211
elderberry and blackberry wine 145
elderberry wine 17, 20, 131
elderflower wine 132
esters 54–5
export ale 245

fermentation 57–8
  and brewing 257–8, *257*, *268*
  and cider 310–11
  in early winemaking 14
  of juice 89–91
  length of 87
  and mead 327
  records 240
  and wines 169, 172, 183, 185, 194, 205–6, 214, 223, 229
fermentation bin 15, *22*, 23, 32, 34, 248, *249*, 304, *309*
fermentation-on-the-pulp 66, 85–7
ferments, stuck 77, 106
fig and rosehip 'sherry' 203
fig cordial 348

fig, raisin and prune 'sherry' 202
filtering 27, 94–5, *95*, 141
fining 28, 94, 112, 141
flavour
  lack of 115
  in table wines 138
flavourings 28, 54, 196, 221, 342
flower wines 166–7
flowers 40, 41, *41*, 68
food
  and cider 316
  and liqueurs 350
  and mead 336
  and wine 236
fortified wines 218–21
fruit cordials 348–9
fruit juice wines 5, *38*, 40, 168–9, 170–71
fruits
  bottled and canned 38, *38*
  citrus 69, *69*
  contents of 44–5
  crushing 64
  and dessert wines 205
  dried 38–9, *38*
  fresh 35–6, *36*, 37
  from freezer 36–7
  and hygiene 30
  in liqueurs 342
  maceration 68
  peeling 69–70
  poisonous 46
  straining 31, 70
fungal amylase 43
funnels *22*, 23, 34, *249*

Gay-Lussac notation 220
ginger and marrow wine 161
ginger beer 295
ginger wine 159
glasses 234–5, *234*, 298–9, *299*
glycerine 54, 342
Golden Shred marmalade aperitif 176
gooseberry wine 132
grain-mashed beers 280–90, *283*

grains 42–3, 64
grape juice *22*
grape varieties 227
grape wines 226–30
grapefruit and apple juice wine 224
grapes
  buying 229
  in table wines 139
greengage jam wine 175
greengage wine 148

heating ingredients 66–7
herbs 42
home brewing 244
honey 6, 13, 48, 320–21, 325–6
honey and pineapple wine 171
honey beer 335
hops 251–2, *283*
hydrometer 15, *22*, 23–4, 71–9, *73*, *249*, 250, *309*
hygiene 30, 250, 305, 339, 355
hypocras 334

immersion heater 25, *249*, 250
isinglass 28

J tube 26
jam wines 39–40, 172–3, 174–6
jars
  cleaning 23
  receiving 27
  storage 24
  trial *22*, *73*, *249*, 250
  see also demijohns
jelly wines 39–40, 173, 175
juice extractors 29, 67, *67*

labelling 8, *22*, 25, 26, 101–2, *102*, 185, *260*, 357
lager 247, 276, 289
law and alcoholic beverages 8–9
lead poisoning 15
leaves 41–2, *41*
lemon balm wine 160

INDEX · 383

light ale 245
liqueurs 9, 20, 337–50, *341*
liquid measures 5

maceration 68
madeira-style wines 213–17
mail order 366
malic acid 28, 49
malt 251
malt syrup beers 271–9
marmalade wines 172, 176
marrow and ginger wine 161
mashing bin *249*, 250
maturation 169, 173, 183, 194, *194*, 206, 214–15, 223, 259–60, 312, 357
mead 6, 9, 13, 318–36, *326*
    see also honey
medium sherry 199
medium-sweet wines 18
melomel *326*, 332
meniscus 72, *73*
metheglin *326*, 334
mild ale 247, 273
mincers 29
mint wine 162
mixed soft fruit wine 149
morello cherry ale 296
muscatel cordial 349
must
    acid in 28
    clean 62–3
    pectin in 28
    preparing 168–9, 172, 183, 194, 204, 213–14, 325
    protection from infection 30
    surplus 5

neck collars 26
nettle beer 296
nitrogen/acid deficiency 106–7
nutrients 52, 140, 322

oak 50–51
orange and carrot wine 158

orange and pineapple wine 170
orange aperitif 170
orange 'fino sherry' 201
orange gin 347
orange juice wine 225
orange wine 133
orchard and autumn harvest rosé 155–6
original gravity 256
oxidation of cider 314–15

paddle, stirring 248, *249*, *309*
pale ale 245, 284
parsley wine 163
parsnip wine 20, 134
pasteurizing 353, 357
peach brandy using Polish spirit 344
peach brandy using vodka 343–4
peach wine 150
Pearson's Square 219–20
pectic enzyme 28, 30, 51–2, 85, 122, 205, 307, *309*, 323
pineapple and honey wine 171
pineapple and orange wine 170
pineapple juice wine 225
pineapple wine 151
plum and apple wine 153
plum jam wine 175
plum wine 135, 152
poisonous plants 41, 46
port-style wine 204–12
pouring beer 298
presses, fruit 29
pressing 31, 70, 87, *88*, 89, 155, 308, *309*, 310
priming 258–9, *269*
prune cordial 349
prune 'madeira' 217
prune, raisin and fig 'sherry' 202
pulp fermentation
    see fermentation-on-the-pulp
pumps 27
pyment *326*, 333

racking 14–15, 91–4, *92–3*, 230, 240, 258, 312, 327
    see also storage
raisin and rice wine 164
raisin, prune and fig 'sherry' 202
record-keeping 27, 238–41, *239*
red wines 20
redcurrant jelly wine 175
rhubarb wine 154
rice and raisin wine 164
rosé wines 19
rosé petal wine 136
rosehip and fig 'sherry' 203

sealing containers 77, 94
second-run wines 155–6
sediment 185–7, *186*
selling produce 8
serving
    beer 298–9
    cider 316
    mead 336
    wine 32, 173, 188, 196–7, 207, 215, 231–7
sherry-style wines 193–203, *194*
shops 365–6
shredders 29
sieve, nylon *22*, 23
siphons and siphoning *22*, 26, *27*, 32, 91–2, *92*, *103*, *249*, 250, *269*
skimming *257*, *268*
sloe gin 347
sloe wine 137
social wines 20, 157–67
solera
    commercial 193
    home-made 195, 196
sparging 250, *283*
sparkling apple wine 189
sparkling cider 313
sparkling fruit juice wine 190
sparkling gooseberry wine 190
sparkling mead 330
sparkling strawberry rosé wine 191

sparkling whitecurrant
    wine 192
sparkling wines 19,
    183–92, *186*
specific gravity 71–2, 75,
    76, 78, 310, 340–41
spices 43
spruce beer 297
stabilizers 55–6
stains, coping with 31–4
sterilizing *11*, 30
stirring 23
stock items 27–8
storage
    bulk 95–6
    of equipment 30
    of mead 327
    of wine 26, *102*, 169,
        173, 183, 185, 194,
        206, 214–15
stout 246
    dry 278, 288
straining bag 23, 32, 34,
    88
straining pulp 23, 31, 70,
    88
strawberry rosé 174
strong ale 279
sugar
    adding 74–5, 90
    in beer 254, 258–9
    in cider 307, 312
    in country wines 121
    and diabetics 222
    in history 13, 14
    as ingredient 47–8
    in liqueurs 340
    problems 106
    quantity needed 72, 229
    record of 240
    volume of 78
    and yeast 59
suitability of wine 231–2
sulphite 7, *11*, 23, 24, 30,
    52, 85, 94, 307
    see also Campden
        tablets

suppliers 365–6
sweet mead 329
sweet sherry 200
sweet wines 18
sweetening 53, 166, 188,
    195
sweetness in table wines
    138–9

table wines 19–20, 138–54
tannin 28, 50, 140–41, 322
tartaric acid 28, 49, 122,
    322
tea wine 165
temperature 76, 86, 90,
    106, 232–3, 257, 280,
    298, 316, 336, 350
thermal belt 25, *25*, 250
thermal pad 24, *25*, 250
thermometer 24, 249, *249*
titration kit 81–2, *82*
treacle ale 297

vegetables *36*, 43
vine cultivation 13–14,
    226–7, *228*
vinegar 7, 263, 314, 351–8
vodka
    and fortified wines 218,
        219, 220
    and liqueurs 340

warming devices 24–5, *25*
washing glasses 235
water as ingredient 47,
    85–6, 140, 252, *268*
white wines 19
wine
    appreciation 237
    classification 18
    history 13–17
    as intoxicant 16, 17
    kits 21, 116–20
    in liqueurs 341–2
    as medicine 16, 17
    as vehicle 16
wine boxes *103*

wine problems
    bloom 113
    browning 113–14
    hazes 111–12
    lack of taste 115
    ropiness 111
    unpleasant-smelling
        108–10
    unpleasant-tasting
        110–11
winery, the 30, 31
wines
    country 121–37
    dessert 20, 204–17
    for diabetics 222–5
    dry 18–19
    fortified 218–21
    madeira-style 213–17
    medium-sweet 18
    port-style 204–12
    sherry-style 193–203,
        194
    sparkling 19, 183–92,
        186
    suitability 231–2
    sweet 18
    table 19–20, 138–54
wort 253, 257, *257*, 258,
    259, 262, *268*, *283*

yeasts
    activating 61–2
    bite 262
    buying 61
    in cider 307
    correct type 7, 43, 253
    development 15
    in future 63
    how yeast works 58–9
    in mead 322–3
    needs of active yeast 62
    nutrient for 28, 322
    problems 106–8
    quantity 5
    in table wine 140
    wine 60
    see also fermentation